To Andy Wong, fellow RHS-58 classmate,
From the daughter of the author,
Patricia Beckman
October 6, 2013
Bellows Beach

CRISIS

President Franklin Delano Roosevelt broadcasting from Navy League dinner, Oct. 27, 1941, his last important address before Pearl Harbor. "Our Navy is ready for action."

Crisis

*The Japanese Attack on Pearl Harbor and
Southeast Asia*

By Allan Beekman

Heritage Press of Pacific
1279-203 Ala Kapuna Street/ Honolulu, Hawaii 96819

Copyright © 1992 by Allan Beekman

All rights reserved

Library of Congress Catalog Card No. 92-081919

ISBN: 0-9609132-3-8

Published and distributed by:
Heritage Press of Pacific
1279-203 Ala Kapuna Street
Honolulu, Hawaii 96819

Also by Allan Beekman

HAWAIIAN TALES
THE NITHAU INCIDENT

Printed in the U.S.A.

CONTENTS

Alphabetical List of Photos

FOREWORD

This book attempts to trace the causes that culminated in the Japanese attack on Pearl Harbor and Southeast Asia, beginning with the three bullets discharged from an assassin's gun at Sarajevo, June 28, 1914.

By the time the events had coalesced into the situation on the eve of the Japanese attack, Dec. 7, 1941, seven titans dominated the world. On the Allied side were Franklin Delano Roosevelt, Winston Churchill, Josef Stalin and Chiang Kai-shek. On the Axis side were Adolf Hitler, Benito Mussolini and Hideki Tōjō.

I have sought to weave the actions of these titans into a suspenseful story told in layman language, including sufficient background to show the cause and significance of the Japanese attack.

Japanese names are written in the Western style – given name first. In accordance with Japanese use of roman letters, Japanese names are rendered with a macron over prolonged vowels. The pronunciation of the more important Japanese names, and of some of the place names, is given, usually the first time the name is mentioned. The pronunciation is also given in the list of Principal Characters, page 381.

He who writes of this subject today bears an enormous debt to the scholars who, over the years, have ferreted out the pertinent details. For the benefit of readers who may choose to explore further some aspect of the case, I include a bibliography of some of the books and materials I have consulted.

Allan Beekman
1990

1

The Ominous Portents

It was after 9 p.m., Dec. 6, 1941, in the Oval Study on the second floor of the White House. Abroad, giant armies were locked in combat. In the seesaw battle against the British in North Africa, German Field Marshal Erwin Rommel had restored the siege conditions around Tobruk to those existing before 28 November. On the Eastern Front in Europe, the Finns had taken Hanko, the base at the entrance of the Gulf of Finland, which the Russians had occupied the previous year. Advancing to within 23.5 miles of Moscow's Red Square, the Germans had driven the Russians to the wall. Having scraped up all the human and material resources possible, the Russians had launched a general counter-offensive all along the front - especially the Moscow front. In the freezing weather, 88 infantry divisions and 15 cavalry divisions, with 1500 tanks, had hurled themselves on the Germans.

In Southeast Asia, Japanese transports were moving towards British positions along the Kra Isthmus. Having declared war on Finland, Hungary and Rumania the preceding day, and having their resources strained to the limit by the 18-month-old war with Germany, Italy and their allies, the British faced the dread prospect of fighting another formidable foe, Japan.

Though the study of the President might have been considered the focal point of the nation, indeed of all the war- racked world, it was quiet. Skillful operators diverted urgent telephone calls from the President to some other lower in the government hierarchy.

As he nursed a sinus cold and conversed with his
companion and adviser Harry Lloyd Hopkins on subjects
removed from the harshness of war, the President, as he
often did at such moments, relaxed with his stamp
collection.

The room in which he sat resembled a naval museum
painted a flat battleship gray. Photographs, a vast
collection of ships' models and hundreds of books lined
the study shelves. Personal mementoes covered the
President's massive oak desk, made from the timbers of
H.M.S. *Resolute*. A cabinet radio, two breakfronts full
of books and a big green rug contributed to the
furnishings.

If the President lifted his head, he could see on
the walls his old naval prints, portraits of his wife
and one of John Paul Jones. There was also a portrait
of his mother, Sara Delano Roosevelt, who had died three
months earlier.

Sara Delano came from a long line of seafaring men.
Her father, Warren Delano II, born in 1809, had a
comfortable inheritance, but he too went to sea. While
still in his twenties he became captain of his own ship
and entered the China trade. By his thirtieth birthday
he was senior partner in a company whose main enterprise
was the export of tea from China. He directed the
enterprise from the China end. In his early thirties he
became owner of a magnificent estate in Macao.

In 1843 he visited New England and returned to the
Orient with an 18-year-old bride. After three years the
couple returned to America where he used his capital to
expand and diversify his business interests. His
seventh child, Sara, was born on the family estate on
the Hudson, Sept. 21, 1854.

Then fortune turned against him. In August 1857
the Ohio Life Insurance and Trust Co. failed. National
panic began. By the end of the year nearly 5,000

businesses had failed; 4,000 failed in each of the succeeding years. In the shacks of the miners of copper and coal from whose labor he had formerly profited there was actual starvation through the bitter winters.

In 1850, age 50 and facing bankruptcy, he again looked to China for help in retrieving his fortune. Leaving wife and children in America, he sailed for China and there entered the opium trade. Through this enterprise, of which his descendants would be ashamed, he quickly restored his fortune.

Two years after leaving his family, he charted a clipper to bring it to Hong Kong. Sara, who was to have her eighth birthday en route, would travel much during her lifetime, but this voyage would impress her more than any other.

After 120 days at sea they sighted land. Sara saw a boat being rowed toward her and in it her father, slender and handsome and clothed all in white.

She was to spend 18 months in her father's mansion, Rose Hill. There she observed his relations with Chinese notables.

Stories of these incidents she would tell her son, the future President, would so impress him that he would love to tell them over and over throughout his life. It is easy to trace his lifelong bias for China being formed through these tales learned at his mother's knee.

Warren Delano's transactions in China so prospered that seven years after leaving New York he was able to return, a wealthy man, to live out the remainder of his long life on the family estate at Algonac.

One of his neighbors was James Roosevelt, of an equally early and substantial family, who lived on the family estate at Hyde Park on the Hudson. Delano and Roosevelt were fellow members of some clubs.

When Roosevelt met the 26-year-old Sara, he was a widower twice her age, with a son six months older than she.   He had invested in railroads, coal lands and several speculative enterprises. For years he had been vice-president of the Delaware and Hudson railroad. Unlike Warren, he was a Democrat.

Differing political affiliation being permissable, and the age difference being overlooked, Sara and James married and settled down in the Roosevelt mansion, Springwood, on his estate at Hyde Park.

He had bought Springwood in the spring of 1867. Much of it had been wooded and most had been unsuited to cultivation. Since he wished to continue active farming, he soon added other tracts, until he owned 900 contiguous acres. He expanded his herd of dairy cows, built stables for his riding and driving horses and racing trotters. He established extensive gardens. Through the sale of his milk, produce, hay and grain, he made the estate pay the cost of its upkeep.

At Springwood, Franklin Delano Roosevelt was born Jan. 30, 1882.

Before he could read, Franklin loved to have his mother read to him, especially from books about the sea. He loved to make crude boats and to sail them on the Hudson, on the banks of which he lived. While still a boy he learned to handle a ship moved by either wind or motor. At the family summer home at Campobello, Maine, at the age of nine, he took the wheel of the family 51-foot sailing yacht.

Campobello Island is part of New Brunswick in Canada, but it lies only three miles east of the village of Eastport, Maine, where the Bay of Fundy narrows into Passamaquoddy Bay at the mouth of the St. Croix River. James and Sara had discovered the island when Franklin was one-year old.

James built a house there and bought a boat. From that time Campobello became Franklin's second home. Hiking, swimming, canoeing and sailing, he explored every foot of the shoreline and became an expert navigator of the surrounding currents and tides.

Another facet of Sara's experience that was to affect her son was her early acquired hobby of stamp collecting. Great Britain had adopted adhesive stamps in 1840; America had followed in 1847. Sara acquired some of the earliest issues of British and American stamps. During her residence at Rose Hill, in Macao, she added rare Hong Kong and Chinese issues

Until her early twenties, she found abundant opportunities to pursue this hobby as a complement to her round-the-world travelling. Then she presented her collection to her younger brother, Fred Delano.

Franklin early took up stamp collecting. By the age of ten, he was applying himself to the pursuit with such diligence that his uncle, impressed by such dedication, presented him with his own collection, which he had greatly enlarged over what Sara had given him. Thus, while still a child, Franklin owned a collection that an affluent philatelist might have needed to spend a lifetime to have collected.

Sara had Franklin educated by tutors, both at home and abroad. From the time he had reached three, she had taken him to Europe for most of the year.

Finally she enrolled him in a village school in Bad Nauheim, Germany. There was sown the seed of his anti-German bias.

In his reminiscences about the school he revealed that among the schoolchildren there had been much talk about an inevitable war with France and of building up the German empire into the greatest world power. The teachers taught their charges to disrespect the English and to regard the Americans as barbarians. At 15, while attending Groton, he first read *The Influence of Sea Power Upon History, 1660-1783,* by Alfred Thayer Mahan, the American naval officer and historian. More convincingly than had any earlier writer, Mahan argued the dominating influence of sea power. He saw in Anglo-American naval supremacy the surest hope for peace.

Since sea power was the basis of world power, British naval superiority during the 19th century had enabled that small island kingdom to become a world empire. By the 20th century British sea power, though still superior, was declining in relation to that of other nations. Consequently, the United States needed to develop naval power for its defense, but it should still cooperate with Great Britain to ensure peace by controlling the seas.

Dec. 8, 1900, while Franklin was a freshman at Harvard, his father died, age 72.

At Harvard, Roosevelt began to collect books and pamphlets on naval history. He soon had the nucleus of what would become one of the finest collections in the country of books, manuscripts, pamphlets, articles and prints on naval matters.

At Harvard he had a conversation with a Japanese student that he was never to forget. The student told him of a Japanese plan, conceived in 1889 and that was to cover 100 years, that would lead to Japanese world domination. The plan went as follows:

1. An official war with China to demonstrate that Japan could fight and beat China.

2. The assimilation of Korea.

3. A defensive war against Russia.

4. The seizure of Manchuria.

5. The seizure of Jehol, a region in northeast China.

uncle, President Theodore Roosevelt, gave the bride away.

In 1907, after receiving his law degree, Franklin, passed the bar exams and went to work as an unsalaried clerk for the distinguished law firm of Carter, Ledyard and Millburn, New York. One day he and his five fellow clerks, each at his roll-top desk, began to talk of their personal ambitions.

Roosevelt said he had no intention of making a career of law; he was going into politics. Following in the footsteps of Theodore Roosevelt, whom he greatly admired, he would win a seat in the State Assembly. Continuing in those swift, sure footsteps, he would later secure an appointment to Assistant Secretary of the Navy. Then, as Theodore had done, he would win election to the governorship of New York State.

"Once you're elected governor of New York," he said, "if you do well enough in that job, you have a good show to be President..."

In 1911 he gained the first rung up this ladder toward the Presidency by being elected, as Democrat, to the New York State Senate. From here he looked to the man most likely to be able to help him gain the next rung – Woodrow Wilson, governor of New Jersey, who seemed in line to receive the next Democratic nomination for the Presidency.

In June 1912 Roosevelt came to Baltimore for the Democratic Presidential Convention as leader of 150 members of the New York State Wilson Conference. There he met and favorably impressed many nationally prominent Democrats, including journalist Joseph Daniels and U.S. Representative Cordell Hull, with both of whom he would later be closely associated.

Wilson won the nomination and, in the succeeding election, the Presidency. He appointed Daniels Secretary of the Navy. Daniels chose Roosevelt as

Assistant Secretary, his choice being cleared by Wilson and confirmed by the U.S. Senate.

Roosevelt was then 31, a tall, vigorous, handsome man, with all the promise of a successful political career before him. His private life had suffered a serious reverse.

In 1906, his first child, Anna Eleanor, had been born. Then followed James; Franklin Jr., who died in infancy; Elliott; the second Franklin Jr; and then John. About the time of the birth of John, March 13, 1916, Eleanor learned that Franklin was involved with her social secretary, Lucy Page Mercer.

Eleanor made scenes. His mother supported her. No divorced man had ever held the Presidency on which he had set his heart. An appearance of marital harmony being essential to political success, he finally agreed to break off his relationship with Lucy.

Thereafter sexual relations between him and Eleanor ceased. Though his attraction to Lucy may have precipitated this rift, there may have been a deeper underlying reason. Eleanor was always surrounded by people. Her son, Elliott, was later to write that many of the women who flocked about her were active lesbians.

Roosevelt was never to lose his love for Lucy.

The rage of Eleanor at discovering his involvement with Lucy seems inconsistent with her complacency toward a long-enduring relationship between him and Marguerite "Missy" Lehand, who soon afterward became his secretary.

But to return to him when he still occupied the post of Assistant Secretary of the Navy. He was eager to expand and strengthen the navy. "...the policy of Congress should be to build dreadnoughts until our Navy is comparable to any in the world."

The British navy was stronger than the American, but few Americans, if any, expected to confront it. Congress was concerned with the German and Japanese navies, with Roosevelt preoccupied with the Japanese.

But neither a German nor a Japanese would strike the spark that would engulf the world in war, but a 19-year-old Serbian student, Gavrilo Princip.

June 28, 1914, Princip stood on a street corner in Sarajevo, Serbia seeking an opportunity to kill the visiting Archduke Franz Ferdinand, heir to the throne of Austria-Hungary.

The opportunity came when the car carrying the Archduke, second in the procession, followed the lead car, which had mistakenly made a right turn into a side street instead of continuing straight on. When Ferdinand's chauffeur learned of the error and was told to return to the proper route, he had to stop to put his car into reverse.

He stopped within five feet of Princip. Princip fired twice. The first shot fatally wounded Sophie, morganatic wife of the Archduke, the second fatally wounded the Archduke himself.

Princip was a member of a secret nationalist movement; his weapons had been supplied by the Serbian terrorist organization known as the Black Hand. Insisting that the Serbian Government had instigated the plot, Austria delivered an unacceptable ultimatum to Serbia July 23.

Serbia rejected the ultimatum and began to mobilize. Austria declared war on Serbia July 28.

The various alliances of the opposing bloc of nations began to fall into place. Czar Nicholas II of Russia ordered mobilization in support of Serbia. His first cousin, Kaiser Wilhelm II of Germany, demanded that the Russian army and fleet be demobilized.

France, ally of Russia, mobilized. Germany declared war on Russia August 1. Forty-eight hours later she declared war on France and sent her troops into Belgium to advance through it to confront the

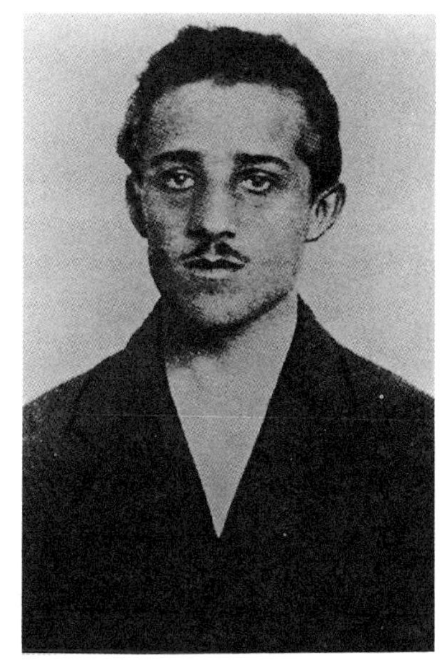

Top. Archduke Francis Ferdinand and consort arriving at Sarajevo, June 28, 1914, a few hours before their assassination.

Right. Gabriel Princip after arrest. His bullets plunged the world into war.

French. Violation of Belgian neutrality caused England to declare war on Germany August 4. Austria declared war on Russia August 6.

The Great War had begun, with the Central Powers led by Germany, the Allies led by France and England.

Though he had failed to grasp the implications of the assassination immediately, Roosevelt perceived the drift of events sooner than most of his colleagues. America became more and more alienated from Germany because of its submarine warfare. Over the objections of Daniels and other important pacifists, Roosevelt insisted that America should intervene.

The situation was similar to one he would meet later in his career when greater personal power would permit him to act on his convictions.

Pres. Wilson called a special session of Congress for April 2, 1917 to hear his plea for a declaration of war against Germany. In the front row gallery seat sat the President's daughter Margaret and his wife, Edith. Elsewhere sat Franklin and Eleanor Roosevelt.

The President said, "...I advise that Congress declare the recent course of the Imperial German Government to be in fact nothing less than war against the Government and people of the United States; that it formally accept the state of belligerent which has been forced upon it." He spoke for a half hour, went into his peroration and ended, looking up and over the heads of his audience, "God helping her, she can do no other."

On the morning of Wednesday, April 4, the Senate began debating the war resolution, continuing far into the night. Eighty-two Senators voted for the declaration; six against. In the House, 80 spoke in favor; 20 in opposition. When the House vote was taken, after 3 a.m., April 6, 353 voted for declaration, 50 against. Among those voting against the resolution was Jeannette Rankin, the first woman to be elected to

Congress, of whom we shall hear again.

After lunch that day, Pres. Wilson signed the War Resolution.

July 9, 1918, Roosevelt sailed on the destroyer U.S.S. *Dyer* for a personal inspection of Navy and Marine operations in the war theater. In France he saw how bombing and shelling had destroyed Dunkirk. During a week spent in Paris he called on Marshal Joseph Joffre, commander in chief of the Allied forces. On the fourth anniversary of the war in the West, Roosevelt went to the front.

He crossed ruined landscapes where shell holes full of water stunk from the rotting corpses of men who had died in them. He saw the village of Mareuil through which the Germans had retreated less than 24 hours before, leaving a number of their dead in the field. "...in one place a little pile of them awaiting burial." He fired one of a battery of 155's toward the German lines. Wearing a gas mask and a French helmet, he crossed the Meuse and was driven across the shell-churned grounds of Verdun where he came under fire a second time.

He went on to Italy, a member of the Allies.

He made a second visit to the front, going westward through the British sector into the tiny portion of Belgium that remained in Allied hands. He watched an encounter between destroyers and U-boats in the Channel, came under prolonged long-range artillery bombardment and in the night experienced two air raids.

He crossed the Channel by destroyer, which was twice attacked by bombing planes before reaching port. In England he conferred, travelled and inspected.

One evening he attended a dinner in London at historic Gray's Inn, the most northerly of the four inns of Justice Francis Bacon, the Inn's most illustrious member. The dinner was in honor of the War Ministers.

Roosevelt was a prominent guest and rated it "a really historic occasion." It was more historic than he was able to realize at the time because at the dinner he met, for the first time, the British Winston Churchill, with whom his destiny was later to be linked.

The political fortunes of Churchill were than at a low ebb, though he was Minister of State for War and Air Minister. Neither man particularly impressed the other.

Roosevelt returned to France. At Brest he boarded the *Leviathan* and collapsed in his cabin bed, suffering double pneumonia and influenza – the same Spanish influenza that would claim 20 million lives. He disembarked at New York, carried down the gangplank on a stretcher.

The Armistice, ending hostilities, was signed Nov.11, 1918.

The fateful year of 1918 had diminished figures who had loomed large at the start of the war. The German Kaiser had fled into exile in neutral Holland. Bolsheviks had murdered the Russian Czar and all his family.

In Austria the Emperor Franz Joseph had sustained the fabric of administration until his death, Nov. 21, 1916. Charles I, who succeeded him, renounced all share in the government of German–Austria. The following day he took similar action concerning Hungary. Refusing to abdicate, he carried his empty titles into exile. In April 1919, the Austrian parliament would depose him.

Jan. 2, 1919 Franklin and Eleanor sailed for Europe aboard the U.S.S. *Washington* along with President Wilson and his advisers. In France, Roosevelt was excluded from the rooms where the representatives of the Allied nations were making history. As he set out for home on the train to Brest, he saw for the first time a copy of the League of Nations Covenant, which Wilson insisted should be part of the peace treaty. He and Eleanor read the Covenant with high hopes that it would be the instrument to prevent future wars.

The Versailles Treaty was signed June 28, 1919.

The following day the Roosevelts sailed from Brest aboard the *Washington* with Wilson a fellow passenger. One day Wilson summoned Roosevelt to the Presidential suite and talked to him privately about the League and what it should mean for mankind.

Alas for his hopes, the Senate refused to accept Wilson's advocacy of the signing of the peace treaty with its provision that America should enter the League of Nations.

The Allies carved up what had been the Central Powers, eliminating Serbia and shrinking Austria and Hungary. They created new nations that ran between a shrunken Germany on the west and a shrunken Russia on the east. The new nations began with Yugoslavia at the south, bordering the Adriatic Sea, and continued on north with Czechoslovakia, Poland, Lithuania, Latvia, Estonia and Finland – nations that appear on a map of Europe like a tongue of flame exacerbating the passions of the defeated powers.

Within the Polish customs union was the Free City of Danzig, serving Poland as an outlet to the sea and separating Germany from a portion of the German nation beyond.

Without American participation, the League would be impotent to enforce its decisions. So the war precipitated by a disgruntled student, which had killed more than 8 million persons, wounded more than 20 million, made missing countless more, achieved untold property damage and inflicted incalculable misery had succeeded only in creating an inflammable situation that needed only a spark to cause it to burst forth in uncontrollable flame.

The French Marshal Ferdinand Foch, appointed to

As Ass't Secretary of the Navy Franklin D. Roosevelt, above, advocated American entry into the European War. After victory in Europe, President Woodrow Wilson, above right with his secretary Joseph P. Tumulty, was unable to persuade the Senate to ratify the Treaty of Versailles, his most formidable opponent being Senator Henry Cabot Lodge, right.

supreme command of all Allied armies March 26, 1918, declared, "This is not peace. It is an Armistice for 20 years."

Adamant in his decision to have American acceptance of the League, Wilson embarked on a nationwide tour to drum up public support. He overtaxed his strength, was stricken and returned to Washington in complete collapse. October 2 a thrombosis impaired control of the brain over the left side of his body.

This was the situation when the Democratic National Convention convened in San Francisco. Many of the delegates opposed the renomination of Wilson because of the tradition limiting the President to two terms, because his prestige had declined, and because he was too ill to campaign. July 5, 1920, the Convention nominated James M. Cox, governor of Ohio, for the Presidency with Roosevelt for the Vice Presidency.

Sunday, July 18, 1920, the two Democratic candidates called at the White House. They found the President, huddled in his wheelchair, on the south portico, which overlooked a wide, lush lawn, The paralyzed left side of his face leaned slackly on his sunken chest.

With tears in his eyes, Cox bent over the President and greeted him warmly.

For the first time the President looked up and whispered, "Thank you for coming. I am very glad you came."

Roosevelt was smartly attired in white shoes, white trousers, dark-blue double-breasted jacket and navy-blue tie. As he bent deferentially to greet the President, Mrs. Wilson was struck by how bright and spruce Roosevelt appeared.

Said Cox, "Mr. President, I have always admired the fight you made for the League."

The President made a painful effort to straighten

up. "Mr. Cox, that fight can still be won."

"Mr. President, we are going to be a million percent with you, and that means the League of Nations."

The President nodded. "I am very grateful."

Aug. 6, 1920, Roosevelt formally resigned as Assistant Secretary of the Navy. He expected a Republican victory; nevertheless he campaigned vigorously, making the League the central theme of most of his speeches.

"Every sane man," he declared, "knows that in case of another world war America would be drawn in...whether we were in the League or not."

Despite his efforts, the voters overwhelmingly elected the Republican team of Warren Harding and Calvin Coolidge. The United States would sign a separate peace with Austria, Aug. 24, 1921; with Germany, August 25 and with Hungary, August 29.

Roosevelt accepted his political defeat with good grace. Times were good; the Democrats would need an economic depression before they could regain the Presidency. He so busied himself with activities disassociated with the election that when he set out for his summer home in Campobello in August 1921 he was dead tired.

Despite his fatigue, he continued the strenuous pace. One hot day he fell off a fishing boat into the Bay of Fundy. The frigid water shocked his perspiration bathed body. The chill that swept over him astonished, even alarmed him.

Nevertheless, having been helped back aboard, he spent the rest of the day in his wet clothes. Though he felt no better next day, he continued the furious pace. After a strenuous day, he jogged two miles along a narrow, dirt road and, perspiring, plunged into a small lake, Glen Severn. The lake water being warm, he topped off the swim by a dip in the icy ocean.

When he emerged, he did not "feel the usual reaction, the glow I'd expected."

After returning to the cottage, he sat in his wet bathing suit reading the mail. Suddenly a violent chill seized him. In the morning when he tried to swing his legs out of bed, his left leg dragged. When he tried to stand up, the leg almost collapsed under him.

There would be complications and misdiagnoses, but eventually he would be discovered to have been stricken with poliomyelitis, commonly known as polio.

He became totally helpless. He had had faith in God as a beneficent Creator who had chosen him for a major role in the great drama of history. Now helpless and in pain, he felt God had forsaken him.

He began to feel his way back to life. Still unable to sit up under his own power, he was discharged from the hospital Oct. 28, 1921. Though he would become able to wheel himself about in a wheelchair, he would never be able to stand again without the support of steel braces on his atrophied legs.

Dr. Robert W. Lovett assured him that many polio patients had made a marked improvement through swimming. He also told Roosevelt that the improvement was greater among those who swam in warm water.

Roosevelt learned of a hot spring resort in Merriwether County, Georgia, about 70 miles southwest of Atlanta, near the village of Bullochsville. The resort had once been famous but had fallen into decay. It had an outdoor swimming pool 50 by 150 feet, fed by a thermal spring gushing from a huge fissured rock — 800 gallons of water a minute at a constant temperature of 89 degrees.

He also learned that a young man, Louis Joseph, had gone to the resort three years before almost totally crippled by polio. By constant swimming in the heated pool and doing walking exercises in the buoyant water, he had so improved that he was now able to walk the streets on unbraced legs, supported only by an ordinary cane.

The Roosevelts went there. He and Louis Joseph entered the pool. Roosevelt stayed in the pool an hour, luxuriating in its warmth and the energizing buoyancy of the highly mineralized water. He emerged feeling more refreshed than he had in years.

He set about transforming this shabby, moribund resort into a health spa, to be renamed Warm Springs. With his encouragement, and he being the most prominent resident, the resort became a Mecca for polio victims.

He increased his weight to 187 pounds. Through a regimen of exercise, he so developed his muscles from the hips up that when sitting he seemed an unusually powerful man.

Formerly he had projected an image of a handsome, healthy aristocrat untouched by misfortune. Many less fortunate may have found it hard to believe he could understand their situation.

Physical disability did not diminish his desire for political power. His gallant effort to surmount his affliction may have won the voters' sympathy. He was elected Governor of New York in 1928.

As governor he instituted a progressive administration that so met with the approval of the electorate he easily won re-election in 1930.

He responded to the onset of the economic depression of the 1930's by establishing the nation's first state relief agency.

At this time he came to know Harry Hopkins well. Hopkins was a social worker who had become a favorite of Eleanor who was interested in various charitable works. In 1931, Roosevelt appointed Hopkins head of the State's Temporary Emergency Relief Administration.

In the Presidential campaign of 1932, the economic

depression was the only issue of consequence. The incumbent President Herbert Clark Hoover was held to be responsible for the economic depression that made millions unemployed. His proposals for countering it, made with habitual glumness, seemed less persuasive than those of Roosevelt who campaigned with smiling buoyancy and confidence. November 5, Roosevelt was overwhelmingly voted the Presidency.

He was to take office March 4, 1933. In the meantime he concentrated on formulating the measures he expected to take and on gathering around him the team he intended to use to execute them.

The economic depression that had begun in 1929, being worldwide, had exacerbated international relations. Japan was one of the nations most affected. Being a nation without natural resources and dependent upon export for survival, when her overseas market had vanished she had turned to China as the last potential market available.

China was unamenable to the move. Having been plundered by Japan and other powers, China was striving to regain her sacrificed sovereign rights; she opposed Japan's attitude toward Manchuria. From this situation sprang the first overt step up the stairway to global war.

At that time the U.S. Secretary of State was Henry Lewis Stimson. Since he will cut a considerable figure in our story, it is appropriate at this point to give something of his background and of his attitude toward these ominous events.

Born in New York City Sept. 21, 1867, Stimson, like Roosevelt, came from an old New York family. Dissatisfied with the curricula of the New York schools, his father, a socially prominent, successful banker and physician, took him out of school for two years and taught him himself.

When Henry was 13, his father sent him to Phillips Academy at Andover, Mass. From this first escape from city life he learned to love the outdoors with which he became acquainted.

In 1885 he had an opportunity to visit the vast wilderness of western America, then still a frontier. Thereafter, for nearly 20 years, he would spend a portion of each year exploring, hunting, and traveling by horse, foot or canoe through the western or Canadian Rockies.

Though of a Republican family, Stimson first mixed in politics as a Democrat. But finding the corruption there more than he could stand, he reverted to the Republican party. During these years of hard political work he met Theodore Roosevelt. Their friendship lasted from 1894 until the death of Theodore in 1919.

When America went to war with Spain in 1898, though over 30 and without military training, Stimson enlisted in Squadron A of the National Guard. His troop was not called to combat duty, but he remained in the squadron for nine years, rising from private to 1st lieutenant.

In December 1905, Theodore Roosevelt, now President, invited Stimson to Washington. Up until this time Stimson had been in private law practice. His chief previous connection with outdoor-man Theodore had been as a fellow member of the Boone & Crockett Club of New York. Seated across from Stimson in the White House, the President asked him to serve as U.S. Attorney for the Southern District of New York.

Stimson accepted. It was his first public office. All his later opportunities derived from it.

He became closely associated with Theodore Roosevelt who, in 1910, persuaded him to run for governor of New York.

Stimson ran and lost, but the following year President William H. Taft appointed him Secretary of

War. He served until 1913.

During World War I he served for a short time in France as colonel of field artillery. From 1918 to 1926 he enjoyed a lucrative law practice, but was called back into public service. Appointed governor general of the Philippines in 1927, he returned to America in 1929 to become Secretary of State under President Herbert Hoover.

Stimson headed the U.S. delegations to the London Naval Conference in 1930 and the Geneva Disarmament Conference in 1932. But the major problem of his four-year term derived from the Japanese invasion of Manchuria.

Manchuria, in northeast China, was the original home of the Manchus who subjugated China and founded the Manchu dynasty, which lasted from 1644 to 1912. Both Russia and Japan coveted Manchuria. In 1907 China set up a civil administration there, and it became increasingly the destination of Chinese immigration.

The Japanese government took no effective measures to counter the worldwide economic depression that had set in when Franklin Roosevelt was governor of New York On the contrary, toward the end of the administration of Giichi Tanaka in 1929 there were free-for-all brawls in the Diet and repeated exposures of party scandals. The Japanese became convinced that their parliamentary representatives were rotten and corrupt.

At the same time the Japanese became incensed over the inability of the government to curb rising Chinese nationalism, which threatened Japanese interests in China.

Popular disgust with the political parties strengthened the military and right wing groups in Japan. When the London Naval Disarmament Treaty of 1930 limited the number of cruisers for Great Britain, the United States and Japan on a 10-10-7 basis, with Japan

on the short end, it gave the Japanese militarists a cause
to use against the political party cabinets. Already some
militarists had demonstrated the extreme length to which
they were ready to go to force the government in the
militarists' chosen direction. June 24, 1928, a Japanese
Kwantung Army staff officer commanding men from an Engineer
regiment dynamited the special train of the Chinese warlord
Chang Tso-lin, fatally injuring him. This coup had been
plotted by Maj. Kanji Ishiwara (kän'jē -e shē wä' lä) and
Col. Seishirō Itagaki (sä ē shē'lō ē tä gä' kē) who hoped
the assassination would speed the making of Manchuria into
an autonomous state under Japanese control.

The naval treaty led to the formation of such
ultranationalist groups as the Blood Brotherhood (Ketsumei-
dan). Radical groups of young Army officers coalesced
around Ishiwara and Maj. Kingorō Hashimoto (kin'gō lō
hä shē mō' tō) of the Army General Staff. In the fall of
1930 they formed the Cherry Blossom Society (Sakurakai).

In league with Ishiwara and men under his command,
Hashimoto, Sept. 18, 1931, blew up the Manchurian railway
at Liut'iaokou and blamed the Chinese for the incident.

Having manufactured the requisite incident, the
Japanese immediately occupied all strategic points in
Manchuria. They justified the move "as necessary measures
of self-defense" taken "to protect the lives of Japanese
civilians."

Stimson tried to cope with the complex situation. To a
degree the special rights of Japan in Manchuria were
sanctified by treaty. In its victory in the Russo-Japanese
war of 1904-5, Japan had wrested the region from Russia.
In the treaties of Portsmouth and Peking of 1905, Japan was
recognized as the successor to czarist Russia in South
Manchuria.

But during the first three decades of the 20th century, 30 million Chinese had poured into Manchuria. There they continued to think of themselves as Chinese in Chinese territory. The few hundred thousand Japanese there goaded the rising nationalist pride of the Chinese.

America advocated the principle of the Open Door in China, meaning that it insisted that the territorial integrity of China was to be respected and that all nations should have free access to its commerce. The Nine Power Treaty signed by the United States, Germany and all other nations except Russia holding territory in the Pacific, had enlarged the principle of the Open Door and made it into law.

Further, the American interest in world peace had been formalized in the Kellogg–Briand Pact signed by China, Japan, the United States and every other major nation in August 1928. The treaty renounced war.

Reports from the Far East made clear that the Japanese movement in Manchuria was an act of aggression – a flagrant violation of the Kellogg Pact, the Nine-Power Treaty and the Covenant of the League of Nations to which Japan, but not America was signatory.

The action appeared, however, to have been taken with neither the approval of the Japanese Prime Minister nor the Foreign Minister. The U.S. State Department withheld action in the hope that the liberal leaders of Japan might repudiate the aggression. To the Japanese ambassador, Stimson expressed his desire to avoid complicating any efforts the Japanese Prime Minister might make to improve the situation. At the same time he expressed concern that Japan, Oct. 8, 1931, had bombed the city of Chinchow, Liaoning province, northeast China, on the northwest coast and railroad of the Liaotung peninsula.

September 21, China appealed to the League of

Nations at Geneva, of whose Council both Japan and China were members. Though not a member, the United States recognized that the League, composed of 60 nations, represented world opinion. Consequently, as far as it considered it permissable and appropriate, the United States tried to cooperate with the League in adjudicating the dispute. With the approval of Japan, the League appointed the Lytton Commission, which included an American representative, to go to the Far East to investigate.

In the meantime, Japanese aggression continued. December 11 the moderate Minseitō Cabinet fell and was succeeded by a Seiyūkai Cabinet, which was sympathetic to the aggression. Jan. 2, 1932, Japan occupied Chinchow, destroying the last remnant of Chinese authority in Manchuria.

Concluding that his efforts at conciliation by restraint had failed, Stimson entered a new phase of policy. Pres. Hoover felt that American interests in China were insufficient to justify military action. Believing that anything beyond verbal protest – for example, imposing economic sanctions – might lead to war, Stimson dispatched a note to China and Japan in which he stated he was confident that the Lytton Commission would facilitate an ultimate solution to the difficulties between China and Japan. In the meantime, the United States was unable to acknowledge the legality of any situation, treaty or agreement that might impair the treaty rights of the United States or its citizens in China or the Open Door policy. Neither would the United States recognize something brought about through violation of the Kellogg–Briand Pact.

This principle of non–recognition, which would become known as the Stimson Doctrine, was aimed at Japanese militarism. Stimson hoped that other western nations, particularly Great Britain, would follow his lead with similar declarations.

None did.

Though Great Britain failed to protest vigorously the Japanese seizure of Manchuria, a situation soon arose that caused her to reevaluate her position towards Japan. Indignation over the Manchurian incident led the Chinese to boycott Japanese imports, with Shanghai becoming the center of anti-Japanese agitation. The unrest reached such a pitch that in January 1932 the Municipal Council of the International Settlement proclaimed a state of emergency.

With the Manchurian incident still unresolved, Rear Adm. Kiochi Shiozawa (kē ō'chē shē'ō zä wä), commander of the Japanese forces in the International Settlement at Shanghai, capitalized on the assassination of a Japanese Buddhist priest by landing marines who clashed with the Chinese 19th Army. The Chinese infantry resisted with determination and skill.

Shiozawa retaliated with a bombing attack on the helpless civilians in the area of the fighting.

The first terror bombing occurred in Chapei, a section of northern Shanghai about eight square miles in size, bounded on the south and west by the American sector of Shanghai; on the east by the Japanese. The terminal for trains to Nanking and the coastal area around Woosung, North Station, was within Chapei, which was generally referred to as the Chinese quarter of Shanghai. It contained mostly ramshackle homes.

As the Japanese airmen maneuvered into position, they leaned out of their planes and waved to watching volunteers below. Opening fire from a fair height, they came in lower and lower until at about 300 feet they dropped their bombs on the railroad station. When they had finished, only bare, gaunt walls of outer Chapei remained standing. Thousands of Chinese died. Hundreds of homes were demolished.

250,000 civilians fled from the ruins into the International Settlement.

The Chinese troops continued to resist; the Japanese continued to pour in reinforcements. After a month the Chinese found themselves outflanked by a vastly better-equipped force.

The world press more fully reported the Shanghai Incident than it had the Manchurian. In Shanghai, Western interests, particularly British interests, were more clearly threatened than they had been in Manchuria.

The brutality of the Japanese alienated the West; the gallant defense of the Chinese evoked its sympathy. A cease-fire ensued, but among the Chinese anti-Japanese sentiment had reached crescendo.

In October 1932, the Lytton Commission turned in its report to the League. The Commission unanimously declared that the state of Manchoukuo, which Japan had established in what had been Manchuria, was the artificial creation of the Japanese General Staff; the wishes of the residents had played no part in its formation. The Commission proposed establishing an autonomous Manchuria, which would remain a part of China under the aegis of the League. There should be a comprehensive treaty between China and Japan regulating their interests in Manchuria.

Stimson said of the report: "It became at once and remains today the outstanding impartial authority upon the subject which it covers."

Nevertheless, when the League accepted the report Feb. 24, 1933, the Japanese delegation, led by its spokesman Yōsuke Matsuoka (yō sōo'kä   mä tsōo ō'kä), filed out of the Assembly Hall. The great doors closed slowly and silently behind them. March 27, the Japanese government gave official notice of its withdrawal from the League.

The League had demonstrated that it stood by its

principles, and that it was powerless to enforce them.

This was the situation when Roosevelt prepared to assume the Presidency. Seeking as smooth a transition as possible from the Hoover administration to his own, he sought to confer with Stimson on foreign policy. Finally he succeeded in arranging a meeting.

Monday, Jan. 9, 1933, Stimson went to Hyde Park. He later wrote about the meeting: "The Governor did everything he could to make the interview pleasant, and his hospitality was very agreeable...We both spoke with the utmost freedom and informality."

No others were present, and the talk continued for six hours. After they had discussed about every major aspect of current foreign policy, Stimson found he was in substantial agreement with the president-elect. To Stimson the most important point was Roosevelt's quick understanding and general approval of his Manchurian policy.

January 19, when they met for a second time, Roosevelt said, "We are getting so that we do pretty good teamwork, don't we?" Stimson laughingly agreed.

Coming from similar backgrounds, the two had much in common and, like most visitors, Stimson was susceptible to Roosevelt's charm.

2

THE LONG SHADOW OF THE AXIS

In Washington on the day preceding the inaugural of Franklin Roosevelt as President, the weather was as bleak as the mood of the impoverished country in which banks were shutting down. Hungry, homeless, disillusioned Americans focused their attention on the capital where the leaden skies portended rain.

It was customary for the retiring President to ask his successor for dinner on the night of the third of March, the eve of the inaugural. Hoover declined to issue the invitation. Insisting that the President-elect must be given the opportunity to pay his respects, the White House usher arranged a tea for the afternoon of the third.

At the tea in the Red Room the atmosphere was strained. Realizing that Hoover was indisposed to complete the round of protocol, Roosevelt suggested that Hoover need not return the visit.

Looking Roosevelt in the eye, Hoover said coldly, "Mr. Roosevelt, when you are in Washington as long as I have been, you will learn that the President of the United States calls on nobody."

This barb found its mark in the breast of the usually serene Roosevelt.

Heavy winter clouds hung over the city as the official car, with Roosevelt aboard, pulled into the White House drive the following day to take Hoover to the inaugural. Hoover glumly climbed into the car and seated himself beside his successor.

Both men wore overcoats and held their silk hats in their hands. With lowered gaze and downcast expression, Hoover discouraged Roosevelt's efforts at polite conversation.

Assuming that the occasional cheers from the dejected crowds packing the sidewalks were meant for Hoover, Roosevelt at first avoided responding to them. When it became clear that Hoover was not responding either, it must have occurred that he and his somber companion were making a poor impression. Roosevelt began to smile and wave his top hat to the crowds.

He was unsmiling when he took the oath of office from Chief Justice Charles Evan Hughes. Roosevelt's expression was grim when, as President, he took the rostrum to make the first inaugural address to be broadcast by radio.

In the cultured voice and careful, simple diction that was to become familiar to his countrymen, he said: "First of all, let me assert my firm belief that the only thing we have to fear is fear itself...Rulers of the exchange of mankind's goods have failed through their own stubbornness and their own incompetence."

On foreign relations, which was to be a distraction to his efforts to put the nation again on a firm economic basis, he said: "In the field of world policy I would dedicate this nation to the policy of the good neighbor- the neighbor who resolutely respects himself and, because he does so, respects the rights of others – the neighbor who respects his obligations and respects the sanctity of his agreements in and with a world of neighbors."

He was almost immediately to find that the policy of the good neighbor was easier to enunciate than to fulfill. Japan was not only infuriated by the League censure of her activities in Manchuria, Europe was restless under the inequities of the Versailles Treaty; and two men there were giving direction to that restlessness.

On the one hand there was Benito Mussolini, born in Forli, Italy in 1883 to an impoverished, antireligious, political malcontent blacksmith. Benito's mother was a school teacher. By the age of 18, he too had qualified as teacher. But restless and ambitious he associated with various revolutionary groups, became editor of a small Socialist newspaper and by Dec. 1, 1912 became editor of the *Avanti*, the Socialist Party's official organ.

A strong and effective journalist, he quarreled with the Socialists. He left them and began to publish his own paper, *Il Popolo d'Italia*. He served in the World War as a private, was wounded and returned to his paper.

In 1919 he organized the *Fasci di Combattimento*, a strongly nationalistic association. The party took its name from the *fasces* of ancient Rome – a bundle of elm or birch rods from which the head of an axe projected; the bundle fastened together by a red strap and symbolizing the power to scourge or decapitate. The party took the *fasces* as its emblem. Oct. 24, 1922 a Fascist convention in Naples offered an opportunity for a concerted march on the capital to demand power; King Victor Emmanuel III asked Mussolini to form a government.

Mussolini complied, gradually shaping the government into a dictatorship with him as the head. Therewith he introduced into popular usage the term *fascism* or *Fascism* denoting a governmental system headed by a dictator with complete power, forcibly suppressing opposition and criticism and forcibly regimenting industry and commerce.

Having consolidated his power, he gave the term Fascism a further meaning through the fulfillment of a bellicose nationalism, extending the influence of Italy into the Balkans and Austria.

In Germany Mussolini had an admirer, Adolf Hitler, a man who had risen to power with neither family background nor much formal education. Born April 20, 1889 in Braunau, Upper Austria, Hitler had served through the entire World War with bravery and prudence, but never rising above the rank of corporal. After the war he discovered he had the gift of oratory.

By November 1925 he had used this talent with such good effect by stressing the wrongs he deemed inflicted on Germany and the need for redress that he felt strong enough to attempt to seize control of the government. His plot failed, but at his trial he conducted his defense with such brilliance that he gained considerable favorable publicity.

The court sentenced him to five years imprisonment, which he began to serve in Landsberg prison. There the jailers treated him as an honored guest. He lived in comfort and used his confinement to prepare the first volume of his infamous work *Mein Kampf* (My Struggle).

In *Mein Kampf* he preached a philosophy that seemed ludicrous then, when he was out of power and known as the political clown of Europe, but that would soon pose a sinister threat to mankind. He believed in the inequality between individuals and races as part of the unchangeable natural order. The mythical Aryan race, of which he regarded the Germans as the purest embodiment, was the sole creative element of mankind and thus rightfully should rule the lesser breeds. The natural unit of mankind was the nation, of which Germany was the greatest. The state existed to serve the nation. Morality and truth was to be judged in accordance with the interest and preservation of the nation.

The unity of the nation would be incarnated in the <u>Fuhrer</u> (leader) endowed with absolute authority. The greatest enemy to the nation was Marxism with its emphasis on internationalism and class conflict. Behind

Marxism he placed a mythical figure of incarnate evil, the Jew. Germany must expand; the "race" of "Jews" must be eliminated.

Hitler was released from prison after nine months. During his imprisonment his Nazi Party had disintegrated. He set about rebuilding it.

He was five feet eight and one-half inches in height and weighed about 157 pounds. He had dark hair and piercing blue eyes. His toothbrush mustache resembled that of the famous comedian Charley Chaplin; so it was natural for his detractors to seize on this peculiarity to caricature him as a comic Chaplinesque figure.

Actually he moved with grace, had a commanding presence and a hypnotic personality. His unique oratory and mastery of mass psychology drew to him larger and larger audiences, multiplied many times over by the postwar world of radio and, a little later, talking movies.

He also demonstrated a gift for intrigue and an outstanding ability to use people who sought to use him. He was chancellor of Germany when Roosevelt was inaugurated as President of the United States. Nineteen days later Hitler persuaded the Reichstag, the law-making body of Germany, to give him dictorial powers. Henceforward Hitler symbolized a military Germany. The time would come when he would link his fortunes with those of Mussolini

Then there was Josef Stalin, born Dec. 21, 1879 in Russian Georgia to emancipated serfs and Christened Iosif Vissarrionovich Dzhugashvili. His shoemaker father died while the future Josef Stalin was still a child. His illiterate mother directed him toward priesthood.

Educated first in the local school at Gori, he entered the theological seminary at Tiflis. There he rebelled against the brutal authority of the seminary's

42

Adolf Hitler, of Germany, above, came to power in a Europe dominated by two other strong men, Benito Mussolini, upper right, and Josef Stalin, right

regime and against the religious ideas it embodied. In 1899, by now a member of the Russian Socialist Revolution party, he was expelled.

For the next 18 years he was an underground revolutionary. In 1902 he was arrested. Between that time and 1917 he escaped and was recaptured four times. When in 1903 the party split into factions of Bolsheviks and Mensheviks, he followed Nikolai Lenin and the Bolsheviks. The authorities rejected him for military service on medical grounds. When the Czar fell in 1917 and the prisons opened, he returned in triumph from his exile in Siberia.

From that time he rose rapidly. When Lenin died in 1924, Stalin began to remove his rivals. By 1929 he had become undisputed master of Russia. At the beginning of 1931 he began with utter ruthlessness to transform Russia from a backward agricultural state to an industrial power. Forcibly shifting 25 million peasants from rural areas to the industrial centers he turned them into factory workers by means of intensive training and harsh industrial discipline.

This was the situation when the London World Economic Conference opened June 12, 1933, attended by representatives of 64 nations.

Most of the nations of Europe had left the gold standard. Holland, Belgium, Italy and Switzerland had not. These four nations wanted the conference to stabilize the gold value of currencies. Great Britain had depreciated its pound sterling in 1931; now it proposed to stabilize it at 1933 levels advantageous to her.

Roosevelt felt this movement was inimical to the interest of the United States. Contrary to the pound sterling, the gold content of the dollar was unchanged. If the dollar were fixed at the existing ratio to European currencies, he would find it difficult to raise domestic prices, which he regarded as necessary for the economic recovery of the nation.

At Campbobello, June 29, Roosevelt received a compromise proposal that its originators expected him to accept. The compromise endorsed the principle of stabilization but did not bind countries not then on the gold standard to work for stabilization immediately.

July 3, Roosevelt sent the Conference a message that chastised it for considering stabilization ahead of "larger purposes", and asserting that "the sound internal economic system of a Nation is a greater factor in its well-being than the price of its currency."

Other matters, including the reduction of tariffs, were on the Conference agenda, but the British and French negotiators considered agreement on currency stabilization of primary importance. The delegates to the Conference were so shocked by the Roosevelt message that only the skill of Cordell Hull, the American delegate, kept the Conference from immediate collapse.

Negotiations continued, but the message of Roosevelt obviated any good result coming from them. The Conference ended in failure.

Currencies were unstabilized and tariffs were unlowered. A currency war followed the conference with more tariffs and intensified international competition. There came a recrudescence of rampant nationalism. Great Britain initiated a "Buy British" campaign.

Roosevelt had inadvertently helped the world up to step two of the staircase leading to global war.

The evil effects of the recrudescent nationalism can easily be read in the nascent power of Germany manipulated by the demonic genius of Hitler. Oct. 14, 1933, Germany withdrew from the League of Nations.

Hitler's first move to enlarge the borders of Germany was moderate and lawful and directed at the Saarland, which before the World War had been divided between Prussia and Bavaria. The Treaty of Versailles assigned its coal mines to France and placed the 991 square mile territory, between France and Germany, under the administration of the League of Nations. In a plebiscite held March 1, 1935 the residents responded to the blandishments of the Nazis by voting to return the Saar to Germany.

Japan by its actions in Manchuria had demonstrated the impotence of the League and Hitler and Mussolini had learned from the example. March 16, 1935 Hitler publicly tore up the Versailles Treaty, under which Germany had been disarmed, and reintroduced compulsory military conscription. Oct. 3, 1935, Mussolini, avid for military glory and in search of Empire, sent his troops into Ethiopia, taking the world another step up the staircase to global conflict.

No doubt encouraged by the spectacle of the League being unable to curb Mussolini, Hitler looked to the Rhineland as the next means of expanding his frontiers. The Rhineland had been established on the left bank of the Rhine as a demilitarized zone by Articles 42, 43 and 44 of the Treaty of Versailles. The prohibition was further strengthened by the Treaty of Locarno of 1925, freely negotiated by both sides, in which the signatory Powers, including Germany, guaranteed individually and collectively the permanence of the frontiers of Germany and Belgium and of Germany and France. Article 2 of the Treaty of Locarno promised that Germany, Belgium and France would never invade or attack across these frontiers.

Yet on March 7, 1936 columns of German troops, 35,000 strong, streamed across the boundary of the Rhineland and occupied all the main ethnically German towns. Hitler had found a subterfuge for his action in the Franco-Soviet five-year treaty of mutual guarantee of May 2, 1935. He declared the treaty to be a violation of the Locarno agreement. While the French Senate was still debating ratification of the treaty, Hitler, March 7, repudiated the Rhineland clauses of Versailles and Locarno and announced that German troops had entered the demilitarized zone.

France, with the greatest army in Europe, was pledged to drive the Germans out but declined the risk. The risk was far more slight than the French and their allies calculated. Knowing his puny force was no match for the French, Hitler had ordered it to withdraw if confronted with force.

Hitler's bluff had succeeded. His belief in himself and his contempt for his opponents grew. He set about militarizing his new territory. He had led the world up step four of the staircase to global war.

The Spanish Civil War, which began July 18, 1936, brought the holocaust nearer by another step. Now partners, Hitler and Mussolini sided with the Fascist rebel Francisco Franco and used the war as a training ground for their weapons and troops.

Hitler built himself a villa on a mountain top at Berchtesgaden, 10 miles south of Salzburg in the Bavarian Alps. Known as Berghof (Eagle's nest) this hideout was reached over ten miles of hairpin road cut into the mountainside, leading to a long underground passageway drilled through the rock from which an elevator carried visitors 370 feet to an elevation over 6,000 feet from where the window presented a breath-taking view of the panorama of the Alps and giving the viewer a feeling of being suspended in space.

The French Ambassador Andre Francois-Poncet who visited the Berghof later wondered "was this edifice the work of a normal mind or of one tormented by megalomania and haunted by visions of domination and solitude?"

At the Berghof Oct. 25, 1936 Mussolini signed a pact with Hitler aligning the policies of Germany and

Italy. Mussolini returned to Italy to report the significance of the new alliance. In a speech at Milan November 1, he said "...this vertical line between Rome and Berlin is not a partition but rather an axis round which all European states animated by the will to collaboration and peace can also collaborate.

He thereby bequeathed a name to the Fascist nations, who thereafter became known in the world press as the Axis.

Nov. 23, 1936 Hitler took his first overt move towards including Japan in his scheme of conquest when he inveigled Japan into signing an Anti-Comintern pact against the spread of Communism. The Comintern, against which the pact was directed, also known as the Third International and as the Communist International, was an ultraradical and Communist organization founded in Moscow for the purpose of uniting Communist groups of various countries. It was said to advocate the attainment of its ends through violent revolution

The Anti-Comintern Pact committed Germany and Japan to exchange information on Communist activities and to collaborate closely on preventive measures. A secret supplementary protocol identified the Soviet Union as the common enemy of the signatories. The signatories also secretly agreed not to conclude with the Soviet Union, without mutual consent, political treaties opposed to the spirit of the pact.

Italy would join the pact in 1937; Hungary, Spain and Manchukuo in 1939. In 1941 the five-year pact would be renewed for another five years.

Alarmed by the coalition of Fascist nations, known as the Axis or Have Nots, who had become more and more hostile and threatening toward the Democracies, known as the Haves, Roosevelt, Jan. 11, 1938, through the British ambassador in Washington, approached British Prime Minister Neville Chamberlain with a proposal to ease the situation. The President would take the initiative in securing peace by inviting the representatives of certain nations to Washington to discuss their differences. He pledged that only if the suggestion met with "the cordial approval and wholehearted support of" the British government would he then approach the governments of France, Germany and Italy.

Son of a prominent British statesman, and born at Edgbaston, Birmingham March 18, 1869, Chamberlain had been educated for a business career. After graduating from Mason College, Birmingham, he had gone to Andros Island in the Bahamas where for seven lonely years he strove unsuccessfully to prosper his father's sisal plantation. Then he returned to Birmingham and entered business.

In his 50th year he entered Parliament. He held cabinet posts and on May 28, 1937 he succeeded Stanley Baldwin as Prime Minister. In office, he took what, for a Prime Minister, was an unusually large and personal part in diplomatic negotiations. He sought to detach Italy from Germany and to appease Hitler, a policy most of his countrymen supported at that time.

Accordingly, Chamberlain, Jan. 22, 1938, formally rebuffed the proposal of Roosevelt: Roosevelt might find it worth considering whether the proposal might cut across British efforts.

Since the British were contemplating direct negotiations with the Axis, Roosevelt agreed to postpone acting on his proposal. But in his reply to the rebuff, he added that he was concerned that the British suggestion to accord recognition to the Italian position in Ethiopia, which Mussolini had fully subjugated, would not only be regarded unfavorably in America but would further encourage the militarist policy of Japan in the Far East.

The reply inspired Chamberlain to send two more

messages. Chamberlain was unable to unqualifiedly accept Roosevelt's suggested procedure; to do so would not only irritate the European dictators but Japan as well.

Despite the soothing tones of Chamberlain, Hitler went his way. March 13, 1938, Hitler forcibly annexed Austria to the German Reich. By doing so he changed the map of Europe so that it now portrayed Germany as a wolf with gaping maw about to bite off half of Czechoslovakia.

The Sudetenland portion of Czechoslovakia,. totalling 8,719 square miles and ringing the eastern borders, contained many ethnic Germans. To dismember this portion of Czechoslovakia to add to the German Reich, Hitler threatened war. Among the objections of the Czechs to parting with this portion of their country was that the region encompassed the nations natural defenses as well as housing arms and munitions factories.

Hitler's generals were appalled at the prospect of going to war in such a situation. Czechoslovakia had a first-class army of a million men. France was bound by treaty to assist her if she were attacked. If the French marched, the Franco-British agreement required Great Britain to march with her.

The proposed attack on Czechoslovakia seemed so fraught with peril that Hitler's generals sought to dissuade him. He would have none of their objections.

Hoping to avert war, Chamberlain flew to Europe and conferred with Hitler at the Berghof Sept. 15, 1938, at Godesberg, Sept. 22, 1938 and at Munich where Edouard Daladier, Premier of France joined with Chamberlain and Mussolini joined with Hitler. The Czechs were excluded.

Hitler insisted that his demand for the Sudetenland was his last territorial claim in Europe. By Sept. 29, 1938 the Allies had capitulated, providing for German occupation of the Sudetenland between October 1 – 10.

The Allies told the Czechs that if they chose to fight they must fight alone. France and Great Britain would guarantee the new frontiers.

France had guaranteed the last frontiers, which had been incomparably easier to defend. Of what value was a French guarantee now!

Czechoslovakia's neighbors quickly manifested their contempt for such guarantees. As the Czech government staggered, her neighbors attacked like ravening wolves. Bulgaria and Poland demanded the same rights for their minorities in Czechoslovakia as the Czechs had conceded to the Germans. The Poles demanded that the Czechs evacuate Teschen, an area of about 419 square miles on the West bank of the Olsa River. The Czechs had to yield.

Hitler made his triumphal entry into the Sudetenland October 3. Eduard Benes resigned as President of Czechoslovakia. Hungarian troops invaded Czech border towns.

France and Great Britain stood by while Hungary annexed the Slovakian territory and Poland annexed Teschen of the now defenseless nation. Unmindful of his pledge that he had no more territorial demands in Europe, Hitler, March 15, 1939, made a triumphal entry into Prague, the capital of Czechoslovakia. The following day he made the Bohemia-Moravia section a German protectorate

March 22, 1939 he caused Lithuania to cede to Germany Memel, a long strip of land along the right bank of the river Niemen on the frontier of Prussia, comprising about 976 square miles and a population of 150,000, among which the German-speaking residents predominated.

Seven days later the Spanish Civil War ended with the Fascist rebels triumphant. With the backing of France, Great Britain now offered guarantees to Poland, Greece, Turkey and Rumania.

After the signing of the Munich agreement, Chamberlain had returned to London waving a sheet of

Flourishing the document he believes to symbolize "peace in our time", British Prime Minister Neville Chamberlain, above, returns from his negotiations with the Axis dictators. Winston Churchill, below, excoriated the Chamberlain agreement with the Axis as "a total and unmitigated defeat."

paper signed by both him and Hitler in which they agreed that consultation would be the method concerning differences between Great Britain and Germany.

Facing a large crowd that had pressed into Downing Street, Chamberlain, from a second-story window of the Prime Minister's residence, said:

"My good friends, this is the second time in our history that there has come back from Germany to Downing Street peace with honor. (He referred to Disraeli's return from the Congress of Berlin in 1878). He flourished the paper. "I believe it is peace in our time."

Roosevelt had not been fooled. He had recognized the Munich Pact as a step up the staircase to war.

April 15, 1939, Roosevelt sent identical notes to Hitler and Mussolini asking their assurance that neither would invade 31 independent nations of Europe and Asia for at least ten years. Mussolini dismissed the request as an absurd proposal based on "pyramidal errors of geography."

April 17 Mussolini invaded Albania.

Hitler felt that the request rendered Roosevelt vulnerable. It had: since Hitler had broken his word so many times, what point was there in asking him for another assurance!

Hitler delayed his reply so as to include it in his address to the Reichstag, scheduled for April 28. In the meantime he worked on his address, one of the longest he was ever to make, and that would require more than two hours to deliver.

When he made the address, he heaped ridicule on Roosevelt, naming one by one the countries for which Roosevelt had asked assurance against invasion, but slyly avoiding mention of Poland.

He ended with an implied comparison of Roosevelt's failure to end unemployment in America with Hitler's success in Germany.

> I once took over a State which was faced by complete ruin, thanks to the trust in the promises of the rest of the world and to the bad regime of democratic governments...I have conquered chaos in Germany, re-established order and enormously increased production...developed traffic, caused mighty roads to be built and canals to be dug, called into being gigantic new factories and at the same time endeavored to further the education and culture of our people.
>
> I have succeeded in finding useful work once more for the whole of the seven million unemployed...Not only have I united the German people politically, but I have also rearmed them. I have also endeavored to destroy sheet by sheet that treaty which in its four hundred and 48 articles contains the vilest oppression which peoples and human beings have ever been expected to put up with.
>
> I have brought back to the Reich provinces stolen from us in 1919. I have led back to their native country millions of Germans who were torn away from us and were in misery...and, Mr. Roosevelt, without spilling blood and without bringing my people, and consequently to others, the misery of war...

Recognizing the need for Soviet neutrality for the success of his military plan against Poland, Hitler had his foreign minister, Joachim Von Ribbentrop, negotiate a non-aggression pact. The pact was signed in Moscow Aug. 23, 1939. Hitler paid the heavy price required: recognition of the Soviet sphere of influence extending to Finland, Estonia and Latvia and the Soviet right to annex eastern Poland and Bessarabia. In return for such concessions, Germany was to gain a steady supply of vital strategic minerals and foodstuffs in exchange for deliveries of industrial equipment and machinery. A secret protocol provided for the partitioning of Eastern Europe.

Except that it would alienate Japan by violating its treaty with her, the treaty with Russia scored as a brilliant diplomatic coup for Germany. Great Britain and France tried to counter with a formal alliance with Poland, March 31, involving automatic intervention by either country in case of aggression by any other.

At 4:45 a.m. September 1, 1939, without a formal declaration of war, the German army crossed the Polish frontier at several points, with 53 divisions under command of Gen. Walther von Brauchitsch. The German troops overwhelmed the Polish defenses in a few hours. German tanks penetrated deeply into Polish territory.

Simultaneously the Germans bombed several Polish cities, including Warsaw, Lodz and Krakow. In the port of Danzig, the control of which was the German manufactured cause of the dispute, the German training ship *Schleswig-Holsteinan* armored cruiser, opened a murderous fire on the fragile defenses of the Westernplatte, where the Polish navy's arsenal was situated.

Hitler annexed Danzig to the Reich, though the official act would be delayed.

The German air force destroyed most of the Polish air force on the ground. The Germans advanced with such speed they bequeathed a descriptive term to modern warfare – *blitzkrieg* – lightning war.

Now having permitted Hitler to rearm Germany and to gain by bluff what they could have prevented with a show of force, having given away their defenses with

Czechoslovakia, so that Hitler no longer needed to bluff, Great Britain and France took up arms on behalf of Poland who had followed the lead of Hitler in grabbing a slice of Czechoslovakia.

September 3 Great Britain, France, Australia and New Zealand declared war on Germany. South Africa followed suit the next day, Canada September 9.

Even before declaring war, Chamberlain approached Winston Churchill to become a member of the British Cabinet. At this point it is appropriate to say something about this man who was destined to play a star performance in the unfolding drama.

Winston was the son of Jeannette Jerome, an American beauty, through her marriage to Lord Randolph Henry Spencer Churchill, the third son of John, 7th duke of Marlborough. Randolph served as chancellor of the exchequer and leader of the House of Commons in 1886. His son Winston was born to him Nov. 30, 1874 at Blenheim palace in Oxfordshire.

In recognition of his brilliant exploit in routing the French and Bavarians at Blenheim on the Danube in West Germany Aug. 13, 1704, the grateful British nation had given Blenheim to John Churchill, the first Duke of Marlborough.

In early youth, Winston seemed so unpromising that his father determined on a military career for him. Winston entered the Royal Military college, Sandhurst, where he applied himself and graduated 8th in a class of 150. The following year he entered the 4th hussars but took leave to report the Cuban War of Independence for the *Daily Graphic*, (London). Thereafter he pursued a joint career as soldier and journalist.

His dispatches attracted such wide attention that five years after leaving Sandhurst he entered politics. He lost the election and went to report the South African War, also known as the Anglo-Boer War, for the

Morning Post (London).

In South Africa he won fame for helping to rescue an ambushed armored train and for escaping from a Boer prison. He returned to England where he was elected to Parliament. He laid the foundation of private income by earning 10,000 pounds on lecture tours in Great Britain and the United States.

In 1908 he entered the Cabinet as president of the Board of Trade. In 1911 he became First Lord of the Admiralty – a position analogous to the U.S. Secretary of the Navy. Though he did an excellent job of preparing the Navy for the World War that erupted in 1914, it was in this position that he suffered a check to his hitherto meteoric career.

The circumstance that was to lead to his discreditation began in January 1915 when Great Britain's ally, Russia, appealed to Great Britain for urgent diversionary activity against Turkish naval bombardments and land attacks. Churchill backed a plan to capture Istanbul and join Russia through an offensive from the east. For by command of the Dardanelles waterway, which linked the Black Sea with the Mediterranean, Turkey was able to prevent the Allies from joining forces. The British hoped that the capture of Constantinople would bring the then neutral nations of Italy, Rumania, Bulgaria and Greece into the war on the side of the Allies.

The plan was bungled and failed. Each side lost about 250,000 men. Churchill was held largely responsible for the failure; he was demoted from the Admiralty.

In November 1915 he resigned from the government and returned to soldiering. He returned to politics in June 1916.

In periods when he was out of office or out of power he found solace in painting and writing. In the years 1922–24 he completed a war history, which was also an autobiography, in six volumes, *The World Crisis*. The history netted him 20,000 pounds with which he purchased Chartwell, his country home in Kent.

Though he remained in Commons from 1931, he was excluded from the Cabinet and thus from the source of power. Both major parties thought him lacking in judgment and distrusted him. He applied himself to writing. Among other important literary achievements he wrote *Marlborough: His Life and Times*, in four volumes. He had begun it as a refutation of the criticisms of his great ancestor in the *History of England*, by Thomas Babington Macauley.

During the period when he was engaged on the Marlborough history he was also concerned about the growing menace of Nazi Germany. Before a supine government and skeptical opposition, supported only by a small personal following, he argued the seriousness of the German threat and the need to prevent the Luftwaffe from gaining parity with the Royal Air Force.

When Stanley Baldwin became Prime Minister in 1935, he continued the policy of excluding Churchill from Cabinet office, but he offered him membership on the secret committee on air defense research. In this position Churchill was able to work on some vital national problems.

When Neville Chamberlain succeeded Baldwin, the gulf between Churchill and those in power widened. Chamberlain advocated appeasement; Churchill militant preparedness.

When Chamberlain returned from Munich waving his sheet of paper and declaring it meant "peace in our time," Churchill went before Commons and excoriated the agreement.

"We have sustained a total and unmitigated defeat," cried Churchill.

Events had now proved him to have been correct. It fell to Chamberlain to acknowledge he had led his country down a grievously wrong path.

At 11:15 A.M., September 3, Chamberlain, in an address to the German people, summarized his reasons for finally leading his people into war. He said of Hitler:

> He gave his word that he would respect the Locarno Treaty; he broke it. He gave his word that he neither wished nor intended to annex Austria; he broke it. He declared he would not incorporate the Czechs into the Reich; he did so. He gave his word after Munich that he had no further territorial demands in Europe; he broke it. He has sworn to you for years that he was the mortal enemy of Bolshevism; he is now its ally. Can you wonder that his word is, for us, not worth the paper it is written on?

After concluding his address, Chamberlain met with Churchill and, in addition to membership in the War Cabinet, offered him the same post he had held at the outbreak of the World War — First Lord of the Admiralty. Churchill accepted.

September 11, Roosevelt dispatched a message to the First Lord of the Admiralty:

> My dear Churchill:
> It is because you and I occupied similar positions in the World War that I want you to know how glad I am that you are back again in the Admiralty. Your problems are, I realize, complicated by new factors but the essential is not very different. What I want you and the Prime Minister to know is that I shall at

all times welcome it if you will keep me in
touch personally with anything you want me to
know about.   You can always send sealed
letters through your pouch or my pouch.
      I am glad you did the Marlboro volumes
before this thing started – and I much enjoyed
reading them.

Thus began a long and fruitful correspondence that
was to have historic consequences.

Churchill was now operating in the same room he had
left a quarter century before, sitting in the same chair
and devoting all his energies, as he put it, to cope
with the "might and fury of the valiant, disciplined and
ruthless German race."

The German juggernaut had swiftly made its way
through Poland.   September 17 the Russians invaded
Poland from the farther border to claim their share of
the spoils. On the 18th the Polish government fled to
London. On the 20th the Polish army surrendered.

Russia demanded that Finland cede several forward
posts on Finnish territory to the U.S.S.R.   Finland
declined. November 30, 1939 Russia attacked at various
points on the Russo-Finnish frontier. The conflict
would end in Russian victory in February of the
following year.

In central Europe a breathing spell followed the
German conquest of Poland.   Though Germany and the
Allies were technically at war there was so little
conflict the situation became known as the Phony War,
Twilight War and *Sitzkreig* (sitting war).

The quiescence could be attributed to the French
commitment to defensive warfare symbolized in her
Maginot line facing Germany and thought by many to be
impregnable. Named for Andre Maginot, a French Minister
of War, this line of concrete and steel fortifications

stretched from Luxembourg to Switzerland along the
French border with Germany.   Though the Germans might
circumvent the defense by advancing through Belgium as
they had in 1914, and though the Allies feared the
execution of this strategy, the fortifications were
discontinued along the Franco-Belgian frontier.   This
neglect sprang from the Belgian objection that extending
it would consign Belgium to Germany in the event of war,
because a group of French strategists held that the
Germans could not penetrate the Ardennes, the wooded
plateau covering most of the Belgian province of
Luxembourg, part of the Grand Duchy of Luxembourg and
occupying the Meuse valley in the French department of
Ardennes.

Inside the Maginot line, equipped with heavy
artillery enclosed in bombproof casements, the French
awaited the expected German attack while restricting
their own operations to occasional patrols and probing
and intelligence missions.

The Germans were inactive because the bulk of the
Army had been deployed in Poland; the Germans had only
23 divisions to fight the 100 of the French.
Redeploying and refitting the German army took time.
But by spring the Germans were ready for action; April
9, 1940 they invaded Denmark and Norway.

May 10, 1940 the German army penetrated the assumed
impenetrable Ardennes area and rolled through Belgium,
Netherlands and Luxembourg. At this point, the British,
already persuaded of the folly of Chamberlain's
appeasement of Hitler and dissatisfied with the conduct
of the war, pressured him into resigning.

May 10, 1940, Churchill replaced him as Prime
Minister.

Roosevelt had recoiled from the brutal excesses of
the Nazi regime. There had been the purge of June 30 to
July 2, 1934 when Hitler had murdered 200 persons, many

of them innocent of even opposing him, as he sought to
eliminate the opposition led by Ernst Rohm. There were
the Nuremberg laws adopted Sept. 15, 1935 that sharply
limited citizenship for Jews and, according to the
irrational Nazi definition, persons alleged to be Jews,
and that restricted relations between Jews and alleged
Jews with the mythical Aryans. There had been the
campaign of terror the Nazis had launched against the
Jews and alleged Jews Nov. 9 - 10, 1938, known as
Crystal Night because of the shattered glass (valued at
six million marks) resulting from unbridled window
smashing.

On Crystal Night the Nazis plundered 267
synagogues, wrecked 815 shops and arrested 20,000
persons.

Roosevelt had been responding to the world drift
toward general war in accordance with his preconceived
biases, but well aware, as a master politician, that his
views were unshared by many of his countrymen. Though
most Americans disapproved of the saber-rattling of
Germany, Italy and Japan their disapproval stopped short
of encouraging a situation that might involve America in
another foreign war. They tended to think in terms of
former wars where the Atlantic and Pacific Oceans
safeguarded America. They were unable to recognize that
a situation might occur in Europe that might put America
in reach of enemy planes. Unlike Roosevelt, they
disregarded the agents of Hitler already in South
America preparing the site for the time when Hitler's
plan for world conquest might enable him to turn on a
United States stripped of all allies.

Among the unpersuaded were militants who came to be
known as isolationists. For the most part these were
American nationalists who felt it to be to the advantage
of the nation to disassociate itself from foreign
entanglements. The internationally inclined Roosevelt

accordingly moved cautiously in regard to European and Asian affairs lest he alienate those Americans who feared involvement in foreign quarrels.

Though he had undermined the World Economic Conference during his first term in office, after January 1934 he had the Treasury Department work toward the relative stabilization of the dollar in relation to the British pound and French franc. In November 1933, in the vain hope of stimulating trade, he had broken with national policy followed since 1917 and recognized the Soviet Union. In the next five years Cordell Hull tried to beat down the barriers to international trade by negotiating agreements with 21 nations and lowering the tariff approximately 20 percent in return for concessions to U.S. exporters.

Fear of impending war led Congress, with the approval of Hull and Roosevelt, to enact a series of neutrality laws intended to keep America out of the conflict. When in response to the arms race going on in the rest of the world Roosevelt began strengthening American defenses, the isolationists gave small opposition as long as he restricted his rearmament to the Western Hemisphere.

When Japan refused to renew the naval limitation treaties that expired Dec. 31, 1936, Roosevelt persuaded Congress to authorize the construction of two 35,000-ton battleships. When war broke out between Japan and China July 7, 1937, he forbade government-owned ships to transport arms and munitions to China and Japan and warned that other American ships did so at their own risk.

When Germany tumultuously welcomed Mussolini on his visit in late September 1937 it seemed clear to Roosevelt that the Axis nations were growing closer in common cause. Oct. 5, 1937, in Chicago, Roosevelt made what was to become known as his Quarantine Speech. He said:

> Innocent peoples, innocent nations, are being cruelly sacrificed to a greed for power and supremacy which is devoid of all sense of justice and humane considerations...If those things come to pass in other parts of the world, let no one imagine that America will escape, that America may expect mercy, that the Western Hemisphere will not be attacked and that it will continue tranquilly and peacefully to carry on the ethics and arts of civilization...There must be a return to a belief in the pledged word, in the value of a signed treaty.
>
> It seems to be unfortunately true that the epidemic of world lawlessness is spreading.
>
> When an epidemic of physical disease starts to spread, the community approves and joins in a quarantine of the patients in order to protect the health of the community against the spread of the disease...

The speech showed an alteration in his course from advocacy of nonintervention to a plea for collective action. The peace-loving nations, he said, must make a concerted effort against the growing international anarchy "from which there is no escape through mere isolation or neutrality."

If he had hoped for public endorsement of his changed policy, he must have been disappointed. The isolationist press charged him with "warmongering." Liberals and conservatives alike were alarmed by the belligerence he had expressed. Only the confirmed interventionists seemed cheered by his words.

Appalled that he had let himself get so far ahead of public opinion, he backed off from the furor he had created. He said he had made no moves. "We are looking for some way to peace," but the speech represented an attitude not a program. He was searching for a program.

Behind his speech there had been more than a search for public attitude. He wished to encourage those already resisting aggressors. He hoped he might awaken a will for united action among the frightened and mesmerized peoples of Europe.

To reorient American neutrality in anticipation of another conflict in Europe, Congress had enacted Neutrality Acts in 1935, 1936 and 1937. Roosevelt had come round to thinking that these acts operated in favor of the Fascist nations he opposed and were a danger to the security of America. Within three months after Munich he switched his political strategy, with its emphasis on domestic reforms, to one of achievement of a foreign policy of collective security.

In a note approved by the President, Hull, April 8, 1939, denounced the Italian invasion of Albania as a "threat to the peace of the world." In a press conference April 11, the President implied that if a general war broke out the United States would become involved.

When war had broken out in Europe in 1914, President Wilson had urged his country to be "neutral in fact as well as in name...impartial in thought as well as in action." Roosevelt took a different position.

When Germany invaded Poland, Roosevelt took to the air waves for one of his communications referred to as "fireside chats", in which he pledged that America would remain neutral. Nevertheless, he added: "but I cannot ask that every American remain neutral in thought as well. Even a neutral cannot be asked to close his mind or conscience."

He had come to realize that the Neutrality Act of 1937 favored the attacker over the attacked. The statute permitted all countries to purchase arms in time of peace, but proscribed their sale once war had broken out. After Munich both France and Great Britain, anticipating hostilities, had placed large orders for airplanes and other material. Now that war had broken out, the delivery of these orders was supposed to be prohibited.

Roosevelt felt the prohibition was contrary to the national interest. Having given lip service to neutrality, he thereafter applied himself with zeal and great skill to aiding the beleaguered democracies against the Axis.

Sept. 8, 1939 he proclaimed a limited national emergency. In November 1939, after the outbreak of war in Europe, he secured a relaxation of the law in order to permit belligerents – actually France and Great Britain – to obtain arms from the United States on a cash and carry basis. He denounced the invasion of Denmark and Norway.

He asked Congress for $1,182 million for defense. He announced that the Army and Navy should be equipped with 50,000 planes. He ordered the recommissioning of 34 more of the destroyers that had been laid up since the World War. Then he asked Congress to authorize the creation of a naval air force of 10,000 planes and 15,000 pilots. May 31 he asked for another billion for defense.

At least Mussolini was unintimidated by these bellicose moves. June 10, 1940, when he found the Allies staggering under the German onslaught on France, he declared war on France and Great Britain.

Referring to this act of Mussolini, Roosevelt, speaking at the University of Virginia, said, "The hand that held the dagger has plunged it into the back of its neighbor."

Yet though he recognized the situation in Europe as the major threat to America, the President was also concerned about events in the Far East. There the Japanese militarists with unbridled ambition and utter ruthlessness were seeking to reshape the world into a form more acceptable to Japanese concepts and less acceptable to the views of Roosevelt.

Secretary of State Henry L. Stimson, above, left, appointed Joseph Clark Grew Ambassador to Japan.

Shown with wife, Grew was predisposed to like his assignment, but he embarked on his duties in a period of particular stress.

3

JAPAN – POWDER KEG OF THE ORIENT

The embassy in Tōkyō of American Ambassador Joseph Clark Grew had begun June 6, 1932. It had been a troublesome period with the civilian leadership of Japan of the preceding decade nearly eclipsed, the influence of the militarist extremists ascending and anti-American sentiment rife.

In America anti-Japanese sentiment was equally strong. As Grew was to write later:

> **Whatever may have been the merits of the case for Japan and of the incentive which led to the seizure of Manchuria, the methods adopted to achieve her ends placed her, legally and logically, out of Court so far as the United States was concerned...**

At what were supposed to be welcoming functions for the new American ambassador, his hosts expressed their views and feeling on the subject of the alleged American arrogance and obtrusion into Far East affairs, sometimes in highly discourteous terms.

Birth and training had fitted Grew to cope with this difficult situation. Born in Boston May 27, 1880 of a patrician banking family, Grew, like Roosevelt, had attended Groton and Harvard. He had graduated from Harvard in 1902, two years ahead of Roosevelt.

Grew then began a world tour, spending most of his time in the Far East. In a published account of his travels, *Sport and Travel in the Far East*, he recounted an incident involving a tiger that attracted the attention of the then President Theodore Roosevelt. The President's interest resulted in his finding a clerk position for Grew in the consulate in Cairo. From this position, Grew soon advanced to become deputy consul general.

During the next several years he served in a number of consulates in Mexico as well as in St. Petersburg, Vienna and Berlin.

In 1918 he returned to Washington as chief of the State Department Division of Western European Affairs. The following year he attended the Versailles Peace Conference. After a series of diplomatic assignments of increasing responsibility, he became, in 1924, undersecretary of state. In 1927 he became ambassador to Turkey.

In 1932, Stimson, then Secretary of State, appointed Grew ambassador to Japan, which he had last visited in 1902.

Grew was predisposed to like his new assignment. His wife had been brought up in Japan and spoke the language. Further, as the granddaughter of Commodore Matthew Calbraith Perry, a towering figure in Japanese-American relations, she conferred prestige on her ambassador husband.

In 1853, President Millard Fillmore had sent Perry to Japan to persuade that nation to open its ports to American ships. The mission was delicate and difficult. Japan had closed its borders to the world in 1640 and henceforth resolutely prohibited entry to foreigners.

Behind Perry's mission was the accumulated resentment at the mistreatment of shipwrecked Americans cast up on Japanese shores and of the rebuffs and

insults that Japan had inflicted on American civilians
and naval officials who had called at Japanese ports.
There was also the pressure of American transcontinental
expansion, American interest in the present and future
market of China and the potential market of Japan. And
the recent application of steam to ocean-going vessels
made necessary coaling stations to service them

Japan's first known contact with the West had
occurred about 1542 when a storm drove a Portuguese
vessel to the island of Tanegashima off the southern
extremity of Kyūshū. The Portuguese introduced
firearms.

The situation was particularly favorable for the
reception of these weapons; the nation was embroiled in
internecine warfare. Warlords vied with each other to
maintain their domains, or to enlarge them with the
hope, among the more powerful, of unifying and ruling
the country.

Jesuit missionaries followed the first Portuguese
traders. With zeal and tact they converted members of
the ruling class. By 1595 there were 137 Jesuits in
Japan and 300,000 converts.

In the meantime, other Europeans had encroached on
the original Portuguese-Jesuit monopoly. Spanish
Franciscans entered the country where they pursued their
own brand of proselyting. Quarrels between the two
factions ensued. Hating both Portuguese and Spaniards,
Protestant Dutch discredited the Catholics.

The country became unified after 100 years of civil
war; the rulers began to think of the Europeans, and
particularly the Catholic Europeans, as a political
threat. In 1565, 1568 and 1587 they issued anti-
Christian decrees. In 1640 they closed Japan to all
Europeans except a handful of Dutch who were permitted
to trade, under strict supervision, from the artificial
island of Deshima in Nagasaki Bay.

After receiving his assignment, Perry studied the situation from such accounts as were available to him. In November 1852, determined to demand of Japan "as a right, and not to solicit as a favor, those acts of courtesy which are due from one civilized country to another," he sailed in command of a squadron.

He arrived in the bay of Edo (now Tōkyō) in July 1853. Threatening to land a force if necessary, he demanded an interview with the highest possible official in order to deliver the President's letter.

Recognizing their inability to resist Western arms, the Japanese reluctantly acceded to his request. Promising to return for the reply, Perry left.

He returned in February 1845, distributed gifts and accepted a treaty, signed March 31, 1845, which provided for fueling and supply privileges at two Japanese ports and for hospitable treatment of shipwrecked sailors.

Other Western nations quickly insisted upon rights equal to those granted America. Japan was powerless to deny them.

Perry had mistakenly believed he was dealing with the Emperor. But at that time the Emperor, shorn of secular power, was residing in Kyotō. The country was ruled by the same Tokugawa family that had issued the 1640 order for expulsion and prohibition of entry to foreigners.

Over two-and-a-half centuries, the rule of the Tokugawa had decayed. Its inability to repel the American squadron dramatized its weakness.

The disaffected began a movement to restore the Emperor. The insurgents ousted the Tokugawa and handed the reins of government to the Emperor.

The Emperor, who would become known to history as Meiji, moved from Kyotō to Edo. Surrounding himself with intelligent, progressive advisers he quickly modernized the country. As we have seen, within less than a century after opening her doors to the West, Japan had emerged as a world power.

Events and short-sighted Western statesmanship had meantime so estranged Japan that she was turning away from the nations that had first been her mentors. She had modelled her modern Navy on the British and had forged an alliance with Great Britain from which both nations had benefited. At the Washington Naval Conference in 1922 America pressured Great Britain into abrogating the alliance. Japan interpreted the abrogation as a spurn from the Western powers.

The Conference allotted an inferior naval ratio in capital ships to Japan by the formula of 5,5,3, the first two figures being the allocations for the United States and Great Britain and the third for Japan. It can be argued that this ratio worked for the benefit of Japan as having spared her a naval armament race while leaving her with sufficient forces with which to defend herself.

Some Japanese concurred in this view, conceding that Great Britain had several oceans to guard, America two and Japan only one. Many Japanese rejected the argument, perceiving the disproportionate ratio as a humiliating discrimination.

On some other matters even the most liberal of the Japanese could hardly deny the discrimination against Japan. Most nations of the New World accepted European immigrants. But Canada, Australia and New Zealand made plain they accepted only white immigrants.

There had been a time when America had encouraged immigration, but only from Europe or for the importation of black slaves from Africa. Since Perry had knocked on its doors, Japan's population had doubled. Now though the United States had a population density of only 31 persons per square mile compared to Japan's 400, anti-immigration fever had seized the United States.

The United States had long barred the Chinese from immigrating. In 1924 a bill was introduced in Congress that would set quotas on immigration based on the number of any nationality already in the United States. Under the quota system Japan would be allowed no more than 150 immigrants in any one year. Some of the sponsors then inserted a clause excluding "Asiatics" from any quota whatever. Since the Chinese were already barred, the clause was obviously directed at Japan.

At the invitation of Secretary of State Charles Evans Hughes, who opposed the restrictive clause, Japanese Ambassador Masako Hanihara (mä sä' kõ   hä nē hä' lä) wrote him a personal letter outlining the serious effects that the passage of the bill would have on Japanese-American relations. If the Japanese were barred as "undesirables", the bill would result in "serious consequences" to Japanese-American relations.

The letter circulated in the Senate with an explanation of how it came to be written. All went well until isolationist Henry Cabot Lodge, who had been a key figure in sabotaging President Wilson's effort to secure acceptance of the Versailles Treaty and consequent membership in the League of Nations, took umbrage at the phrase "serious consequences."

Did the phrase mean, asked Lodge, that Japan was threatening war. Hanihara denied that it did. Lodge was unappeased.

In a subsequent debate Lodge characterized the Hanihara statement as "interference" in American domestic affairs. The bill, with its gratuitous insult to Japan, passed and was signed into law.

The grave consequences ensued as Hanihara had predicted; the bill discredited America's friends in Japan and credited her foes who regarded American protestations of equality as hypocrisy.

For years there had been anti-Japanese activity on

the West Coast of America with discrimination and even
violence against Japanese nationals and also against
their American-born descendants. To these wrongs America
now added insult.

In the Japanese press appeared a rash of articles
about the divine heritage of the Imperial line,
traditionally ascribed as descendants of the Sun Goddess.
The people must dedicate their lives to the Emperor and
die for him if necessary.

When a school building caught fire, a schoolboy went
to save the Emperor's picture; unable to escape, he died
clutching it. A young Army lieutenant who made a slip of
the tongue while reading an Imperial rescript, apologized
to his men by falling on his sword. Having elevated the
Emperor to the status of a god, the militarists used his
name in attempting to cleanse the government of
corruption.

The rightists harbored vengeance against Prime
Minister Yukuō Hamaguchi (yōo'kōo ō hä mä gōo' chē) for
having the Emperor, over the objections of the Naval
General Staff, sign the treaty that gave Japan an
unfavorable ratio of naval craft.

On his way to attend special Army exercises in
Okayama prefecture, on the morning of Nov. 14, 1930,
Hamaguchi was awaiting his train on the platform of Tōkyō
station when a shot rang out. Hamaguchi sank to the
ground. His bodyguards grappled with the gunman, who was
dressed in kimono.

Hamaguchi was half-carried down the stairs. Six
months later he would die of his wounds.

The assault had occurred when tension was at its
height between Hamaguchi's policy of international
cooperation and that of the "positive" moves advocated by
the military.

The assassin, Tome Sogaya, was a member of a rightist
organization that resented Hamaguchi's approval

of the naval limitation pact.   In the wake of the
shooting, the Hamaguchi cabinet fell.

The worldwide economic depression had hurt Japan
perhaps more than any other nation.   Poor in natural
resources, Japan looks to foreign trade for survival.
The markets of the West shut against her, she had nowhere
to turn for profitable markets except East Asia.
Consequently the public tended to applaud military
adventurism there.

This was the situation when Grew presented his
credentials to the Emperor June 6, 1932.

The reigning Emperor was Hirohito (hē lō hē' tō),
then 30. His grandfather, Meiji (mā'-e jē), had died in
September 1912 when Hirohito was 11. Hirohito's father,
who would become known as Taishō (tī' shō) became
Emperor, a role for which he soon demonstrated he was
unfit.

Taishō was given to fits of eerie laughter and
outbursts of ungovernable rage, tantrums that sometimes
ended in tears. For a few months in 1914 and 1915 he had
been sane and reasonable, but when he arrived back in
Tōkyō after performing his devotions to his ancestors at
the shrines of Ise (ē' sā), he gave evidence that his
sanity was slipping.

He fell off his horse at parades.   He whipped
soldiers he was inspecting;   on one occasion, going to
the opposite extreme, he suddenly embraced a young
officer

His advisers gradually began to withdraw him from
public life. At what was to be his farewell performance,
he was supposed to read a speech to the assembled members
of the Diet. He rolled up the speech and used it as a
telescope to owlishly observe them.

Thereafter he retired to the palace on the beach at
Hayama.   His Empress treated him considerately and
catered to his whims to the last.

So Nov. 3, 1916 a photograph of Hirohito clad in the uniform of a naval captain appeared in the newspapers accompanied by the announcement that he had been installed as Crown Prince and Regent. He was 15 years old, 5-feet six-inches tall and wore thick glasses to ease his myopia.

He was supposed to be the 124th descendant of Jimmu who, according to tradition, had founded the Empire in 660 B.C. In the more sober light of historical perspective he was the head of an ancient and distinguished family.

He had already acquired his hobby of marine biology. At 20 he embarked on a grand tour of Europe. He returned with the memory of his stay in England as the happiest period of his life. He was to be married in 1923, but the Great Kantō (kän' tō) earthquake of September 1 that year caused postponement of the royal nuptials.

When the residents were cooking the midday meal on open stoves, the earthquake toppled the tinder-dry flimsy houses. Fire broke out. Gas mains broke and the escaping gas ignited. Oil tanks spilled rivers of gasoline into streets where they burst into flames.

Days later when the fires were brought under control, three-quarters of Tōkyō and four-fifths of Yokohama had been destroyed. In Tōkyō 107,000 persons had died; in Yokohama 33,000.

The royal wedding, to Nagako, took place Jan. 26, 1924.

Taishō expired Dec. 26, 1926. Hirohito immediately succeeded to the throne.

He was 25. The era of Taishō had passed. The era of Shōwa (shō' wä) (Enlightened Peace), by which Hirohito's reign would be known, was beginning.

The heralded peace proclaimed by his era name failed to ensue. The Peace Conference of Paris had confirmed Japan in the possession of the former German properties in Shantung, the coastal province in northeast China.   China objected; she declined to sign the Versailles Treaty and began a nation-wide boycott of Japanese goods.

In 1927 revolutionary Chinese troops advancing north clashed with Japanese troops in the Shantung capital, Tsinan.   The Japanese occupied the city.   After a settlement was reached at Nanking the following year, the Japanese troops withdrew, but the incident had produced a deep gulf of bitterness between the Chinese government and Japan.   Anti-Japanese sentiment had taken root and it began to flourish.

At home in Japan rightist lawlessness continued.

Tadashi Konuma, a young member of the Blood Brotherhood, having been assigned a target, practiced shooting on a deserted beach.   Then catching his target, Finance Minister Junnosuke Inoue (jōōn nō sōō' kā   ē nō' yōō ā), who often opposed the mounting Army appropriation, he shot him dead on a sidewalk.

Inoue was married to a daughter of the Iwasaki (ē wä sä' kē) family, which owned the great Mitsubishi (mē tsōō bē' shē) financial interests.   This link seemed to prove to the militarists that he was a greedy politician seeking to advance his personal goals by selling out the nation and usurping the powers of the Emperor.

Less than a month later, Baron Takuma Dan (tä kōō'mä dän), president of Mitsui (mē tsōō'-ē) financial interests, stepped out of his car and felt the pistol of a Blood Brotherhood member shoved into his back.   The member Gorō Hishinuma, pulled the trigger.   Dan died.

May 15, 1932, ultranationalists planning a reform, and helped by 42 young military officers, early in the morning arrived at the official residence of the Prime Minister. They carried revolvers and hand grenades.

They entered the building and broke into the

quarters of Prime Minister Tsuyoshi Inukai (tsoo̅ yō'shē ē'noo̅ kī). His daughter-in-law, carrying her baby, was with him. They ordered her to leave; she refused. Unruffled by the intrusion, the 77-year-old Prime Minister led them into another room, asked them to remove their shoes and to sit down and talk it over. On his appointment to the Prime Ministership he had made plain he would brook no nonsense from Army fanatics and would curb their ambitions by cutting their budget at home. Now he lit a cigarette.

Another group, led by Lt. Masayoshi Yamagishi, carrying a dagger, burst in.

"No use talking," said Yamagishi, "Fire!"

All the intruders began firing. The Prime Minister sank to the matted floor.

The conspirators then panicked and fled, killing one guard and wounding another as they left. The revolt of which they were a part came to nothing except that it secured for the revolutionists their object of removing civilian control of the government.

But when the search began for a successor to Inukai, the Army made plain that no War Minister would be nominated unless the Army approved the new Prime Minister. By law the positions of War Minister and Navy Minister could only be filled by serving or ex-service officers. Since a serving officer had to be approved by the High Command, either Army or Navy, these ministries could prevent the formation of a Cabinet. They could also bring about the fall of a Cabinet by having either of their nominees resign.

Nine days after the assassination of Inukai, Manchuria became Manchoukuo, with Army generals in all positions of power and the area openly exploited as a Japanese colony. In Shanghai the Japanese Army and Navy had taken over all but the International Settlement.

This was the situation when Grew presented his

credentials to the Emperor. The tall, handsome, distinguished-appearing Grew towered over the Emperor. In a high, singsong voice the Emperor read his speech of welcome in Japanese. Then, according to protocol, he shook hands with the new ambassador.

Then, with Toshio Shiratori, director of the Bureau of Information and Intelligence of the Foreign Office interpreting, the Emperor asked two or three formal questions. Grew was deaf and had so informed Shiratori. But by rule no one was to raise his voice in the presence of the Emperor.

So though Grew wore a hearing aid, he could hear only one word in four of Shiratori's translation. In this awkward situation, he did his best to answer the questions.

Later he had the same trouble when introduced to the Empress. This time his wife came to the rescue.

Yet it would not be his deafness but the increasing bellicosity of the militarists that would impede the efforts of Grew to foster good relations between his government and that of Japan. He strove to stem the growing conflict between Japan and American claims in the Far East, but the situation steadily deteriorated.

Having rejected the League finding on Manchuria, Matsuoka returned from Geneva a hero, his popularity so great he even thought of becoming Prime Minister.

When in a lecture at Kyotō University in 1933 Prof. Yukitoki Takikawa (yōō kē tō' kē   tä kē kä' wä) suggested that the Constitution of Japan wa more important than the Emperor, Minister of Education Ichirō Hatoyama demanded his immediate dismissal.

The faculty members threatened to resign if their colleague was forced to leave. Hatoyama said: "Let all the professors resign if that is how they feel. We do not mind closing the universities altogether."

The Army resurrected the former Manchu Emperor of

China, Henry Pu-yi. He had lost his post when China became a republic in 1912, and he had been living under Japanese protection. March 1, 1934, the Army made him Emperor of Manchoukuo.

Dec. 19, 1934, Japan denounced the Washington treaties of 1922 and 1933, which consequently were abrogated, leaving Japan to enter into naval building competition with the other powers. Japan had a good start. She had built up to the limit of the treaty; America had not.

Nevertheless, the Navy-minded Roosevelt would support about every Navy request for expansion. The saber-rattling of the Japanese militarists encouraged his bent for rearmament. Their lawlessness continued.

Lieut. Col. Saburō Aizawa (sä' bōō lō   ī zä'wä) of the 41st Regiment in Fukuyama, called on Maj. Gen. Tetsuzan Nagata (tā'tsōō zän nä gä'tä) and advised him to resign because Nagata had been a key figure in having extremist Gen. Jinsaburō Mazaki, Inspector General of Military Education, transferred to the less influential post of Military Councillor. Prime Minister Keisuke Okada (kā ē sōō'kā ō kä'dä) held Mazaki responsible for assisting in fomenting agitation in the Army.

Nagata not only refused to resign but ordered Aizawa transferred to Taiwan.

On the morning of Aug. 12, 1935, Aizawa again called at the War Ministry. When he entered the office of Nagata, he found him with Col. Hideo Niimi, chief of the Tōkyō Military Police.

When the two caught sight of Aizawa with his razor-sharp sword in hand, they leaped to their feet.

Aizawa sprang at Nagata and slashed him with the sword. Niimi tried to engage Aizawa while the wounded Nagata tried to escape toward the door. Aizawa slashed the fleeing general in the back. Nagata fell dead.

Aizawa left the room, arm bleeding and hat missing, but striving to regain his composure. Sirens howled; military police rushed into the building. To the apparent surprise of Aizawa they put him under arrest.

The Nagata assassination shook the public and even the hardened military; it was the first time a field-grade officer on active duty had murdered his superior.

The incident gained for the Imperial Way (Kōdōha) faction the removal of its chief adversary; moreover, public indignation hurt War Minister Senjurō Hayashi who had appointed Nagata and was responsible for discipline.

Gen. Sadao Araki (sä dä' ō ä lä' kē), as Supreme Military Councillor, quickly reminded Hayashi that"it is traditional in the Army for a War Minister to resign over such an incident." Hayashi resigned Sept. 4, 1935.

The authorities granted Aizawa a public court-martial at the headquarters of the First Division in Tōkyō. To prevent the Young Officer members of the Imperial Way from profiting from the Aizawa trial and from personnel changes in the War Ministry, the General Staff decided in late 1935 to send the Division to Manchuria for a tour of duty beginning in 1936.

At his trial, which began Jan. 28, 1936, Aizawa attacked statesmen, politicians and the family business combines known as *zaibatsu*, charging all with corruption. Pleading guilty to the charge of murder, he claimed he had only done his duty as an honorable soldier of the Emperor.

His defense counsel said, "If the court fails to understand the spirit that guided Col. Aizawa, a second Aizawa and even a third will appear."

On the evening of the day, Feb. 25, 1936, when the defense counsel spoke these prescient words, Grew was giving a private showing of *Naughty Marietta*, starring Jeanette MacDonald and Nelson Eddy. Grew described the film as "full of lovely old Victor Herbert music, beautiful scenes, a pretty, romantic story and no vulgarity whatever..."

Among his guests was Viscount Makoto Saitō (mä kō' tō sī'tō), recently cashiered as Prime Minister and appointed lord keeper of the Privy Seal. Another was the retired admiral, Kantarō Suzuki (kän'tä lō sōō zōō'kē), grand chamberlain to the Emperor. Two blocks away, Prime Minister Keisuke Okada (kā ē sōō'kē ō kä'dä), also a retired admiral, was hosting a banquet at his official residence in celebration of the victory, five days earlier, of the government party (Minseitō) in the general election for the House of Representatives. Before dawn all three of these Japanese would be targets for assassination.

At the American embassy the guests were enjoying the entertainment. Though he ordinarily left parties at 10, Saitō not only stayed for refreshments at the ending of the first half of the film, he remained until the end. It was 11:30 when he and his wife arose to leave.

Several days after the assassination of Nagata, three members of the Young Officers Movement, and one cashiered officer who was still a member, met and decided to kill the three chief "villains" of the state: the Marquis Kimmochi Saionji (kēm mō' chē sī ōn'jē), a former Prime Minister who was the sole survivor of a small, revered group of political leaders known as genrō (elder statesmen) who had participated in the restoration of the Emperor in 1868; Lord Keeper of the Privy Seal Count Nobuaki Makino (nō bōō ä'kē mä kē'nō) who, like Saitō, had opposed the withdrawal of Japan from the League of Nations; and the new inspector General of Military Education Gen. Jotarō Watanabe.

The Young Officers' Movement consisted of a loosely-connected organization of company-grade officers, mainly of the Army, burning with the frustration of the rural areas from whence many of them

80

had sprung. They professed allegiance to the Emperor and intended to overthrow the government, which they alleged to be usurping his power.

They were influenced by the teachings of Ikki Kita (ēk' kē kē' ta͡y), a former socialist, who wrote that the Meiji constitution, promulgated after the restoration of the Emperor to power, should be set aside in favor of a revolutionary regime advised by "national patriots" and headed initially by a military government. This revolutionary government would nationalize major forms of property, limit wealth, end party government and peerage systems and then prepare to grasp the leadership of a revolutionary Asia. The plots of the Young Officers, which he encouraged, were supposed to create such great disorder that military government must follow. The naive young officers believed that having achieved so much the Army would know what further steps to take.

Amid falling snow, 300 soldiers surrounded the official residence of the Prime Minister, across the street from the Diet building. At gunpoint they forced the guards to open the gate. As the soldiers entered, other guards opened fire. The insurgents returned the fire, killing three policemen.

The shooting awoke the residents of the house. The alarm bell rang. The Prime Minister's brother-in-law, Col. Denzō Matsuo (den'zō mä tsōō' ō), assisted by a policeman, rushed the 74-year-old Prime Minister out of the house and hid him in a storage shed in the garden.

When Matsuo and the policeman tried to reenter the house the insurgents fired on them, killing the policeman. Matsuo halted.

The soldiers hesitated. A lieutenant arrived, and believing that the old man before him was the Prime Minister, ordered them to shoot. They fired.

Matsuo cried, "Banzai!" and fell dead.

While the insurgents were toasting his assassination, Okada, unable to bear the cold outside, quietly returned to the house. Two maids discovered him and hid him in a closet in their quarters. Later his supporters would identify him as a mourner overcome with grief, smuggle him out of the house and spirit him away.

The insurgents broke into the home of Suzuki and shot him down. As he bled on the floor, his wife kneeling at his side, an officer drew his sword to deliver the death stroke. Mrs. Suzuki pleaded that the privilege be hers. Assuming that the old man was dying anyway, the officer agreed.

The officer apologized to Mrs. Suzuki, explaining that her husband had been shot for the future of Japan. He saluted Suzuki and ordered his soldiers to do likewise.

Insurgents broke into the suburban home of Watanabe. They found him lying on a cushion with his young daughter. An intruder fired his pistol at the recumbent man; another drew his sword and slashed at Watanabe's head.

Another group ranged through a mountain resort in search of Makino. Unable to locate him in the hotel in which he seemed to be lodged, they set fire to the building to drive him out. His 20-year-old granddaughter, Kazuko, led the old man out a rear entrance. As the two struggled up a steep hill, soldiers at their heels fired a fusillade.

Kazuko stepped before her grandfather, spreading her kimono sleeves as if to conceal and protect him. An insurgent cried, "Success!" and persuaded his mates to leave.

A third group, assigned to kill Saionji, never left Tōkyō. At the last moment the officer in charge refused to go; he was unable to persuade himself to inflict violence on the last genrō.

Legend identified Japanese Emperor Hirohito (above), posthumously known as Emperor Shōwa, as descendant of the Sun Goddess. Though they otherwise treated him with the reverence befitting his supposed divine origin, his advisers made the important decisions, which he was expected to approve.

The abortive coup d'état of February 26, 1936; rebel troops surround the Diet building.

(Left) Insurgents surround the Japanese Diet in the Young Officers revolt of Feb. 26, 1936.

The Young Officers abortive coup d'etat led to Foreign Minister Kōki Hirota, right, being promoted to Prime Minister.

The insurgents failed in their object of capturing strategic public buildings. So after assassinating Matsuo they took refuge in the Prime Minister's residence and in the Sanno Hotel.

At the American Embassy, near the edge of the insurgent zone, Grew cabled the first news of the revolt to the State Department:

THE MILITARY TOOK PARTIAL POSSESSION OF THE GOVERNMENT AND CITY EARLY THIS MORNING AND IT IS REPORTED TO HAVE ASSASSINATED SEVERAL PROMINENT MEN. IT IS IMPOSSIBLE AS YET TO CONFIRM ANYTHING. THE NEWS CORRESPONDENTS ARE NOT PERMITTED TO SEND TELEGRAMS OR TO TELEPHONE ABROAD. THIS TELEGRAM IS BEING SENT PRIMARILY AS A TEST MESSAGE, TO ASCERTAIN IF OUR CODE TELEGRAMS WILL BE TRANSMITTED. CODE ROOM PLEASE ACKNOWLEDGE IMMEDIATELY UPON RECEIPT.

Observers on the roof of the American Embassy could see the insurgent banner waving from the Prime Minister's residence and the Sanno Hotel. Though Grew assured his wife that the last thing the insurgents wanted was trouble with the United States, Mrs. Grew became so nervous that she insisted on sleeping in a different room.

The Emperor had been angered by the assassination of Marshal Chang Tso-lin and the unauthorized action in Manchuria. Now he was angered by the unauthorized use of his troops and the attacks on his advisers.

The Emperor declared, "If the Army cannot subdue the rebels, I will go out and dissuade them myself." By midnight martial law was declared.

Though apathy gripped the authorities, the position of Army versus insurgents began to polarize. Swayed by the Emperor, the nation's highest authority, the Army at 5:06 A.M., February 28 issued an edict ordering the insurgents to "speedily withdraw" from their present position and return to their units. Residents of the danger zones would be evacuated. If the insurgents had not withdrawn by 8 A.M. of the following day, the Army would fire on them.

Despite the edict, all but a few insurgents refused to withdraw. From outlying cities Army reinforcements invested Tōkyō. The Combined Fleet steamed into Tōkyō Bay. Landing forces took positions outside the Navy Ministry and other naval installations, manned by men seething with anger over the attack on three of their senior officers.

At 6 A.M. February 29 the Army announced: "We are positively going to suppress the rebels who caused disturbances in the neighborhood of Kojimachi in the imperial capital." This was the first time the insurgents had been officially branded rebels.

The Army brought tanks to assault positions. Other tanks clanked up to rebel barricades bearing placards invoking the insurgents to "respectfully follow the Emperor's order." Fully loaded bombers droned overhead. Other planes dropped leaflets addressed to noncommissioned officers.

Above the Aviation Building floated a large balloon, its long trailer emblazoned with large characters: **IMPERIAL ORDER ISSUED. DON'T RESIST THE ARMY FLAG.** Loudspeakers brought up to strategic places informed the enlisted men that the rebel leaders had deceived them. "If you continue to resist, you will be traitors for disobeying the Emperor's order."

The solidarity of the ranks began to crack. Thirty noncoms and soldiers walked away from their positions carrying machine guns and rifles. By noon almost all the enlisted men had returned to their detachments. At

2 P.M. the insurgent banner came down from the Prime Minister's residence. An hour later Army headquarters announced by radio that the insurgents had surrendered without a shot being fired.

Loyal troops made no effort to capture the leaders of the insurgency who remained at the War Ministry and the Sanno Hotel. Gen. Araki asked them to commit hara-kiri. The Young Officers considered the request; only one acceded to it. The others decided to submit to court-martial where, like Aizawa, they could alert the nation to the corruption besetting Japan.

What had been planned as a national revolution ended with only seven persons killed. Okada had escaped, Makino was untouched, Suzuki was to recover from his wounds.

The martial law invoked during the rebellion would continue month after month, with voices of dissent silenced and the press rigidly controlled. The insurgents were swiftly tried in private. Thirteen officers and four civilians, including Ikki Kita, were sentenced to death. July 12 they were bound to racks, bull's-eyes marking their foreheads above the blindfolds. Most gave three banzais for the Emperor before the shots rang out.

The mutiny was to be recorded in history as the 2-26 Incident (February 26 Incident).

Though executed as rebels, the Young Officers had won their point: though Okada had escaped with his life, he was removed from the Prime Ministership; and it became evident that if the social reforms the rebels advocated were unfulfilled, the policy of permanent expansion would be fulfilled – the expansion being in the direction of China.

The Emperor ordered Foreign Minister Kōki Hirota (kō' kē hē lō' tä) to form a new Cabinet.

Son of a stonemason, Hirota took the post of Prime

Minister reluctantly. He recognized the formidable
difficulties facing him.

On the other hand, Grew was pleased with the
appointment of Hirota. He wrote in his diary:

> I am very much pleased because I believe
> that Hirota is a strong, safe man and that
> while he will have to play ball with the Army
> to a certain extent, I think he will handle
> foreign affairs as wisely as they can be
> handled given the domestic elements which he
> will have to conciliate. I think, too, that
> he wants good relations with the United States
> and will do what he is able to do in that
> direction...If I had the pick myself, I know
> of nobody whom I would have more gladly chosen
> to head the government, with American
> interests in view.

Again Grew wrote:

> For me there are no finer people in the
> world than the best type of Japanese. I am
> rather inclined to place Hirota among them; if
> he could have his way unhampered by the
> military I believe he would steer the country
> into safer and saner channels.

Of course, Hirota was not to have his way
unhampered by the military. Under his administration
Japan signed the Anti-Comintern Pact with Germany.

The drift toward pro-Germanism among the Japanese
Army leaders had begun almost from the time Japan had
opened its doors to the West. At first Japan had
engaged French military instructors for its fledgling
Army. But after the defeat of France in the Franco-

Prussian War of 1871–1872, the Japanese deduced that German arms were superior and switched to the German manual of arms. Thereafter the Army sent promising officers to Germany for further instruction. Consequently a tradition of pro-Germanism had grown up in the Japanese Army officer corps.

When Japan signed the Anti-Comintern Pact, Hitler had already won his gamble of occupying the Rhineland. Mussolini had invaded Ethiopia and proclaimed a Rome–Berlin Axis. Hitler had denounced the Versailles Treaty. The failure of the democracies to curb these warlike actions encouraged those in Japan who sought territorial aggrandizement.

Henceforth the Japanese militarists were to regard with awe the transformation of Germany from a bankrupt, isolated nation to a military power that threatened the peace of the world. The Anti-Comintern Pact was the first tangible step by which the Japanese Army leaders began their march toward outright military alliance.

In the end Hirota was unable to cope with the military. Gen. Count Hisaichi Terauchi (hē sä ē'chē tā'lä ōo'chē) resigned his post of War Minister, thus causing the fall of the Cabinet. Hirota returned to private life. Prince Fumimaro Konoye (fōo mē mä'lō kō nō'yä) succeeded him June 1, 1937.

An ancestor of Konoye, Nakatomi no Kamatari, in A.D. 645, gave signal assistance in restoring the Emperor to power by overthrowing the mighty Soga clan. In reward the Emperor bestowed on him much preferment and a new name, Fujiwara

By marrying their women into the imperial lineage where they bore sons who would become Emperor, the Fujiwaras came to control the imperial institution. They ruled the country from about the 10th to the 13th centuries, the period of their rule being one of grandeur and exquisite taste.

Of the 115 Emperors, 65 were of Fujiwara birth. Though the House of Fujiwara split into several branches, the main house still existed. Konoye was the nominal head of all. His father had been president of the House of Peers.

Born in 1891, Fumimaro was educated at the Peers' School and the First Higher School. He entered Tōkyō Imperial University but soon transferred to Kyotō Imperial University, which had a freer intellectual atmosphere.

At Kyotō he came under the influence of Dr. Hajime Kawakami, then one of Japan's leading socialists. In 1914 Konoye translated Oscar Wilde's *The Soul of Man Under Socialism* and published it the student magazine *Shinshisho* (New Current of Thought). The authorities banned the publication.

In 1916 Konoye became a member of the House of Peers. Graduating from Kyotō University Law School in 1917, he found a position in the Home Ministry where he worked for passage of a universal male suffrage law. During the Paris Peace Conference in 1919 he served as secretary to Kimmochi Saionji, the Japanese representative. In 1932 Konoye became president of the House of Peers.

The Emperor appointed Konoye Prime Minister because he seemed the one man who could bring about the cooperation of the political, military and bureaucratic factions of the government. The first great test of whether he would be able to achieve this object came at what history knows as the Marco Polo Bridge Incident, which had been at least part of the inspiration for Roosevelt's Quarantine Speech.

The Marco Polo Bridge was an ancient stone structure at a place called Lukouch'iao in the suburbs of what had been Peking, renamed Peiping after Nanking became the central capital of China in 1928. Japanese troops had been stationed in the Peiping area ever since an international expeditionary force, which included

Prime Minister Fumimaro Konoye, left, headed a family that had ruled Japan from about the tenth to the 13th centuries, a period that for the nobles had been one of grandeur and exquisite taste.

The Japanese attack on the American gunboat Panay, above, exacerbated American hostility towards Japan.

Europeans, Americans and Japanese, suppressed the bloody, xenophobic Boxer Rebellion in 1900.

In Peiping, Chinese students had launched an anti-Japanese movement. In 1929 the Kuomintang Party of China, led by Chiang Kai-shek, joined the Communist Party in Sian to form a common anti-Japanese front. After the occupation of Manchuria, the Japanese militarists planned to invade North China.

This was the situation when on the night of July 7, 1937 a Japanese company was holding maneuvers about a mile from a large Chinese unit near the Marco Polo Bridge. As a bugle signalled the end of the operation, bullets came from the Chinese lines. The Japanese returned fire, but within a minute the skirmish was over.

After the skirmish the Japanese found a member missing. They demanded the right to search the Peiping suburb of Wanping for the missing soldier; the Chinese denied them.

The Japanese launched an infantry and artillery attack. The Japanese Foreign Office, then under Hirota, was disgusted with this new military incident; it agreed that the incident should be prevented from spreading and that a swift local solution should be achieved. Despite the efforts of the Foreign Office the fighting escalated into an undeclared but full-scale war.

The Japanese strategy included capturing all ports to shut off foreign aid to China, to be followed by the destruction of the Chinese field armies. The Japanese poured into North China from Manchuria and occupied Peiping July 28 and Tientsin the following day.

The Japanese assault against the Chinese included peripheral offenses against Western representatives. August 20 a stray Japanese artillery shell struck the U.S.S. *Augusta*, moored in the Whangpoo River, killing one seaman and injuring 17. August 26 Japanese airmen fired on the motorcar carrying the British ambassador.

As the Japanese poised to capture Nanking, they
committed offenses against the Western powers that could
not be excused as accidental. Near the town of Wuhu, the
same Kingorō Hashimoto who had helped to manufacture the
Manchurian Incident, and who had been reactivated as
colonel of artillery, laid out a two-mile gauntlet of
heavy field pieces along the river bank to cut off escape
from Nanking. December 11 he shelled a ferryboat of
British refugees as well as a British gunboat, the
Ladybird, killing a British sailor.

On the morning of December 12 he learned that three
Socony–Vacuum tankers and the little U.S. gunboat *Panay*
were waiting out the occupation of Nanking at an anchorage
downriver, halfway between the battery and the beleaguered
city. He may also have learned that the *Panay* carried key
parts from the newest Japanese aircraft.

Hashimoto commanded a squadron of naval aircraft,
attached to his unit to help him blockade the river. He
ordered the naval pilots to attack the U.S. ships.

Though noncommissioned officers, the pilots
questioned the orders and took off only after a long
argument.

At 1:38 P.M. three twin–motor Japanese planes
approached the *Panay* from the southwest. Those aboard the
Panay were observing an ordinary Sunday routine. The
bright sunlight glittered off two huge American flags
painted on the deck. As the Japanese planes passed over
the gunboat they released bombs.

One bomb scored a direct hit on the bow; a second
stove a hole in the starboard side. The explosions
demolished pilot house, sick bay and radio shack, knocked
out the engine and disabled the three–inch gun. A piece
of shrapnel struck the captain in the throat and rendered
him mute.

The captain coped with his disability as best he
could by writing orders. Six single–engine biplane

fighters bore in from the south and unloaded antipersonnel bombs. The biplanes wheeled and returned for a second and third run of dive bombing.

The crew of the 30–caliber machine–gun on the afterdeck began to return fire. The enemy planes replied. After 20 minutes of bombing and strafing the *Panay* was listing to starboard and slowly settling.

The attacking planes then directed their attention to the tankers.

As the wounded from the *Panay* were being ferried ashore, a Japanese plane returned and strafed the open lifeboat. By 3 P.M. when the decks of the *Panay* were awash, two mates rowed back and took off provisions and medical supplies.

A Japanese launch approached the *Panay*, swept her decks with machine–gun fire and put aboard an inspection crew. A moment later the inspection crew leaped back into its boat, which quickly drew away. Five minutes later the *Panay* rolled on its side and sank.

Two of the tankers were burning; a third had been grounded on a mud bank. The Japanese had killed three men and wounded 48, including five civilian passengers.

The survivors hid out for three days in the rushes of the riverbank. Finally the U.S.S. gunboat *Oahu* rescued them.

On his own account, Hull instructed Grew to impress upon the Japanese government "the gravity of the situation and the imperative need to take every precaution against further attacks on American vessels and personnel."

"Deeply shocked," Roosevelt told the State Department to render a protest to the Japanese Emperor.

Far more bellicose than Hull, Roosevelt told Secretary of the Treasury Henry Morgenthau Jr. that there are lots of ways of declaring war. In the old days, sinking an American naval vessel would in itself have constituted a cause of war. In the end, the President decided to act on a suggestion offered by Morgenthau's subordinate, Herman Oliphant.

The President could proclaim a national emergency and issue regulations prohibiting or restricting exchange transactions...expressly prohibiting banking and foreign exchange transactions and monetary exports in which the Japanese government was directly or indirectly interested.

Hoping for the cooperation of Great Britain, Roosevelt dispatched an envoy to London. He also sent Capt. Royal E. Ingersoll of the U.S. Navy to investigate "with the British Admiralty...what we could do if the United States and England would find themselves at war with Japan."

Son of an admiral, Ingersoll had returned to the Chief of Naval Operations office to direct the War Plans Division and to participate in the London Naval Conference of 1935-36. Now at age 54 he was to arrange with the British for "parallel action in the Far East."

He was to inform the British that Roosevelt had decided to renounce the London Treaty on naval arms and press for more and bigger ships. Despite the critical situation in Europe, the assumption was that Great Britain and the United States would eventually find themselves at war with Japan at the same time and would need to coordinate command relationships.

The *Panay* Incident of Dec. 12, 1937 had reminded Grew of the situation in 1915 when the Germans had sunk the *Lusitana*, causing the loss of 1,198 lives, 125 of them American. At that time Grew had been 1st secretary of the American Embassy in Berlin. War between America and Germany threatened. The *Panay* Incident seemed equally ominous; he ordered his servants to pack his bags.

Grew was able to unpack his bags. Japan accepted responsibility for the incident, made formal apologies, promised indemnities and appropriate punishment and gave assurances for the future. Hull accepted these assurances

92

and thus closed the incident.

Navy Vice-Minister Isoroku Yamamoto (ē sō lō'kōō yä mä mō'tō) said of the incident, "the Navy can only hang its head." He immediately replaced Rear Adm. Teizō Mitsunami (tā'ē zō mē tsōō nä'mē) who, as commander of the Second Combined Air Force, was held to be responsible.

Yamamoto assumed that the Army would follow suit by dismissing Hashimoto; this expectation went unrealized. On the contrary, grosser breaches of Army discipline were in the offing.

Japan delivered its formal apology for the *Panay* Incident Dec. 24, 1937. The following day Japan took over Nanking. For two weeks Japanese soldiers ran amok, destroying one-third of the city, slaughtering more than 200,000 civilians and raping, and then murdering, 20,000 women. Their bestiality disgusted the whole world.

Japan continued her conquest of East Asia. Feb. 14, 1939, Japan took over the Spratleys in the South China Sea, which France had formally claimed in 1933. Japan moved strategically closer and closer to the time when she would be most favorably situated to strike at the British in Malaya, the Dutch in the East Indies and the Americans in the Philippines.

Roosevelt had more and more in the Far East with which to be concerned.

4

JAPAN SIGHTS AT AN AMERICAN TARGET

By the time Roosevelt had denounced the Italian declaration of war against France the battle for that nation and for Continental Europe had fallen to Hitler. Hitler had conquered France and driven the British into the sea at Dunkirk. From that beach the fleeing British had ferried 338,226 men, 120,000 of them French, to England, though they left much of their equipment behind.

June 17, 1940, France sued for peace. The United States informed Germany, Italy, France and Great Britain and Holland that it "would not acquiesce...in the transfer of any geographic region of the western hemisphere..."

In this perilous situation, Roosevelt moved to strengthen his Cabinet.

His Secretary of State, Cordell Hull, had served him since 1933. Born Oct. 2, 1871 in Overton County, Tennessee, Hull attended Montvale College in Celina, Tennessee. An ardent Democrat before he was 20, he graduated from Cumberland University Law School and was admitted to the bar in 1891. In 1903 he was elected a Tennessee circuit-court judge. From 1907 to 1931, except for one term, he served in the U.S. House of Representatives, focusing on tax and tariff problems.

Hull advocated the League of Nations. By 1919 he had become convinced that lowering tariffs and removing other trade barriers would promote world peace. Elected to the Senate in 1931, in 1933 he had become Roosevelt's Secretary of State. In this position he helped to form a united hemispheric front against aggression in case of war with any European nation.

Sept. 1, 1939, Roosevelt appointed Gen. George Catlett Marshall Army chief of staff. Marshall took the oath of office a few hours after Hitler attacked Poland.

Born in Uniontown, Pennsylvania, Dec. 31, 1880, Marshall graduated from Virginia Military Institute, served in the Philippines, attended the Army's School of the Line and in 1908 graduated from the Command and General Staff School. During the World War he served in high planning and administrative posts with the Allied Expeditionary Force. From 1919 to 1924 he was an aide to Gen. John J. Pershing. He served three years in China. His colleagues greatly respected him for his integrity and ability.

It now became necessary for Roosevelt to fill the post of Secretary of War, left vacant by the resignation of Harry H. Woodring and that of the Secretary of the Navy vacated by Charles Edison, who planned to run for governor of New Jersey.

Roosevelt wanted the best men possible for these posts, but he also wanted men who would be political assets. For because of the perilous state of foreign affairs, Roosevelt was preparing to run for an unprecedented third term in the presidency, contrary to what had otherwise been his inclination to retire from political life. As an active politician he consequently found it particularly important to consolidate public opinion behind him. Some prominent Republicans who opposed his domestic policies supported him in his opposition to the Axis. Among them was Frank Knox, publisher of the *Chicago Daily News*, who had been the Republican candidate for vice president in 1936.

Born Jan. 1, 1874 in Boston, Massachusetts, he was christened Franklin (William) Knox. He served in the Spanish-American War with Theodore Roosevelt's Rough Riders. During the World War he served in France as a colonel in the 365th field artillery. In 1931 he became publisher of the *Chicago Daily News*.

Politically a nonconformist, Knox began as a Republican but broke away from the party in the 1912 election to join the Progressive Republican, or "Bull Moose", party, which had as its Presidential candidate Theodore Roosevelt. Knox's friendship with Theodore Roosevelt continued through the lifetime of that dynamic man.

The President called Knox on the long-distance telephone and invited him to take over the Navy Department. Knox accepted but expressed the belief that it would be unwise to announce his appointment until after the Republican Convention, which was about to assemble in Philadelphia. He wanted to attend the convention and fight for a nonisolationist policy and a nonisolationist candidate, Wendell Wilkie.

Roosevelt insisted that the announcement should be made before the Convention. If the Republican Party at the Convention espoused an isolationist policy and nominated an isolationist candidate, a delayed announcement of Knox's appointment would make him appear a disgruntled loser. On the other hand, if Wilkie and the nonisolationists won out at Philadelphia, Knox would be unable to gracefully desert the candidate and the principles for which he had fought.

If Knox accepted the post of Secretary of the Navy before the convention, the public would interpret his act as one of simple patriotism – an act animated by the belief that the conduct of the defense effort and of foreign policy should be placed above partisan considerations.

Stimson was the man Roosevelt wanted for Secretary of War. After the Hoover administration left the White House, Stimson returned to private life, but he maintained his interest in foreign affairs. Several times he visited the White House. When he spoke out there against Roosevelt's domestic programs, the President always listened with

Roosevelt wanted the best available man for Secretary of the Navy and he wanted one who would also be a political asset. Frank Knox, above, seemed to qualify.

Greatly respected by his colleagues for his integrity and ability, Gen. George Catlett Marshall (left) took the oath of office as chief of staff a few hours after Hitler attacked Poland. Here he confers with Secretary of War Henry Lewis Stimson.

interest. On foreign affairs, Stimson continued to find the President's views basically the same as his own.

Stimson was opposed to economic isolationism and believed that American tariffs must be reduced. So in April 1934, when the Democratic sponsored Reciprocal Trade Agreement Bill was before the Senate, he made a radio address strongly supporting the measure.

Pleased with the address, Roosevelt a few weeks later invited him to the White House for lunch. In what Stimson felt was the friendliest chat with the President so far, they talked for an hour and a half. At this meeting, Roosevelt reminisced about the Japanese plan for world conquest the Japanese student at Harvard had revealed to him 32 years before.

Roosevelt commented on how many particulars of this revealed plan had been confirmed by succeeding events. Japan had easily beaten China in the war of 1894-95; she had beaten Russia in the war of 1904-05; she had annexed Korea in 1910; she had acquired many islands in the Pacific as the result of the World War – Marshall and Carolines; she had taken over Manchuria 1931-1932 and Jehol in 1933.

Of this reminiscence, Stimson would write that nothing that happened in the seven years since he first heard it would weaken the aptness of this strange and well-remembered conversation in Cambridge.

June 18, 1940, the day after France sued for peace, Stimson made a radio address in which he said: "The United States today faces probably the greatest crisis in its history." He stated that a totalitarian victory would mean the end of freedom throughout the world, for individuals as for nations. Only the British Fleet remained between the Nazis and the Western Hemisphere. If it should be lost, America, almost unarmed, must stand alone against the world. America must support the British Navy and support and encourage the people of Great Britain. He made some recommendations:

First, we should repeal the provisions of
our ill-starred so-called neutrality venture
which have acted as a shackle to our true
interests over five years.

Second, we should throw open all of our
ports to the British and French naval and
merchant marine for all repairs and refueling and
other naval services.

Third, we should accelerate by every means
in our power the sending of planes and other
munitions to Britain and France on a scale which
would be effective; sending them if necessary in
our own ships and under convoy.

Fourth, we should refrain from being fooled
by the evident bluff of Hitler's so-called fifth-
column (Nazi sympathizer) movements in South
America...they are attempts to frighten us from
sending help where it will be most effective.

...Finally, we should at once adopt a system
of universal compulsory training and service
which would not only be the most potent evidence
that we are in earnest, but which at the present
moment is imperative if we are to have men ready
to operate the planes and other munitions, the
creation of which Congress has just authorized by
a practically unanimous vote.

In these ways, and with the old American
spirit of courage and leadership behind them, I
believe we should find our people ready to take
their proper part in this threatened world and to
carry through to victory, freedom and
reconstruction...

Though the speech fell short of asking for a
declaration of war, it put Stimson ahead of Roosevelt and

most published opinions in recommending a more bellicose attitude toward the Axis.

On the afternoon of June 19, Stimson received a telephone call from the White House. Roosevelt offered him the position of Secretary of War. Roosevelt told him that Knox had already agreed to accept the position of Secretary of the Navy.

Surprised, Stimson pointed out that he was approaching his 73rd birthday. Roosevelt already knew this, and he said Stimson would be free to appoint his own Ass't Secretary of War. After thinking it over for several hours, Stimson called back and asked if Roosevelt had seen the radio speech. Roosevelt had and was in full accord with it. In the end, Stimson accepted.

The Senate confirmed the nominations of both Stimson and Knox.

The two took office at a perilous time. June 21, 1940, the German and French representatives met in a freight car at Rethondes in the Compeigne Forest, the same car on the same spot where a battered Germany had signed the 1918 armistice. This time the Germans dictated the terms and they were harsh: three-fifths of French territory would be under occupation; prisoners of war would not be released; the costs of occupation would be assessed by Germany; the French Army would be reduced to 100,000 men.

The crux of the armistice treaty was the disposal of the French Navy. The armistice agreement stipulated that the French fleet would be demobilized and disarmed and the ships laid up in their home ports.

The Franco-Italian armistice was signed in Rome two days later. Mussolini was able to occupy only what his troops had conquered – a few hundred yards of French territory – and was only able to impose a 50-mile demilitarized zone opposite him in France and Tunisia. Great Britain withdrew its recognition of the new French government, known as Vichy (vish'-ē) from the site of the new capital. In London a French committee led by Gen. Charles Degaulle formed a "free" French force to assist in the liberation of the motherland.

In America the Republicans nominated Wendell L. Wilkie for President. This lawyer turned business tycoon was known as the "most articulate" of the critics against Roosevelt's domestic policies. Nevertheless, in the face of the threat to America posed by the Axis nations, he advocated national unity.

The Democrats nominated Roosevelt for the Presidency on the 1st ballot.

Two days later, July 20, 1940, he signed a bill appropriating $4 billion for a two-ocean navy. On the 25th he tightened the economic noose around Japan that he had begun as a moral embargo in 1938.

The abrogation of the United States-Japan treaty Jan. 26, 1940 opened the way to mandatory embargoes. Now Roosevelt restricted the issuance of export licenses for aviation motor fuel and lubricating oil, tetraethyl and heavy melting scrap, which equalled about 20 percent of scrap exports to Japan.

September 16 he signed a selective service bill.

These measures failed to deter Japan, which had its own means of exerting pressure. In Indo-China, September 22, the French governor having no alternative, considering the fallen French regime in Europe, agreed to permit Japan to establish three air bases in Tonking, in the northern area of Indo-China, and to maintain a small force at the seaport of Haiphong that, through the railway there, had been a principal supply route to Chiang Kai-shek's government in Kunming in southern China.

September 26, Roosevelt manifested his displeasure at the move of Japan into Indo-China by embargoing the shipment of steel and iron scrap outside the western hemisphere, except to Great Britain, effective October 16.

Beginning to strangle in the economic noose fashioned

100

by Roosevelt, Japan at this point took a step that was to complete the alienation of America — the step taking her closer to Hitler who was seeking a dramatic means to divert attention from his apparent impasse with the British.

For after his lightninglike victories on the continent of Europe, the war had ceased to prosper for Hitler. Across the English Channel stood the stubborn British led by the indomitable Churchill.

Hitler's military advisers had told him, and he evidently concurred, that an invasion of England could only succeed if he first gained control of the skies. In charge of the campaign for mastery of the air, henceforth to be known as the Battle of Britain, was Field Marshal Herman Goering.

Goering joined the Nazi Party in 1932 and was wounded in the uprising that led to the imprisonment of Hitler. Goering succeeded in fleeing to Austria. His wound having become gangrenous, he was given morphine to which he became addicted.

His notoriety as a Nazi rendering him objectionable to the Austrians, he moved to Italy and then to Sweden. In 1927 a political amnesty was declared in Germany and he returned there and rejoined Hitler.

By 1939 Goering had made himself so useful that Hitler declared him his "successor", thus making him the second man in Germany. In the Polish campaign, Goering's Air Force (Luftwaffe) continued the terror bombing introduced by the Japanese at Chapei, not only attacking Polish airfields, hangars and fuel dumps but battering central Warsaw and leaving its buildings empty shells.

Success continued to attend him in the battles of Flanders and France, but when he launched his bombers against the British he found himself confronted with a problem for which he had failed to plan. It was not only that the British refused to quail, his own impetuosity was opposed by the cool professionalism of British Air Marshal

Sir Hugh Dowding in the first battle in history to be fought entirely in the air.

Though the battle was to continue beyond that date, it had become apparent to Hitler by the end of September that he had not achieved air superiority over the British and so could not risk an invasion attempt, at least during that year. With his admirable showmanship, he attempted to divert attention from his military reverse through a carefully staged signing of a treaty in Berlin September 27.

By the Tripartite Pact, as the treaty became known, Japan recognized German and Italian leadership in the creation of a "new order in Europe"; Germany and Italy recognized the creation of a new order in "the greater East Asia". The three powers agreed to assist one another with military and other means if one of them were attacked by any power not then involved in the European or the Sino-Japanese War

Ambassador Saburō Kurusu signed for Japan. Born in Yokohama in 1886, Kurusu had studied for a diplomatic career. He entered the foreign service in 1910 and served as consul in Chicago, New York city, the Philippines and Honolulu. He had been ambassador to Belgium before being assigned to Berlin. He was married to an American, and not only she but his two daughters as well spoke English perfectly and were very American in their outlook.

It is said of him that as he sat down to sign, as if forgetting that he was surrounded by German agents, some of whom understood Japanese, he turned to his counselor of embassy and said, "I don't think I am rendering my country a service by signing this."

A Japanese-speaking German overheard the remark and promptly reported it to Hitler. Kurusu was soon recalled to Japan.

The pact seemed directed against America; Roosevelt responded accordingly. October 2, the U.S. Navy began organizing a patrol of 125 ships in the Atlantic supported by planes. October 8, the State Department advised the U.S. consuls in the Far East to advise all Americans to leave Japan, Manchoukuo, China, Indo-China, Korea, Formosa and Hong Kong. Next day Churchill announced that the Burma Road, closed July 17, would be reopened October 17.

The Burma Road was the main route for war supplies to China. This motor highway from Lashio (at the railhead from Mandalay), East Burma ran 681 miles to Kunming in Yunnan, China. The total length, counting the railroad section, and extending from Rangoon, Burma to Chungking, China, was 2100 miles. During the rainy season when the weather reduced the road to minimal usefulness and the British had their hands full repelling the German assault on England, Churchill, at the behest of Japan, had closed the road.

London also announced that British citizens had been advised to leave Japan and Japanese-occupied territory.

November 5, Roosevelt was reelected by 449 electoral votes to 82 for Wilkie. The Democrats retained control of Congress. On the 8th Roosevelt announced that about one-half the planes and other war materials produced by the United States would be allotted to Great Britain.

November 30, Japan signed a treaty in Nanking, formally recognizing the puppet government of China under Wang Ching-wei. Born in Kwantung and educated at Hōsei University in Tōkyō, Wang had joined the revolutionary T'ung Meng Hui and was imprisoned in 1910 for trying to bomb the Manchu prince regent in Peking. After Sun Yat-sen died in 1915, Wang served briefly as president of the Nationalist government; his arch rival, Chiang Kai-shek ousted him.

Wang quit the Nationalists in late 1918, fled the new capital of Chungking and with Japanese aid began creating a "reorganized" national government of estranged Chinese

Nationalists at Nanking.

America countered his recognition by Japan by announcing that the United States would advance $100 million to the government of Chiang Kai-shek.

December 17, Roosevelt announced a plan to lend arms to Great Britain without immediate payment. In his annual message to Congress, Jan. 6, 1941, he said that the United States should act as arsenal to supply all war materials to democracies defending themselves against aggressor nations.

It was about this time that a new career began to open for Harry Hopkins through the esteem in which Roosevelt held him. To Wendell Wilkie, his opponent in the recent election, Roosevelt gave perhaps the most cogent reason for the trust he had in Hopkins.

Roosevelt wanted to send Wilkie abroad on a fact-finding mission. When they conferred in the White House, Wilkie asked:

"Why do you keep Hopkins so close to you? You surely must realize that people distrust him and they resent his influence."

Roosevelt replied, "I can understand that you wonder why I need that half-man around me." He was referring to Hopkins chronic and serious ill-health. "But someday you may be sitting here where I am now as President of the United States. And when you are, you'll be looking at that door over there and knowing that practically everybody who walks through it wants something out of you. You'll learn what a lonely job this is, and you'll discover the need for somebody like Harry Hopkins who asks nothing except to serve you."

Hopkins had come a long way since that first meeting with Roosevelt in the 1928 campaign. Then Hopkins had only represented another handshake to Roosevelt. Hopkins, on the contrary, had been impressed.

Harry Hopkins was born Aug. 17, 1890 in Sioux City, Iowa, the fourth of five chidren of David Aldona Hopkins, a harness maker. A charming, but somewhat erratic and shiftless man, the elder Hopkins had been prospecting for gold in South Dakota when he met and married Anna Pickett, a school teacher.

Shortly after the birth of Harry, the family moved to various new homes in Nebraska and then, for two years, Chicago, a residence as close as possible to the center of the area where the elder Hopkins was then traveling as salesman for a wholesale harness concern. In Chicago, Harry suffered a severe attack of typhoid, the start of the ill-health that would dog him all his life.

About this time a horse-drawn truck ran down the elder Hopkins who sued and collected $10,000 damages. Half of the amount went to Hopkin's lawyer, but enough remained for the victim to buy a harness store of his own in Grinnel, Iowa.

Harry entered Grinnel College with the class of 1912. When he was about to graduate he was offered a post, which he accepted, as counselor for that summer at the Christadora camp for poor children near Bound Brook, New Jersey.

At the camp he was bewildered by the products of the East Coast slums who became his charges. He had known poverty in childhood but it had been of a blander type than that of the hunger, squalor and degradation these children had experienced. After two months in the camp he became the champion of the underprivileged he was always to remain.

His first marriage ended in divorce. His second, to Barbara Duncan, was happy but ended with her death in 1937. Of this marriage a child, Diana, was born in 1932.

Hopkins became a national figure with the election of Roosevelt to the Presidency when Roosevelt made him aadministrator of the Federal Emergency Relief Administration. With his record marred only by a few insignificant scandals, he spent a total of $8,500,000,000, aiding about 15 million persons.

Not only was Roosevelt lonely, though gregarious he concealed his thoughts and feelings. Since Hopkins respected this reticence and shared the Presidential outlook, Roosevelt found him particularly congenial.

So convinced was Roosevelt of the similarity of Hopkin's outlook with his own he began grooming Hopkins to succeed to the Presidency, making him Secretary of Commerce to take the "social worker" stamp off him. But Hopkin's poor health extingished the plan to make him President. He had to have part of his stomach removed and for six months failed to attend a Cabinet meeting. His political ambition thereby annulled, he thereafter devoted himself solely to serving Roosevelt.

On the evening of May 10, 1940, the same day Germany invaded Holland, Luxembourg and Belgium, Hopkins went to dinner at the White House. Since Hopkins was ill, Roosevelt persuaded him to remain overnight. He was to remain for three and a half years.

Roosevelt lodged Hopkins in the "Lincoln's office" guest room on the second floor in the southeast corner. The suite had a large bedroom with a huge four-poster double bed, a small bedroom in which Hopkins at first quartered his secretary to use as an office, and a bath.

Originally the suite had been one room, which Abraham Lincoln used as a study. A plaque over the fireplace stated that the Emancipation Proclamation had been signed here. The Roosevelts considered it the best guest room and had assigned it to King George VI of England when he had visited the White House in 1939. Diana lived on the third floor next to the sun porch.

At the White House, Hopkins worked in his room. After breakfast, after dinner and at odd times during the day he talked with the President. Hopkins ate dinner with Roosevelt on trays in the study and worked with him there until late at night. On Sundays they cruised on the

106

Presidential yacht, the U.S.S. *Potomac*.

Hopkins knew politics and social welfare; he knew some economics and was an energetic administrator. An apt pupil, he rapidly learned Roosevelt's lessons in international affairs.

Towards the end of 1940, Roosevelt said to Hopkins, concerning aid to the beleaguered British, "You know, a lot of this could be settled if Churchill and I could just sit down together for awhile."

Hopkins offered to go to London as intermediary. At first Roosevelt demurred. Later he changed his mind; at a press conference, Jan. 3, 1941, he announced his intention of sending Hopkins.

Hopkins left for London January 9. Scarce had he gone than a telegram dated Jan. 27, 1941 brought ominous news to the State Department.

The telegram from Grew in Tōkyō read:

> A member of the Embassy was told by my Peruvian colleague that from many quarters, including a Japanese one, he had heard that a surprise mass attack on Pearl Harbor was planned by the Japanese military forces in case of 'trouble' between Japan and the United States; that the attack would involve the use of all the Japanese military facilities. My colleague said he was prompted to pass this on because it had come to him from many sources, although the plan seemed fantastic.

5

HAWAII PREPARES AGAINST JAPANESE ATTACK

Grew's warning had originated with Dr. Ricardo Rivera–Schreiber, the Peruvian envoy to Tōkyō. At a diplomatic party, a drunken Japanese interpreter employed by the Peruvian legation had exclaimed to Rivera–Schreiber, "The American fleet will disappear."

Rivera–Schreiber gently questioned the interpreter concerning the place of the attack that would cause the American fleet to disappear. At San Diego? No. San Francisco? No. South Pacific? No. At this point the interpreter pulled himself together, fell silent, bowed and left.

After pondering the incident, Rivera–Schreiber said, "By a process of elimination I decided that Pearl Harbor must be the spot."

These details of the origin of the warning were unknown to Washington where Grew's message wound through the State Department and on to the Navy Department. In neither department did the warning evoke much interest. However, the Chief of Naval Operations daily staff conference decided to forward the message to the Commander in Chief of the Pacific Fleet in Hawaii. The chore fell to Comdr. Arthur H. McCollum, chief of the Far Eastern Section, Office of Naval Intelligence.

The idea of a Japanese attack on Pearl Harbor was not new to McCollum. Born in 1898 in Nagasaki, Japan, of Southern Baptist missionary parents, he had served as assistant naval attache in Tōkyō from 1928 to 1930. He knew that Japanese writers of fact and fiction had for years intrigued readers with stories of such a projected attack. He had first read such an account in a Japanese-language paperback in 1924.

Even earlier a book on the subject had appeared in America. In 1921 Hector C. Bywater, naval correspondent for the *London Daily Telegraph* had his book *Sea Power in the Pacific* published in the United States. Four years later he expanded the book into a novel entitled *The Great Pacific War*, in which he described a Japanese surprise attack on the United States Asiatic Fleet in Pearl Harbor, with simultaneous assaults on Guam and the Philippines and landings on Luzon at Langayen Gulf and Lamon Bay in the Philippines. In September 1925 the *New York Times Book Review* featured the book on page one.

In that same year, while being tried for insubordination in a sensational court-martial, Col. William Mitchell predicted a Japanese aerial attack on Pearl Harbor. Mitchell had been born of American parents in Nice, France, Dec. 29, 1879. He grew up in Milwaukee, was educated at Racine College and at Columbian (now George Washington) University. He left Columbian before graduating to enlist for service in the Spanish–American War. In 1915 he was assigned to the aviation section of the Signal Corps. He learned to fly. In the World War he proved a highly effective air commander. In October 1918 he was promoted to brigadier general.

Mitchell returned from the World War convinced of the overwhelming significance of aviation in any future wars. He called for research, for industry, for building until the American air force reached the strength of any in the world. He even declared that a powerful bomb dropped from the air could sink any ship, even a battleship.

Early in 1921 the Navy supplied former German warships for the express purpose of being used as targets for bombing experiments. Mitchell and his colleagues attacked the vessels and sank them one by one, sinking last

the most unsinkable of all ships, the German battleship
Ostfriesland.

Criticism of Army and Navy brought him demotion from
general to colonel. Four years after the warship bombing
test, on a peaceful mission over Ohio, the huge dirigible
Shenandoah exploded in a storm, breaking into three parts.
It fell 7,000 feet and killed 14 persons, including its
commander. It also injured two of the crew of 28.
Mitchell attributed the loss of the dirigible "to the
incompetence of the Navy Department and the criminal
negligence in ordering this trip." Then came court-
martial.

Mitchell was tried by a panel of Army officers, many
known for outspoken opposition to his campaign. Among them
was Maj. Gen. Douglas MacArthur who had returned from the
Philippines. In the Philippines, among other things,
MacArthur had drawn up a plan for the defense of the Bataan
Peninsula, which encloses Manila Bay on the Western side.

The court found Mitchell guilty and suspended him
from rank, command and duty, with forfeiture of all pay and
allowance for five years.

By late 1939, however, war had come in Europe and the
Axis had been formed; it now appeared that war with Japan
would involve a coalition of enemies. So a new plan called
the *Rainbow* series emerged.

Of the five plans advanced under Rainbow, the
planners settled on the fifth. Rainbow 5 assumed that the
United States would be allied with Great Britain and France
and provided for offensive operations by American forces in
Europe, Africa or both.

The Pacific would be a defensive theater until the
Allies achieved success in the Atlantic area. War in the
Pacific would be between Japan on one side and the Chinese,
Americans, British and Dutch on the other.

In part on the basis of his personal background and
knowledge of Japan plus the most recent information

available to him in the Office of Naval Intelligence, McCollum, January 31 prepared a message for the signature of his chief, Capt. Jules James, acting director of Naval Intelligence.   Capt. James signed it "by direction"-meaning with the approval of the Chief of Naval Operations. February 1, the message went to Adm. Husband E. Kimmel, C-n-C of the U.S. Fleet, whose headquarters was at Pearl Harbor.

The message paraphrased Grew's telegram, but added a second paragraph: " The Division of Naval Intelligence places no credence in these rumors. Furthermore, based on known data regarding the present disposition and employment of Japanese naval and army forces, no move against Pearl Harbor appears imminent or planned for in the forseeable future."

By his misspelled **forseeable** future McCollum meant a projection of no more than a month.

On the date the message was dispatched, Kimmel was at Pearl Harbor taking over command of the fleet from Adm. James O. Richardson.   Richardson had assumed command Jan. 6, 1940. In the ordinary course of events, he would have been expected to continue in this post for two years. But the activities of Japan, as an Axis partner, had created an extraordinary situation.

In the early spring of 1940, Navy Headquarters had dispatched him to Hawaii for maneuvers.   His ships stood into Lahaina Roads off the Island of Maui on April 10. Before that date the only Naval force of consequence in the area had been a small unit at Pearl Harbor composed of a carrier, heavy cruisers and destroyers and called the Hawaiian Detachment. The exercises having been concluded May 9, Richardson expected to take his armada, minus the Hawaiian Detachment, back to its permanent base at San Pedro, California.

But the Chief of Naval Operations, Adm. Harold R. Stark, ordered him to remain in Hawaii because "of the deterrent effect which it is thought your presence may have on the Japs going into the East Indies."

Stark was born at Wilkes-Barre, Pa., Nov. 12, 1880. He graduated from the Naval Academy in 1903 and was commissioned ensign two years later. From 1903 to 1917 he served on various ships and at various naval stations. During the World War he was on the staff of Adm. William S. Sims, commander of the U.S. naval forces in European waters. From 1934 to 1937 he was chief of the naval bureau of ordnance. March 15, 1939, Roosevelt appointed him chief of naval operations with the rank of admiral.

After this appointment Stark pleaded for a larger Fleet. He appeared a number of times before congressional committees to urge larger appropriations, usually succeeding.

Though he did not share the view of Stark as to the deterrent effect of keeping the fleet in Hawaiian waters, Richardson could only obey. In the spring of 1941 the War Department came up with an additional reason for keeping the Fleet there.

Japan had been embroiled and preoccupied with its traditional enemy, Russia, the dissension coming to a head in May 1939 at Nomonhan, a town in Inner Mongolia, Northeast China, on the border of the Mongolian People's Republic, east of Pei-erh. After a minor clash between Japanese and Russian-officered Mongolian forces, the Japanese claimed certain regions occupied by Russian troops. The confrontation grew and grew.

Moscow summoned Gen. Georgi Zhukov and within hours dispatched him to the battlefield in Outer Mongolia. The tough, self-educated Zhukov had risen from the ranks. Anticipating the Japanese offensive by four days, he launched his own enveloping attack 20 August. He drove back the Japanese, inflicting 53,000 casualties. The Russians suffered 10,000 killed and wounded.

The dispute was settled by treaty Sept. 15, 1939, but

112

the rancor remained. But Japanese Foreign Minister Yosuke
Matsuoka, returning from a visit to Mussolini and Hitler,
stopped off at Moscow where he concluded a neutrality pact
April 20, 1941. The pact gave the War Department an
additional reason for keeping the Pacific Fleet in Hawaiian
waters: the neutrality pact with Russia freed Japan to
attack Oahu following the departure of the U.S. Fleet from
Hawaiian waters.

Richardson did not share this fear. "...I felt there
was absolutely no danger at that time of an attack by the
Japanese fleet. I feared that there was, at any time, a
possibility that some fanatical, ill-advised officer in
command of a submarine or a ship might attack. "So
Richardson objected to keeping his fleet in Hawaiian waters
because he believed that his ships "could be better
prepared for war on a normal basis on the west coast."

July 8, 1940 he conferred with the President in
Washington. Richardson felt his command was not yet ready
for war. In October when he again conferred with Roosevelt
he said that he felt the Japanese knew too much about the
Pacific Fleet to regard it as a deterrent. Roosevelt
replied that the presence of the Fleet in the Hawaiian area
has had and was now having a restraining influence on
Japan.

Richardson said, "Mr. Roosevelt, I still do not
believe it, and I know that our fleet is disadvantageously
disposed for preparing for or initiating war operations."

As Commander in Chief of all armed forces, Roosevelt
might have been taken aback at this blunt contradiction.
Worse was forthcoming.

Richardson continued: "Mr. President, I feel that I
must tell you that the senior officers of the Navy do not
have the trust and confidence in the civilian leadership of
this country that is essential for a successful prosecution
of a war in the Pacific."

Roosevelt replied mildly, but he was evidently

displeased by the statement that came close to violating the taboo against an officer of the Armed Forces interfering in national policy making.

Though Richardson disapproved of keeping the Fleet in Hawaiian waters, he expressed no fears for the safety of the ships anchored in Pearl Harbor, despite the success the British had scored against the Italians at Taranto, Italy, Nov. 11, 1940. Yet astute observers on both Axis and Allied sides saw similarities to the situation at Taranto and the threat to the American naval base at Pearl Harbor.

Taranto, the Italian naval base in the Gulf of Taranto at the tip of the Italian boot had been a thorn in the side of the British Fleet, which had the task of guarding British Mediterranean convoys. The British attack, undertaken after careful planning, had the dual purpose of providing cover for several Mediterranean convoys and crippling the Italian battleship fleet, usually based at Taranto.

On this clear, moonlit night, the British launched 21 Swordfish torpedo planes in two waves from the carrier *Illustrious*, about 170 miles from Taranto. Twelve of the Swordfish carried torpedoes, the remainder flares or bombs. The British had chosen to attack at night because of the slow speed and poor defensive capability of the Swordfish that during daylight made them especially vulnerable to the more modern Italian fighter planes. A recent storm had swept away many of the barrage balloons protecting the outer harbor of Taranto where five Italian battleships were moored. The torpedo-net defenses of the harbor were incomplete; moreover, they extended only down to the maximum draft of the battleships, not to the bottom of the harbor.

The British had perfected a new type of torpedo that could pass under the nets and detonate under the keel of the target vessel.

Attacking at an altitude of under 35 feet, the six

torpedo planes of the first wave damaged the battleship *Littorio* and sent the *Conte de Cavour* to the bottom. The second wave further damaged the *Littorio* and put a torpedo into the *Caio Duilio*. Against one battleship sunk and two crippled, the British losses were two aircraft lost and two damaged. The action assured British naval supremacy in the Mediterranean for the next six months.

It also marked a turning point in naval warfare by demonstrating that the carrier and its planes might be the decisive weapon. Again there were many on both sides who failed to recognize that the battleship might be relegated to a minor role.

One who recognized the potential of the carrier that had been demonstrated at Taranto was Capt. Richmond Kelly Turner, chief of U.S. War Plans. Turner submitted a letter for signature to Stark, which Stark dispatched to Richardson Nov. 22, 1940. The letter mentioned that "By far the most profitable object of a sudden attack in Hawaiian waters would be the Fleet units based in that area." Might it not be desirable "to place torpedo nets within the harbor itself..."

Accepting the view of the ordnance experts that torpedoes would be ineffective in Pearl Harbor, Richardson only thought of enemy torpedoes being launched against Pearl Harbor from ships or submarines. He replied that torpedo nets within the harbor were "neither necessary nor practicable. The area is too restricted and ships, at present, are not moored within torpedo range of the entrance."

Since by normal procedures Richardson should have remained CINCUS for at least another year, he was astonished when at 11:30 a.m. Sunday, Jan. 5, 1941 he received orders relieving him of his command. Yet there had been portents of this action that he must, at least unconsciously, have perceived. The correspondence of Stark had cooled since Richardson, in October, had taken issue with the President.

When Richardson reported to Knox in Washington March 24, he told him: "In my experience in the Navy, I have never known of a flag officer being detached from command of the United States Fleet in the same manner that I was, and I feel I owe it to myself to inquire why I was detached."

Knox replied, "The last time you were here you hurt the President's feelings."

On the day Richardson was relieved of his command, as Kimmel returned from the golf course a member of his staff told him to report to the Fleet flagship *Pennsylvania* to read a just-received communication. The dispatch informed him he had been promoted to Commander in Chief effective Feb. 1, 1941.

Kimmel knew that in the present circumstances the post of C-n-C was largely honorary. The Fleet had been divided into three: the first part in the Atlantic to deal with what Washington considered the most dangerous foe, Germany; the second part in Hawaiian waters; the third in the Far East.

Handsome, physically fit at 5'10" and 180 pounds, his blond hair flecked with gray, Kimmel had been born in the small town of Henderson, Kentucky, Feb. 26, 1882. His father had been a major in the Confederate Army. He graduated from Annapolis in 1904, 13th in a class of 62. He went round the world with the fleet in 1908 as a junior officer.

Jan. 31, 1912 he married Dorothy Kinkaid, daughter of an admiral and sister of a Navy officer. Two of his sons by this marriage would serve as Navy officers.

In 1917, during a Panama Canal celebration, he served briefly as aide to the then Ass't Secretary of the Navy Franklin Roosevelt.

During the World War he served on the staff of Adm. Hugh Rodman who commanded the American battleships operating with the British Grand Fleet. In the Asiatic Fleet from 1923 to 1925, Kimmel did additional duty in the Philippines and China.

He steadily mounted the ladder to higher rank and commanded the battleship *New York* in 1933 and 1934. The following year he served as chief of staff to Adm. Thomas Craven, commander battleships of the Fleet.

In 1939 he was type commander of the cruisers in the Battle Force. From this position Roosevelt promoted him over 46 senior officers to make him C-n-C U.S.Fleet and Pacific Fleet.

Though Kimmel knew his superiors regarded him highly, he was surprised by the promotion. He esteemed his old friend Richardson and recognized the irregularity in relieving him of office. He hastened to Richardson's quarters to tell him he saw no justification for his relief, to assure him that he had known nothing about the impending move and to tell him that he had made no effort to replace him. At that time the United States Navy was a homogeneous organization. Most of the enlisted men were extended service personnel who found navy life superior to the unemployment they would risk if they left it. During the economic depression that had dogged the earlier years of Roosevelt's administration, the reenlistment rate had climbed to around 90 percent. Applicants so outnumbered available openings that only one of every 18 aspirants was accepted.

Virtually all the officers were graduates of Annapolis. All important commands were held by Annapolis men.

Now a full admiral and successor to Richardson, Kimmel received Grew's report of a rumored attack on Pearl Harbor. Jan. 24, 1941, Knox had signed a letter to Stark based on the lesson of Taranto coupled with the increasing menace in the Far East.

The letter read:

The security of the U.S. Pacific Fleet while in Pearl Harbor, and of the Pearl Harbor Naval Base itself, has been under renewed study by the Navy Department and forces afloat for the past several weeks. This examination has been, in part, prompted by the increased gravity of the situation with respect to Japan, and by reports from abroad of successful bombing and torpedo plane attacks on ships while in bases. If war eventuates with Japan, it is believed easily possible that hostilities would be initiated by a surprise attack upon the Fleet or Naval Base at Pearl Harbor.

In my opinion, the inherent possibilities of a major disaster to the fleet or naval base warrant taking every step, as rapidly as can be done, that will increase the joint readiness of the Army and Navy to withstand a raid of the character mentioned above.

The letter listed the dangers "in their order of importance and probability of which "Air bombing attack" and "Air torpedo plane attack" ranked first and second...Both types of air attack are possible. They may be carried out successively, simultaneously, or in combination with any of the other operations enumerated"

Along with other suggestions, Knox urged that the Army and Navy forces in Oahu, at least once weekly, prepare against surprise aircraft raids. Oahu is the island on which the Navy and Army headquarters were based. It had achieved its geographical importance in the Hawaiian archipelago not because of its size – two of the other islands are larger – but because it has the best harbor, Honolulu.

A few miles west of Honolulu is Pearl Harbor, a

Chief of Naval Operations Adm. Harold R. Stark, above right, ordered the Pacific Fleet to remain at Pearl Harbor. His headquarters at Pearl Harbor, Commander in Chief of the Combined U.S. Fleet Adm. Husband E. Kimmel, right, maintained harmonious relations with his Army counterpart Lt. Gen. Walter C. Short, above.

teeming anchorage and workshop where the Navy anchored and repaired its ships.

Between Pearl Harbor and Honolulu, somewhat inland, is Fort Shafter, where the man with whom Kimmel was expected to coordinate these exercises had his headquarters. The Army man had arrived as Maj. Gen. Walter C. Short three days after Kimmel had assumed his new post. Short formally assumed his command, in a brief ceremony, February 7. That same day he was promoted to lieutenant general.

In some respects Short had a background similar to that of Gen. Marshall, the man who had assigned him. Born the same year as Marshall, 1880, Short graduated from the Univ. of Illinois at the same time Marshall was completing his courses at Virginia Military Institute. Short was commissioned lieutenant a month apart from the time Marshall achieved that rank. They first met at Fort Reno in 1906 and later served together in the 1st Division in France. In 1940 Marshall advanced Short from division to corps command, shortly afterwards giving him the largest U.S. overseas command.

Marshall spelled out to Short the importance of the assignment and the need of close cooperation with the Navy. The Army's mission was "to protect the base and the naval concentration" and the "fullest protection of the fleet is the rather than a major consideration for us."

He directed Short to work closely with Kimmel. So Short could know "with whom you are to deal," Marshall forwarded a statement of Stark's to the effect that Kimmel, though a man of great ability, could be brusque and undiplomatic. "We must be completely impersonal in these matters," advised Marshall, "at least so far as our own nerves and irritations are concerned."

Short took this admonition to heart. In Hawaii he succeeded in fostering excellent personal relations with Kimmel. Soon they were playing golf together.

A War Department survey of Pearl Harbor defenses in January 1938 had included the prediction that in case of hostilities Japan would strike without notice and "there can be little doubt that the Hawaiian Islands will be the initial scene of action." In 1941 the staffs of Kimmel and Short in preparing plans to cover Army and Navy action in case of trouble underscored the possibility of a surprise attack.

Noting the history of Japan, they predicted that without any prior warning from Naval Intelligence a fast raiding carrier force might arrive in Hawaiian waters. They estimated that "the most likely and dangerous form of attack on Oahu would be an air attack" and "would most likely be launched from one or more carriers which would probably approach inside of 300 miles."

Short's air commander, Maj. Gen. Frederick L. Martin, outlining the requirements for air protection in August 1941, declared that the most favorable plan of action for the enemy "upon which we should base our plans of operation," would be to launch his planes "233 nautical miles from Oahu at dawn the day of the attack"; the worst situation that could arise was "the employment of six enemy carriers against Oahu simultaneously, each approaching on a different course."

June 17, 1940, when the Hawaiian command had been under Maj. Gen. Charles D. Herron, Marshall ordered that Herron, without alarming the public, should put his command on full alert. He should bring out his artillery units, issue live ammunition, take adequate precautions against sabotage and prepare to meet the enemy by sea or air. Herron complied.

After two days, Marshall ordered a gradual relaxation of the alert. Several weeks later he ordered a complete relaxation except for precautions against sabotage and for arrangements permitting establishment of air patrols on short notice.

120

Despite this warning, Marshall shared the view of most of his colleagues that the Hawaiian defenders could cope with an enemy raid. In February 1941 he wrote to Short "that if no serious harm is done us during the first six hours of known hostilities, thereafter the existing defenses would discourage an enemy against the hazard of an attack. The risk of sabotage and risk involved in a surprise raid by air and by submarine constitute the real perils of the situation. Frankly, I do not see any landing threat in the Hawaiian Islands so long as we have air superiority."

In late April, Marshall stressed the apparent impregnability of Oahu in a message to Roosevelt. Marshall mentioned that he intended to send Short 35 heavy bombers and additional medium bombers and pursuit planes. He assured Roosevelt that when the build-up of men, planes and weapons was completed there need be no fear of an enemy landing. An invader would face more than 35,000 troops supported by coast defense guns, antiaircraft, artillery and infantry weapons. With an adequate air defense, the American defenders could attack an enemy task force 750 miles away. If a task force came within 200 miles, it would be hit by all types of bombers and most modern pursuit planes. The island's fortifications, garrison and physical characteristics made it "the strongest fortress in the world."

Both Short and Kimmel took to heart the injuction that close Army-Navy relations were essential for the defense of Hawaii. Soon they established a semiweekly golf date for Sunday mornings.

Like any newcomer to Hawaii, Short could have been confused by what he found there. Sugar was the major industry, and the sugar planters had molded the islands in their own image.

Under the Hawaiian monarchy and later, when the whites overthrew the unncooperative native monarch, Queen

Liluokalani, the planters coped with the labor shortage by importing different nationalities to work in bondage on the plantations. They played these nationalities against each other to discourage them from uniting for better pay and working conditions.

Thus they first brought in Chinese. When the Chinese began to agitate, they brought in Japanese. The first group of Japanese were imported in 1868, the venture being only partially successful. Beginning in 1885, the planters recruited in Japan and began bringing Japanese to Hawaii by the shipload under three-year contracts.

Most Japanese left the plantations upon the expiration of their contracts. Most of these returned to Japan, but many sought opportunities in Hawaii.

America annexed the archipelago in 1898 and gave it a territorial government. Washington appointed the governor; the residents elected the territorial legislature. After America annexed Hawaii, the national government abrogated the labor contracts and prohibited immigration of further contract immigrants.

Japanese nationals were barred from naturalization; their children, being born under the American flag, became American citizens at birth. Until 1924 Japan recognized these American-born as citizens of Japan. The local authorities registered the dual-citizen children in the public schools as of Japanese nationality. Even after Japan changed its law so as to recognize as Japanese citizens only those born after 1924 whose parents registered them as such with the Japanese consulate, the local authorities continued to identify the Hawaii-born as of Japanese nationality. Press, radio and other instruments of propaganda cooperated with the official policy, making it appear that for those of Asiatic origin, even though born and reared in Hawaii, American citizenship was only a technicality. In 1940 the sycophantic U.S. Census Bureau listed about 160,000 persons of Japanese

122

ancestry in Hawaii. Though only 24 percent of these were foreign-born, the entire group was listed as Japanese - 37 percent of the total population.

In these circumstances it was understandable that Short, having only a superficial knowledge of the society of the islands, felt that the greatest menace to the defense of Hawaii against Japan was the 160,000 "Japanese" he envisioned as potential spies and saboteurs.

Marshall shared Short's concern about sabotage from some among the 160,000 in Hawaii identified as Japanese. Consequently there was a tendency to prepare for the defense of Hawaii against this supposed enemy at home, even at the expense of preparing for the known enemy in East Asia.

Distrustful of America after being educated there, Yosuke Matsuoka (right) as Japanese Foreign Minister would pursue a pro-Axis policy.

6

HITLER MAKES A FATEFUL MOVE

When Churchill learned of the impending visit of Hopkins and of his close relationship with Roosevelt, he immediately ordered full hospitality for the emissary. On meeting, Churchill and Hopkins immediately liked each other.

Hopkins remained in England, amid falling bombs, for six weeks. He left for home convinced that the British had a magnificent spirit and the will to resist. He also concluded that they desperately needed food, machine tools, planes, ships, gasoline, oil, guns and ammunition.

He returned in time to meet America's new ambassador to London, John Gilbert Winant at the Roosevelt Hotel in New York City. Winant had been born in New York City, Feb. 23, 1889. He studied at Princeton University and served as captain of the 8th Air Observation Squadron in France during the World War. After the war he was elected to the New Hampshire legislature and he served as Governor of New Hampshire in 1915–26 and from 1931 to 1934. He joined the International Labor Organization in 1935, serving as assistant director and then as director.

He had known Roosevelt for years, and on one of his journeys back to the United States from Geneva at the end of 1938 he urged the President to run for reelection. The President took offense. Roosevelt said he had done his part as a liberal and that some of the others should share the burden of carrying forward the things they professed to believe.

Winant protested that the country was facing war:

Roosevelt had a greater hold on the people of the democratic world than any other statesman of his time; it was too late to find a substitute. Though Roosevelt wanted to retire to Hyde Park to enjoy the freedom of private citizenship, he was needed in the Presidency to cope with the danger confronting the world.

The President looked wan and tired. So Winant suggested that Roosevelt should get away where he could be alone and think the matter out by himself. Thereupon Roosevelt made the only reference to his illness and handicap that Winant ever heard from him.

Roosevelt said, "You know, Gil, I can never be alone." He pointed out the window of the Executive Office and added, "I cannot even go out and walk alone under those trees. Always someone has to be with me or near me. I am never alone."

Nevertheless, as we have seen, Roosevelt did run for the unprecedented third term and was elected. February 6, following his reelection, he appointed Winant Ambassador to Great Britain.

At the Roosevelt Hotel, Hopkins gave Winant a brief description of the British statesmen and military and naval chiefs he had met and an accurate estimate of British civil and military needs. Immediately afterward, Winant boarded a plane and flew to England.

Roosevelt had already turned over 50 overage destroyers to Great Britain. March 11, 1941 he signed the Lend-Lease act, actually entitled "An Act to Promote the Defense of the United States." The act provided that the President might "sell, transfer title to, exchange, lease, lend or otherwise dispose of" defense articles to the government of any country whose defense he deemed vital to the defense of the United States.

Within three hours after he signed the Lend-Lease act, Roosevelt issued two directives putting the program into motion. The first declared the defense of Great

Britain vital to the defense of the United States and authorized the Secretary of the Navy to turn over to the British 28 motor torpedo boats and P.T.C.motor boats, together with certain facilities for arming merchant ships. The second declared that the defense of Greece vital to the defense of the United States and authorized the Secretary of War to transfer to the Greeks guns, shells and other infantry equipment.

As Churchill put it, "(Lend-Lease) transformed immediately the whole position. It made us free to shape by agreement long-term plans of vast extent for all our needs. There was no provision for repayment. There was not even to be a formal account kept in dollars or sterling. What we had was lent or leased to us because our continued resistance to the Hitler tyranny was deemed to be of vital interest to the great Republic. According to President Roosevelt, the defense of the United States and not dollars was henceforth to determine where American weapons were to go."

Even before the Lend-Lease bill was passed, Roosevelt, February 18, 1941, told William Averell Harriman, "I want you to go over to London and recommend everything we can do, short of war, to keep the British Isles afloat." Harriman would be the President's personal representative. He would report to the White House, not to the State Department.

He would concern himself with all matters affecting the conduct of the war – Lend-Lease, shipping, strategy- dealing directly with Churchill and his service and supply ministers. The newly appointed Ambassador to the Court of St. James's, Winant, would take care of the normal business of American representation, deal with the Foreign Office and report to Hull.

William Averell Harriman, who was to be known by his middle name through most of his life, was born Nov. 15, 1891, in New York City to Edward Henry Harriman, financier and railroad executive. The elder Harriman left school at age 14 to become a broker's clerk in Wall Street. By 1870 he was able to buy a seat on the New York Stock Exchange. Eleven years later he began his career in railroading, buying up and expanding railroads.

The Harriman family often reserved summers for travel. During the summers of 1903 and 1904 the family toured Europe by motor car. By 1905 Edward had conceived an idea for a round-the-world transportation network. Late that summer he sailed with his family for Japan to negotiate a deal for the reconstruction and operation of the South Manchurian Railroad, which Japan had wrested from Russia in the Russo-Japanese war of 1904-1905.

The Emperor, Japanese bankers and high officials received Harriman with elaborate courtesy. He signed a preliminary memorandum of agreement with the Japanese government. The Foreign Minister Baron Jutarō Komura was still at Portsmouth, New Hampshire, where the peace treaty was negotiated.

Though the nation had defeated Russia in battle after battle, Japan was financially exhausted. Aware of Japan's financial plight, The Russians capitalized on it to rob her of much of the fruits of victory.

Unable to understand this situation, the Japanese man in the street was angered by the terms of the treaty. Since President Theodore Roosevelt had initiated the Portsmouth negotiations, the Japanese tended to hold him responsible for the treaty's unfavorable conditions. Rioting broke out, tinged with anti-Americanism.

Averell, then 13, was never to forget the explosive character of these Japanese demonstrations. Rioters burned to the ground the house of one government minister, who escaped the fury of the mob by climbing over the back fence. To guard the American Minister, Lloyd Gricom and his guests the Harriman family, Japanese soldiers encamped on the lawn of the American Legation.

The Harriman agreement concerning the South Manchurian Railroad was deferred and then broken off. A provision of the Portsmouth Treaty barred any transfer of control over the railroad except with the consent of the Chinese government. The Chinese opposed granting further concessions to foreigners.

Averell graduated from Yale in 1913 and held many high positions in the business world.

Since his school days at Groton, Harriman had known Eleanor and Franklin Roosevelt. There he had been a classmate of Eleanor's younger brother, Hall Roosevelt. In 1934 Harriman accepted the invitation of Franklin to become divisional administrator for the National Recovery Administration. He remained with the NRA for one year. In 1941 he returned to government service and after three months in the Office of Production Management undertook the assignment to Great Britain.

Harriman arrived in England March 15. Churchill's naval aide met him in Bristol and flew him in a special plane to Chequers, an ancient estate 30 miles northwest of London, the official country residence of the British prime ministers since 1921.

Churchill greeted Harriman warmly. He remembered their first meeting in Cannes in 1927 and their meeting two years later in New York. At the time of the second meeting Churchill had been caught in the speculative fever of 1929 and in the Wall Street crash had lost the money he had just received from the publication of a new book.

There was more than such a financial reverse to concern Churchill now. The war was going badly for the British. Though the threat of invasion had diminished since the German reversal in the Battle of Britain, the number of invasion barges still visible along the French coast made it unwise to dismiss the prospect altogether.

Furthermore, the German submarines were taking a terrible toll of British shipping, sinking a huge proportion of desperately needed imports and destroying ships far faster than the British shipyards could replace them.

Churchill was uncomfortably conscious of the baleful glare of the Japanese fixed on this evidence of British weakness while searching for other chinks in her defense. In February Japanese Foreign Minister Yosuke Matsuoka had said a "dangerous situation" might result from Anglo-American defense measures in the Far East and had told the Diet that the "white race must cede Oceania" to the Japanese.

He defined Oceania as a huge area in the Pacific capable of supporting 600 million persons.

This was the same Matsuoka who had led Japan out of the League of Nations when that organization had acted adversely on the Japanese occupation of Manchuria. A curious facet of his career, much of which had been spent in the forefront of Japanese hostility towards the West, is that he had received much of his education in the United States.

Matsuoka had been born in 1880 to an impoverished samurai family in Yamaguchi prefecture. It was at a time when the first Japanese rejection of Westernization had turned into reluctant acceptance and then evolved into a craze for Western knowledge. The government was sending promising youths abroad to study. Some went on their own resources; such a one was Matsuoka.

In 1893, after his father's business had bankrupted, Matsuoka, aged 13, sailed for America. The captain of the ship was his uncle. When the ship reached America, the uncle put him ashore and told him to shift for himself.

Japanese were still uncommon in America. But the white residents of the West Coast had formed a pattern of discrimination and harassment against the Chinese immigrants. They found it easy to apply the pattern to the Japanese.

The year Matsuoka landed, the director of the San Francisco Board of Education introduced a resolution to provide segregated schools for all Nikkei children, all of whom they identified as Japanese, even though born in America.

The Japanese consul protested the proposed segregation; the Board rescinded the resolution. But the proposal was an ominous portent of things to come.

An American family in Portland, Oregon befriended Matsuoka. Profiting from the opportunity, he worked diligently as laborer and in a law office. Converted to Christianity, he even served as substitute minister. Besides earning a living, he acquired an education. He graduated from University of Oregon law school in 1900.

Though he lingered in America for three years after graduation, his attachment to the country must have been mingled with resentment for some of the things he observed and experienced there. Like the Chinese, the Japanese were barred from becoming naturalized American citizens. In some States they were disbarred from marrying whites. The Japanese and Chinese were barred from membership in labor unions. In a false bubonic scare, the Mayor of San Francisco ordered mass inoculation of Japanese and Chinese, but no others. The government seemed bent on subjecting the Japanese to harassment and humiliation.

Possessed of a law degree but, because of his alien status, denied the right to practice law, seeing the anti-Japanese agitation around him mounting, Matsuoka must have concluded his talents were wasting in America. He returned to Japan.

In Japan, being bilingual, it may have seemed the logical first step in his career to take the Foreign Service examination. He took the examination, passed and in 1904 entered the Foreign Service.

Throughout his life he would insist he understood America. Among his compatriots he posed as an expert on

130

the country.   Considering the abuse and discrimination against the Japanese he had observed there and which, as a member of the Foreign Service he would frequently observe being administered to his countrymen, he could not regard America with complete favor.

He applied himself to his vocation.   He became known as an orator of extraordinary ability.   He began to rise in the Service.   As a Foreign Service officer of the nation that considered itself the natural leader of the Far East, he found many problems to engage his attention on the Asiatic continent.   He served as secretary to the Prime Minister, director of the South Manchurian Railway and became its vice-president in 1927.

He gained repute in Japan by leading the Japanese delegation out of the League of Nations.   He became president of the South Manchurian railway in 1935 and Minister of Foreign Affairs in 1940.

As Foreign Minister he was now on his way to Berlin via Siberia and Moscow.   He arrived in Moscow March 24 and lectured both Stalin and his Foreign Minister Vyacheslav Molotov on how the moral Communists of Japan were unalterably opposed to the individualistic ideals of the Anglo-Saxon peoples.   Stalin replied that the Soviet Union had never gotten along well with Great Britain and "never would."

Three days later Matsuoka arrived in Berlin.   Being involved in planning the crushing of Yugoslavia, Hitler was at first too busy to see even this important ally.   He had concluded plans for the invasion of Russia, hints of which fell to the visitor from the German Foreign Minister Joachim Von Ribbentrop.

According to Ribbentrop if the Soviet opposed German interests, Germany would crush her without hesitation.   If it came to war, the Fuehrer was convinced "there would be in a few months no more Russia."

This expression of reckless belligerence caused

Matsuoka to blink and look alarmed. Ribbentrop reassured him; Ribbentrop did not believe that "Stalin would pursue an unwise policy."

In the afternoon, Hitler talked to Matsuoka. "Never in the human imagination," Hitler told his visitor, could there be a better opportunity for the Japanese to strike in the Pacific than now. "Such a moment would never return. It was unique in history."

April 4, Hitler again talked to Matsuoka, who had just returned from Rome. There Mussolini had told him that "America was the Number One enemy and Soviet Russia came only in second place."

Now Hitler kept from his visitor the German plan to attack Yugoslavia and Greece. Concerning America he was more outspoken.

Germany, said Hitler, had made preparations so that no American could land in Europe. Germany would wage a vigorous war against America with submarines and the Luftwaffe. With her greater experience, Germany would be more than a match for America – and this entirely apart from the fact that German soldiers were obviously far superior to the Americans.

Further, if Japan became in conflict with the United States, Germany would at once take the necessary steps. This seemed such a handsome offer that Matsuoka appeared unable to immediately grasp its significance.

So Hitler added that in case of a conflict between Japan and America Germany would promptly participate.

Of Ribbentrop, Matsuoka had asked, March 28, whether on his return trip to Moscow he should "negotiate with the Russians on the Nonaggression Pact or the Treaty of Neutrality." Referring to this question later, Ribbentrop guaranteed that if Russia attacked Japan "Germany would strike immediately." He wanted to give this assurance "so that Japan could push southward toward Singapore without fear of any complications with Russia."

Disregarding the hints that Hitler would welcome war with Russia with Japan a German ally, Matsuoka on returning to Moscow, as we have noted, signed a treaty with Stalin that provided for each country to remain neutral if the other became involved in war.

At the time of this development, Roosevelt had already revealed an agreement with the Danish envoy in Washington that gave the United States the right to build bases in Greenland. On April 14, the day after the signing of the Japanese–Russian pact, Hull and Undersecretary of State Sumner Welles met with Thor Thors, the Icelandic Consul General in Washington and opened negotiations for the sending of the First Marine Brigade "to supplement and eventually replace the British forces...which were needed elsewhere."

After arrangements to land the American marines in Iceland had been concluded, Stark wrote to Adm. Ernest J. King, Commander in Chief of the U.S. Atlantic Fleet, "I realize that this is practically an act of war." Everyone recognized that if the Germans attacked in Iceland the marines would fight.

April 2, Roosevelt had talked about providing U.S. Naval escort for the Atlantic convoys with definite provision for aggressive action by American warships against German submarines and surface raiders in the western Atlantic. But when Washington had learned of the Japanese–Russian pact, the news caused so much concern about the situation in the Pacific that Roosevelt felt constrained to modify his plan for aggressive action in the Atlantic.

The Japanese–Russian pact indicated that Japan had been freed to concentrate on an advance towards southeastern Asia towards British and perhaps American possessions. So Roosevelt abandoned Hemisphere Defense Plan No. 1 and issued another directive April 24. American ships were merely to <u>report</u> movements of German vessels west of Iceland as they observed or detected them. They should shoot only if shot at.

This order may have appeared sufficient to curb open hostilities because up to this point all acts of provocation or aggression in German-American relations had come from the Americans. Hitler had ordered that provocation with America be avoided until he had disposed of his enemies in Europe.

But June 9, 1941, a Brazilian ship picked up 11 castaways from a lifeboat in the Brazilian coastal lanes, whose plight had come about in defiance of the order of Hitler. May 21 a German submarine, the *U-29*, commanded by Kapitanleutnant Jost Metzler had come upon their vessel *Robin Moor*, an American merchant ship on its way from America to South Africa and halted it. Finding it carried contraband according to German definition – steel rails and trucks, an insignificant number of small-caliber target rifles and a trifling amount of ammunition – Metzler gave the eight passengers, male and female, and the 38 crewmen 30 minutes to scramble into the four lifeboats. When they complied he torpedoed the ship, finishing it off with gunfire.

The Brazilian rescue ship radioed the news of the sinking of the *Robin Moor* June 10. A British ship picked up the remaining castaways, but the rescue was not made public until June 17.

The *Robin Moor* was the first American vessel of any kind to be attacked by the Germans. The interventionists in America, including Hopkins and Stimpson, urged Roosevelt to respond to the sinking with strong countermeasures.

Roosevelt preferred to follow public opinion rather than to lead it. May 27, even before he had full word of the sinking of the *Robin Moor*, Roosevelt had found the war situation sufficiently grim to proclaim an "unlimited national emergency" in one of his fireside chats to the nation. For the first time he attacked Hitler by name.

Roosevelt said, "We are placing our armed forces in strategic military position. We will not hesitate to use our armed forces to repel attack."

He responded to the situation by curbing oil shipments from the Atlantic coast to all countries save the Allies and Latin America. He froze German and Italian assets in the United States and directed the German government to close down its consulates and all German agencies in United States territory except the German Embassy itself.

That same day, Hitler told his naval advisers that "incidents with the USA warships and merchant ships outside the closed area" be avoided until Operation Barbarossa, the code name for the invasion of Russia, becomes clearer.

He invaded Russia at dawn the following morning.

As he wrote in *Mein Kampf*, he had always planned the overthrow of Russia. As a matter of expediency he had concluded the 1939 pact with Russia, but he feared Bolshevism and his fears had been stirred further by the actions of Stalin after the signing of the pact.

While Hitler was engaged in the French campaign, Stalin had capitalized on the German preoccupation by occupying three Baltic states. On June 26, 1940, again without notice to Hitler, Stalin had addressed a 24-hour ultimatum to Rumania demanding the restoration of Bessarabia, a 17,151 square mile province in eastern Rumania that had proclaimed its independence from Russia in 1917, joined Rumania and been recognized as Rumanian by the Treaty of Versailles. In addition Russia demanded the surrender of northern Bukovina, a 3,396 square mile province in northern Rumania, which had also joined Rumania in 1918. Rumania yielded, and the Russian forces poured into a region ominously close to the oil fields on which Germany depended.

Though even in *Mein Kampf* Hitler had pointed out the folly of Germany waging war on two fronts, he began to feel he could not afford to subjugate the West before dealing with Russia.

Originally the plan to invade Russia had been scheduled for mid-May. But without consulting Hitler, Mussolini invaded Greece, and his campaign fared so badly that Hitler had to go to his aid with German troops. Then an uprising overthrew the pro-Axis Yugoslavian government, and Hitler was further diverted by being required to send large forces to crush Yugoslavia. Though the Germans quickly overran both countries, the military diversion caused Hitler to postpone the Russian invasion to late June.

As early as January 1941, Roosevelt, informed Stalin by Undersecretary of State Sumner Welles through Russian Ambassador Constantine A. Oumansky that Germany planned to attack Russia. Through his Foreign Minister Anthony Eden, Churchill, April 3, warned Stalin that Hitler was planning hostilities against Russia. The Allies made other friendly gestures towards the Soviet. January 21, Roosevelt lifted the moral embargo he had initiated against Russia during the Soviet war with Finland. Churchill continued to pass on to the Soviet leaders information regarding Nazi plans.

Stalin interpreted such warnings as an attempt to drive a wedge between Russia and Germany, and he publicly said so in a dispatch broadcast June 13 and published in the papers the following day. On June 21 when a German deserter predicted to the Soviets a German invasion the following morning, Stalin ordered him shot as an agent provocateur.

Nevertheless it had been impossible for Stalin to completely ignore the assembling of large German forces on the Russian border. April 22, the Soviet had complained to the German Foreign Office about continuing and increasing violations of the USSR boundary by German planes; Germany countered with a complaint about Soviet planes.

136

By June 21 one hundred and 20 German divisions of the highest quality were assembled in three army groups along the Russian front. When these German hordes poured over the border at dawn the next morning, the Russians were unprepared. Hundreds of Russian planes were destroyed before they could get into the air.

Their unpreparedness was the more painful because of the nature of the warfare Hitler had ordered waged. Hitler said that since the Russians were not signatories to the Hague Convention, treatment of Russian prisoners need not follow the Articles of the Convention. Commissars (Communist party officials assigned to military units) were to be shot.

Though Stalin was surprised and unprepared, the Allies were not. Churchill had arranged to broadcast as soon as the German invasion plan became perfectly clear. He had already cabled Roosevelt that if war arose between Germany and Russia, the British would give all possible aid to Russia.

That weekend Winant, a guest at Chequers, brought Roosevelt's reply. If the Germans struck at Russia, Roosevelt would immediately support publicly "any announcement the Prime Minister might make welcoming Russia as an ally."

On Saturday evening Churchill's private secretary, J.R. Colville, while walking on the croquet lawn with the Prime Minister asked whether the acceptance of Russia as an ally might be a compromise of principle for Churchill, who was known as an arch anti-Communist.

"Not at all," said Churchill, "I have only one purpose, the destruction of Hitler, and my life is much simplified thereby. If Hitler invaded Hell, I would make at least a favorable reference to the Devil in the House of Commons."

Colville was awakened at 4 the following morning by a telephone message from the Foreign Office: Germany had invaded Russia. Since Churchill had given orders he was to be awakened for nothing except the invasion of England, Colville waited till 8 a.m. before imparting this crucial news to him.

"Tell BBC (British Broadcasting Corporation) I will broadcast at nine tonight," said Churchill.

In his speech that night Churchill said:

> **No one has been a more consistent opponent of Communism than I have for the last 25 years. I will unsay no word that I have spoken about it.   But all this fades away before the spectacle which is now unfolding...Behind all this glare, behind all this storm, I see that small group of villainous men who plan, organize and launch this cataract of horrors upon mankind...Any man or state who fights on against Nazidom will have our aid.   Any man or state who marches with Hitler is our foe...It follows, therefore, that we shall give whatever help we can to Russia and the Russian people...**

Up to this point Roosevelt had made Great Britain the primary recipient of Lend-Lease aid, though he had also given some American weapons to China. Now he had to decide what proportion of the aid available he should give to Russia.

7

CHURCHILL AND ROOSEVELT UNITE AGAINST THE AXIS

Though the Allies welcomed the respite to Great Britain caused by the diversion of German forces to the invasion of Russia, neither British nor American military experts expected the Russians to last more than two months. Nevertheless, two days after Churchill pledged to aid Russia, Roosevelt did likewise. Roosevelt not only pledged all possible aid, he released $40 million in frozen Soviet credits; the following day he announced that the Neutrality Act would not be invoked against Russia.

To expedite the new program, Roosevelt sent Hopkins abroad again.

Since all deliberation on all phases of the war at the time, including American production and Lend Lease, depended on how long Russia could hold out, Hopkins sought the answer from Stalin himself. In England, Churchill arranged transportation for him. Hopkins entrained to Scotland and flew from there to Archangel, 469 miles northeast of Leningrad, at the head of the Divina Gulf. Here he transferred to a Russian plane that flew him to Moscow.

When the Germans had invaded, Stalin had fallen into shock. For several days he disappeared from public and political view, locked in his study and showing signs of mental disturbance. Finally he emerged to broadcast to the Soviet people, exhorting them to resist the invaders.

He then pulled himself together and began reorganizing the army commands. When he met with Hopkins, Stalin was fully restored and showed a keenness of intellect that impressed his visitor.

The Russian campaign was now in its fourth week. It had already passed the minimum given Russia by the British authorities and there seemed a glimmer of hope that Russia might hold out until winter set in.

Hopkins stressed the common purpose of the Allies: the destruction of Hitlerism. He asked what Russia most needed that the United States could deliver immediately and what would be the requirements of Russia on the basis of a long war.

Stalin ticked off his needs, which included antiaircraft guns and aluminum for the construction of airplanes. "Give us the antiaircraft guns and the aluminum," he said, " and we can fight for three or four years."

The vastness of Russia with its impenetrable forests had already persuaded Hopkins that the swift victory predicted by the military experts was unlikely.

Despite the new treaty with Japan, Commissar of Foreign Affairs Vyacheslav M. Molotov was concerned that Japan might attack Russia at what it considered a propitious moment. He believed that a warning from the United States might contribute to deterring Japan. Hopkins departed from Moscow with a favorable impression of Stalin. He later wrote about the meeting:

> **It was like talking to a perfectly coordinated machine, an intelligent machine... (Stalin was) an austere, rugged, determined figure in boots that shone like mirrors, stout baggy trousers, and snug-fitting blouse...He's about five feet six, about a hundred and ninety pounds. His hands are huge...His voice is harsh but ever under control. What he says is all the accent and inflections his words need...**

Since Hopkins was ignorant of Russian, he was probably unconscious that Stalin spoke the language with a Georgian accent.

Hopkins enplaned from Moscow August 1. At Archangel, the British plane captain advised that the weather conditions were such that it would be prudent to delay departure for a day.

Hopkins felt he was unable to wait for the weather to improve. Security reasons prevented him from revealing it to the captain, but he had arranged to accompany Churchill to a special conference with Roosevelt in Newfoundland. Churchill was scheduled to leave on the battleship *Prince of Wales*. Hopkins feared that if he failed to leave Archangel at once he might arrive in England after the *Prince of Wales* had sailed.

Hopkins carried the medicine he needed for survival in a small satchel. Somehow the satchel had been left in Moscow. On the return flight, taken despite the bad weather, he was desperately ill.

When he was delivered into the hands of Adm. Sir John Tovey, C-n-C of the Home Fleet, at Scapa Flow, the British naval base in the Orkney Islands off the northern coast of Scotland, Hopkins was so ill the admiral feared he might not live through the night. The doctors gave him medication that put him to sleep for 18 hours. When he awoke he learned that Churchill would not arrive until the following day. Relieved, Hopkins went back to bed for more rest.

Rested after two nights of sleep, but still pale and wan, Hopkins came on deck to greet Churchill. In addition to his chiefs of staff, various officers of the three services and other dignitaries, Churchill had brought Sir Alexander Cadogan, permanent undersecretary of state for Foreign Affairs.

It was rare for Churchill to have leisure, and he made the most of it on the trip across the North Atlantic.

He played backgammon with Hopkins at a shilling a game. It
was apparent, too, that the respite gained from the German
attack on Russia, plus the enforced leisure of the voyage,
gave Churchill occasion to think more about the menace of
Japan.

In the second week of February he had noticed a stir
and flutter in the Japanese Embassy and the Japanese colony
in London. This agitation among a people usually so
reserved had inspired Churchill with the thoughts he had
communicated to Roosevelt Feb. 15, 1941. He had written:

> Many drifting straws seem to indicate
> Japanese intention to make war on us or do
> something that would force us to make war on
> them in the next few weeks or months...the
> weight of the Japanese Navy, if thrown against
> us, would confront us with situations beyond
> the scope of our naval resources. I do not
> myself think that the Japanese would be likely
> to send the large military expedition necessary
> to lay siege to Singapore. The Japanese would
> no doubt occupy whatever strategic points and
> oilfields in the Dutch East Indies and
> thereabouts they covet, and thus get into a far
> better position for a full-scale attack on
> Singapore later on...You will therefor see, Mr.
> President, the awful enfeeblement of our war
> effort that would result merely from the send
> out by Japan of her battle-cruisers and her
> twelve eight-inch-gun cruisers into the Eastern
> oceans, and still more from any serious
> invasion threat against the two Australian
> d e m o c r a c i e s   i n   t h e   S o u t h e r n
> Pacific...Everything that you can do to inspire
> the Japanese with the fear of a double war
> (Japan versus Great Britain and the United

States) **may avert the danger...**

Churchill had also thought it appropriate to express his opinion on ways to improve Japanese–British relations when the Japanese ambassador, Mamoru Shigemitsu, came to call, though in the meantime the agitation among the Japanese in London had subsided.

Churchill told Shigemitsu that the Tripartite Pact was ostensibly so favorable to Germany and so scarcely favorable to Japan that it inspired the suspicion that the pact must have some secret provisions. Japan had left the Allies in doubt about how she would interpret the pact in some eventualities. Japan had made a great mistake in signing the pact. The pact had harmed Japanese relations with the United States and brought Great Britain and the United States closer together.

So close together that Churchill was now on his way to a face–to–face meeting with the American President where such matters were to be discussed. Churchill believed that Japan would not go to war with Great Britain while she was still undefeated, especially if she felt that the United States would join with Great Britain. So it seemed important to him that the United States should let it be known to Japan that an attack on Great Britain would bring the United States into the war on the British side. Such a communication, he assumed, would do much to deter Japan. He hoped for a common policy of resistance.

As they sailed, Churchill spoke of Roosevelt as if he had never met him. Though Roosevelt was to remember the meeting at Gray's Inn during the World War, Churchill, already an eminent statesman at the time, had taken little notice of Roosevelt and had promptly forgotten him. Now Roosevelt was an almost legendary figure. Churchill recognized that Roosevelt outranked him, for Roosevelt was the Head of State, on the level with the King, while Churchill was only the Head of Government.

He plied Hopkins with questions to ascertain what sort of man was the President. What did Roosevelt think of this and that? With a blend of curiosity and awe, he would insist, "Tell me more about Roosevelt."

"You would have thought," Hopkins later commented to friends, "Winston was being carried up into heaven to meet God." Certainly Roosevelt had been a staunch friend of the British in the time of their greatest peril. Many of the things he had done for them he had done against isolationist opposition and in defiance of the advice of his own ambassador to Great Britain, Joseph P. Kennedy. Kennedy believed that Great Britain was beaten and would soon surrender and so supplies sent to her would not only be wasted but would fall into the hands of the Germans. Until the German invasion of Russia, Communists and Communist sympathizers had decried the war as a British Imperialist war. Within hours of the invasion, they had taken the opposite course, as fervently supporting the Allied effort as much as they had formerly decried it. On the other hand, many isolationists took comfort in the invasion as showing that Germany was a champion defending the world against Bolshevism.

Yet Roosevelt continued to resist the Axis. When Vichy France granted military bases in Indo-China, Vichy being unable to resist, Roosevelt joined with the British in freezing all Japanese assets. He put the armed forces of the Philippines under American command. The United States defense agencies froze all stocks of raw silk. July 28 the Dutch East Indies suspended its oil agreement with Japan and froze all Japanese assets. August 1, Roosevelt banned export of aviation gasoline and oil to all points outside the western hemisphere except to the British empire and "countries resisting aggression," thus tightening the economic noose strangling Japan to its last notch.

This done, he prepared to meet his British counterpart.

On a broiling Sunday in Washington, August 3, newspapers announced that Roosevelt was leaving on his yacht, the U.S.S.*Potomac*, for a cruise off the New England coast. Late that morning, accompanied by his physician, Adm. Ross T. McIntire; his military aide, Gen. Edwin "Pa" Watson; and his naval aide, Capt. John R. Beardall, Roosevelt drove up Pennsylvania Avenue to Union Station. There the group boarded a special train that took them to the New London, Connecticut submarine base where the *Potomac* was anchored. After 8 p.m., to the squeal of a bosun's pipe and the snap of the Presidential ensign being run up the mast, Roosevelt boarded the vessel. In a few minutes the *Potomac* was gliding down the Thames Channel to salt water.

After a leisurely cruise up the coast, the *Potomac* dropped anchor for the night at the Harbor of Refuge, Point Judith, Rhode Island. Next morning the ship proceeded to South Dartmouth, Massachusetts. At 10 a.m. Roosevelt took the wheel of a Chris-Craft speedboat and roared in to the dock of the local yacht club.

There several members of Danish and Norwegian royal families-in-exile awaited him. The Department of State had asked that Roosevelt invite these personages aboard the *Potomac* for a short tour.

Though he disliked entertaining royal displaced persons, Roosevelt knew that his doing so would be publicized in the newspapers and so encourage plausibility to his announced purpose of taking a cruise for relaxation.

He dutifully escorted the royal visitors on a tour of the yacht. Late in the afternoon, he returned them to Dartmouth.

As soon as he returned to the yacht, his tiny task force set course for Menensha Bight, Vineyard Sound. When the yacht dropped anchor there that night, the dark waters reflected the lights of a flotilla of American warships.

Towering above the yacht was the heavy cruiser U.S S

Augusta, flagship of the Atlantic Fleet. Present were the destroyers *Madison*, *Moffett*, *Sampson*, *Winslow* and *McDougal*.

From the deck of another heavy cruiser, the U.S.S. *Tuscaloosa*, the principal officers of the United States Armed Forces were waving greetings. They included Marshall, Stark, King and Gen. Henry H. Arnold.

Early next morning, Roosevelt transferred from his yacht to the *Augusta* along with his staff. The two cruisers, escorted by destroyers, put to sea. The *Potomac*, left behind, had been instructed to carry on as if the President were still aboard.

At 9:24 A.M., August 7, the *Augusta* dropped anchor in Berth No. 2, Ship Harbor, Placentia Bay, off the Argentia Peninsula, in southeast Newfoundland, Canada, which the United States had leased in 1940 for an Army and Navy Base and used as aerial base and military training ground. Ensign Franklin Roosevelt Jr., executive officer of the destroyer *Mayrant*, was ordered to report the C-n-C aboard the *Augusta*. The young man went, expecting to report to King, but found that the C-n-C there was his own father.

Roosevelt asked for his second son, Elliott, an Army Air Corps officer stationed at Gander Bay. He made both these stalwart young men junior aides for the occasion.

As he awaited the arrival of Churchill, Roosevelt conferred with his military and naval advisers. Both leaders had put the "increasing menace" of Japan high on their list of matters to be discussed. Among other things, Roosevelt had decided to increase Air Force strength in the Philippines to one group of P-40's, fighter planes, and one group of B-17's, a multi-engine bomber. The B-17 was known as the Flying Fortress, but at this stage of its development was still vulnerable. He had previously resisted such a provocative act.

He made clear that he had recognized American responsibility for safe delivery of cargoes to Great

Der Führer Adolf Hitler

On the voyage to Placentia, Churchill (second from left) plied Harry Hopkins (center) with questions about President Roosevelt.

As *representive* of King George VI, Prime Minister Winston Churchill presents his credentials to President Franklin D. Roosevelt, supported by the arm of his son, Elliott.

Britain and Russia. On a map he drew a line extending from east of the Azores to east of Iceland and outlined the duties and responsibilities of the Navy up to that line.

The following day a four-engine flying boat brought Harriman and Sumner Welles. Roosevelt had chosen Sumner Welles to represent the State Department at the conference.

Welles was born Oct. 14, 1892 in New York City and had numerous family and social ties with the Roosevelts. He had been a page boy in Roosevelt's wedding. Like Roosevelt, he had attended Groton and Harvard.

Welles was secretary of the U.S. Embassy at Tokyo from 1915 to 1917, stationed at Buenos Aires the next two years and continued to become a polished, professional diplomat, tactful but firm. In 1940 he had gone on a fact-finding mission to Europe, where he had conferred with Mussolini, Hitler and Churchill of whom he formed an unfavorable impression.

Welles was six feet three inches tall, had a resonant, precise voice and was always impeccably dressed. Time Magazine said of him, "...he is absolutely precise, imperturbable, accurate, honest, sophisticated, thorough, cultured, traveled, financially established."

Welles was one of the few State Department officials whose abilities and judgment Roosevelt trusted. Welle's easy access to the White House at first antagonized and then alienated his superior, Hull.

Three hours after the arrival of Welles, Churchill and his party arrived.

When the *Prince of Wales* had crossed into the Roosevelt-designated "western hemisphere," Canadian destroyers assumed screening positions and escorted the battleship to its destination. At precisely 9:00 a.m. August 9, the *Prince of Wales* slowed to come to its berth in the dark waters off Argentia. The mist that had obscured vision as the ship had steamed up the desolate inlet suddenly broke and revealed a bay full of other armed ships, all displaying the Stars and Stripes and their decks lined with cheering seamen.

King's chief of staff and Beardall crossed to the *Prince of Wales* and presented a Presidential invitation to Churchill to visit the *Augusta* and to remain for lunch.

When in response to the invitation Churchill set foot on the *Augusta*, a United States Marine Band struck up "God Save the King." In a light-brown Palm Beach suit, and supported by his son, Elliott, Roosevelt waited in an awning below the bridge. As the last notes of "The Star-Spangled Banner" died away, Churchill stepped forward and presented a letter. As representative of King George VI, he was presenting his credentials. The tableau melted into smiles and handshakes.

Later Churchill commented on how pleased he was to finally meet the President in person. Roosevelt was offended that the other did not, as he, recall the meeting in Gray's Inn in 1918. Nevertheless, not only the two leaders but all present got on well.

Sunday morning, August 10, Roosevelt came aboard the *Prince of Wales* with his staff officers and several hundred representatives of all ranks of the United States Navy and Marines and attended Divine Service on the quarterdeck. Churchill felt an especial affinity between the English-speaking peoples; he went so far as to propose a common citizenship. He was deeply moved by the free intermingling of British and American with the Union Jack and Stars and Stripes draped side by side on the pulpit.

Next day the discussion turned to the Far East, particularly to speculation of the result of the embargo on oil. Roosevelt had taken this step against the advice of his military chiefs. Like the British, they felt the primary enemy was Germany; they opposed complicating efforts to defeat her through provoking Japan to war.

Roosevelt himself had previously publicly said that such an embargo might force Japan into the war. So the move had been a considered risk: if Japan stopped short of open belligerency, America would gain; if Japan chose to defy the Allies by taking by force from Southeast Asia and the Indies the essential materials denied her in trade, America would lose.

In the meantime, however, Japan had offered a proposal for extricating herself from the noose with which the President was strangling her. She would advance no farther in Southeast Asia and would evacuate Indo-China on settlement of the China war. The United States, too, would abstain from military preparation in these regions. The United States would also renew trade relations with Japan and help her to obtain all the raw materials she required in the Southwest Pacific.

Both Roosevelt and Churchill considered the Japanese terms unacceptable: they permitted Japan to take much at present and offer nothing for the future. Nevertheless, Roosevelt felt that time gained through negotiations favored the Allies.

Churchill believed that a plain declaration that further Japanese aggression would cause the United States to resort to arms would be the greatest deterrent to Japan. The British and Dutch had loyally followed the lead of Roosevelt in banning the sale of oil to Japan. Now Churchill presented the bill.

Roosevelt suggested that he and Churchill draw up a joint declaration of certain principles to guide British and American policies along the same road. From this suggestion came what was to become known as the Atlantic Charter.

The Charter affirmed that Roosevelt, Churchill and their countries sought no aggrandizement, territorial or other; desired no territorial changes except in accord with the freely expressed wishes of the people concerned; that they respected and insisted upon the right of all peoples to choose the form of government under which they would

live; the right of victor and vanquished to the raw
materials of the world; the fullest collaboration between
all nations in the economic field; and the establishment of
a peace, after the destruction of Nazi tyranny, that would
afford all nations the means of dwelling in safety within
their own boundaries; and that such a peace would enable
all to traverse the high seas and oceans without hindrance.
The Charter further affirmed that all nations must abandon
the use of force.

Churchill insisted that a stiff warning to Japan was
needed to keep her out of the war, to be worded: "Any
further encroachment by Japan in the Southwest Pacific
would produce a situation in which the United States
Government would be compelled to take countermeasures, even
if these measures might lead to war between the United
States and Japan."

At the final lunch, August 12, in Roosevelt's
quarters, also attended by Hopkins and Lord William M.A.
Beaverbrook, the two leaders reached agreement. Their
decisions were passed on to other members of the staff who
were having lunch in the Admiral's cabin.

Thereupon the men relaxed to enjoy the food and
conversation. But soon the mellow mood was marred by news
of the fate of the Selective Service Act. Under the
original Selective Service Act, draftees were required to
give 12 months service. Both Stimpson and Marshall
recommended an additional 18 months for the draftees.
There was opposition from representatives who personally
disliked the President, but even more from those who feared
offending their isolationist constituents. Nevertheless,
Roosevelt had departed for Argentia confident that he had
the necessary support for the extension of the bill.

Now came news that the Selective Service Act had been
passed by the House of Representatives by only a single
vote: 203 - 202. This close vote chilled the conference,
especially the British in attendance.

The British equated the U.S. House of Representatives with the British House of Commons. They interpreted such a close vote on such a vital matter as almost a vote of no confidence in Roosevelt.

The meeting broke up before three o'clock. The President and Prime Minister came out on the *Augusta's* quarterdeck to say formal farewell.

Probably at Roosevelt's behest, King had ordered Destroyer Division Sixteen, less U.S.S. *Trippe* and the U.S.S. *Sims*, to proceed "in company but not formation" with the *Prince of Wales* to Iceland. There they were to refuel and accompany the British flotilla to a point 150 miles east of Iceland. By that time the British flotilla might have air cover; the Americans were to return to Argentia.

One of these American destroyers was *Mayrant*, aboard which was Franklin D. Roosevelt Jr. The President's son was to go on to England with Churchill.

When the British vessels had passed from sight, the Americans completed their own preparations for returning. Roosevelt wanted the activities of the past four days to be temporarily kept secret so as to avoid endangering the Prime Minister and detracting from the joint declarations the two had prepared. Those who must return immediately boarded plane or the *Tuscaloosa*. With his personal staff, including Hopkins, Roosevelt remained on the *Augusta*.

In London at 3 p.m. August 14, Lord Privy Seal Clement Atlee, on BBC, slowly and unemotionally read the charter the two leaders had composed at Argentia. At the same time, the President's press secretary, Steve Early, made a similar announcement in Washington. The same day, the *Daily Herald*, London, referred to the document as the Atlantic Charter and by this title it has come down in history.

Around noon August 14, the *Augusta* anchored in Blue Hill Bay, Maine. Having finished their diversionary cruise through the Cape Cod Canal, the *Potomac* and *Calypso*

anchored close by. Roosevelt crossed to his yacht and the
two ships left Blue Hill Bay, the remainder of the voyage
being a pleasure cruise.

Welles had left Argentia on the *Tuscaloosa* and flown
back to Washington from Portland. During the flight to
Washington, he had rewritten the draft of the statement he
had composed in his final meeting with Cadogan. Much of
the draft was a historical review of Japanese–American
relations, but the final paragraph, set Hull back on his
heels. It read:

> **The Government of the United States,
> therefore, finds it necessary to state to the
> Government of Japan that if the Japanese
> Government undertakes any further steps in
> pursuance of the policy of military domination
> through force or conquest in the Pacific region
> upon which it has apparently embarked the
> United States Government will be forced to take
> immediately any and all steps of whatsoever
> character it deems necessary in its own
> security notwithstanding the possibility that
> such further steps on its part may result in
> conflict between the two countries.**

To begin with Hull resented having Welles selected
over him to attend the Argentia conference. He further
resented having been kept in the dark about the meeting and
not having been consulted for suggestions. He felt Welles
was seeking publicity and openly challenging the supremacy
of the Secretary of State. At an emergency meeting in his
office, Hull stated that the draft "needed toning down."
His two Far East advisers, Joseph W. Ballantine and Stanley
K. Hornbeck concurred.

Welles pointed out that Roosevelt had promised that
"the American and British Governments would both say to the

Japanese substantially what appeared in the last paragraph of that draft."

Hull and his staff worked on the draft until they managed to edit out any open reference to possible military conflict. In addition they wrote another message intended to ameliorate the force of the first and offer hope of settlement. Hull took the statements to Union Station when he went to meet the Presidential party there.

When the *Potomac* anchored at Rockland, Maine, Tilson's Wharf, August 16, Roosevelt had given a summary of the meeting to the horde of newsmen who rushed aboard. He refused to comment on the Far East.

At Rockland he had boarded a train, which arrived at Union Station, Washington at 10:30 the next morning. Among the small crowd of onlookers was Hull.

Pausing only to permit a few photos to be taken, the party, including Hull, entered limousines for the short ride to the White House. As soon as the party arrived at the White House, Hull showed the statements to Roosevelt.

Roosevelt had been ignorant of the State Department's taking liberties with his commitment to Churchill, and he had only a short time to examine the statements before Japanese Ambassador Kichisaburō Nomura (kē chē sä' bōo lō nō' mōo lä) arrived for a 4:30 appointment.

8

ANGLO-AMERICAN OPPOSITION BLOCKS JAPAN

Roosevelt's visitor, Kiichirō Nomura had had a distinguished naval career. Born in 1887, he had fought in the Russo-Japanese War and served as naval attache in Russia and the United States. As naval attache in Washington during the World War, he had become friendly with the then Assistant Secretary of the U.S. Navy Franklin Roosevelt.

Nomura held a number of important bureaucratic posts in the navy. He was a delegate to the Versailles Conference and to the Washington Naval Conference. After resigning from the navy in 1937, he became a member of the Supreme War Council and president of the Peers School. Prime Minister Nobuyuki Abe appointed him Foreign Minister in 1939.

Called out of retirement at 64, and though he had had little diplomatic experience, Nomura was given the difficult post of Ambassador to America. His wartime acquaintanceship with the present President may have contributed to Nomura having been chosen at this critical time to try to bridge the growing gap between Japan and America.

Like Roosevelt, Nomura had a physical handicap. April 29, 1932, when he was attending a celebration in Shanghai, a Chinese terrorist had thrown a bomb into a group of Japanese dignitaries of whom Nomura made one. The explosion not only cost Nomura the loss of his right eye, but so crippled him that he walked with a limp for the rest of his life.

154

When Nomura was appointed Ambassador in November 1940, Matsuoka was Foreign Minister and the second Konoye Cabinet was in office. Konoye had inherited the troubles that had erupted under his predecessors, Baron Kiichirō Hiranuma, Gen. Noboyuke Abe and Adm. Mitsumasa Yonai.

May 12, 1940, Japanese marines had occupied Ku-lan Su island, international settlement in the harbor of Amoy, China; America, Great Britain and France responded by landing naval forces there. After the British refused to surrender four Chinese accused of killing a Japanese puppet custom official, the Japanese blockaded British and French concessions in Tientsin. June 21, after having occupied Swatow, the Japanese naval commander ordered a U.S. destroyer to leave the city with all other foreign vessels; Adm. Harry E. Yarnell, Commander in Chief U.S. Asiatic Fleet, ignored the order.

June 25, the Soviet Union confirmed that there had been fighting between the Soviet-Mongolian and Japanese forces along the Manchoukuan border since May 11. August 11 the British announced they would surrender the four Chinese whose detention had precipitated the Tientsin incident. August 16, Japanese troops occupied territory adjacent to Hong Kong.

A few days later there was consternation in Tōkyō over the signing of the Nazi-Soviet pact of August 21. Tōkyō ordered the Japanese Ambassador to Berlin to protest.

In these troublous circumstances, the Hiranuma cabinet resigned August 28, Gen. Nobuyuki Abe became Prime Minister. September 1, Germany precipitated the European war by invading Poland.

The Soviet Union and Japan agreed to a truce, effective September 16 to end hostilities on the Manchoukuan and Mongolian frontiers. The same day Japan resumed a general offensive in central China.

Feb. 15, 1940 Japan called on Chiang Kai-shek to

155

surrender since the Japanese armies had conquered enough Chinese territory to support the government of Wang Ching-wei. Chiang spurned the demand. March 3, the Japanese Foreign Office described the American loan of $20 million to China as an unfriendly act. March 30 Wang Ching-wei set up his puppet government in Nanking and called on the soldiers of Chiang Kai-shek to lay down their arms. May 10, Germany invaded Belgium, Holland, Luxembourg and France; Chamberlain resigned as Prime Minister and was replaced by Churchill.

By June 4, the Germans had driven the British from the continent. June 22 Germany and France signed an armistice, with Germany occupying about half of France and France moving its capital to Vichy. Henceforth Japan would deal with the debilitated Vichy government.

Enheartened by the success of Germany over the Allies, Japanese Foreign Minister Hachirō Arita announced that Japan favored uniting all East Asia and the South Seas under a single dominating influence. It was on this note of exultation over the victorious Axis arms that Konoye was offered the Prime Ministership.

Before accepting the post of Prime Minister, Konoye held a meeting at his villa at Ogikubo in Tōkyō with Yosuke Matsuoka, Hideki Tōjō and Zengo Yoshida, his prospective Foreign, Army and Navy Ministers. There he secured their agreement on a policy memorandum compatible with the demands of the military. Cooperation between military and Cabinet thus assured, he set about forming his Cabinet, naming Matsuoka Foreign Minister though the Emperor had expressed reservations about him.

Civilians and military chosen shared the same basic values. All believed in what they called The Greater East Asia Co-Prosperity Sphere, a phrase Matsuoka himself had coined. This sphere included territories under Japanese domination as a result of World War agreements and strategic areas now under their control such as industrial regions (Korea, Manchoukuo and China) and sources of raw materials (French Indochina, Malaya , Burma, the Philippines and the Netherlands East Indies). They believed this Co-Prosperity Sphere would contribute to world peace and that the American position threatened Japan's interests.

All realized that Japanese expansion would arouse the antagonism and resistance of other nations and consequently involve risks; some were more willing than others to take these risks.

The Japanese Cabinet had earlier established conferences to provide liaison between the government and the military. These Liaison Conferences were held in a conference room where the participants sat in arm chairs with the Prime Minister at the farther end of the room, somewhere near the center and surrounded by the conferees. There was no presiding officer and everyone spoke freely.

Whenever a major policy decision was reached, it was necessary to have it ratified at an Imperial Conference. The Imperial Conference included the members of the Liaison Conference plus the President of the Privy Council, who spoke for the Emperor. The Conference met in the presence of the Emperor, who sat before a gold screen mounted on a dais at the superior end of the chamber. The others sat at two long, brocade-covered tables, facing each other and at right angles to the Emperor.

Shortly after the Konoye Cabinet assumed its duties, after a single Liaison Conference between the Cabinet and Imperial Headquarters, it adopted a new policy in a document entitled *Main Principles for Coping with the Changing World Situation.*

This policy was an invitation to war and based on expectation of a German victory over the British. In the event of war with the Allies the Japanese had no plan to meet and defeat the main bodies of the Allied forces. Their offensive plans called for the occupation of the

Greater East Asia Co–Prosperity Sphere, developing a defensive perimeter around it extending from the Kurile Islands on the north, southward through the Mariana Islands and Wake Island, the Marshall Islands and the Gilbert Islands to Rabaul, on New Britain of the Bismarck archipelago. They hoped that the quick occupation of this region, coupled with crippling attacks on the U.S. Fleet would lead to a negotiated peace resulting in Japan keeping most of the Co–Prosperity Sphere.

From the time of the adoption of the *Main Principles for Coping with the Changing World Situation* most of the foreign policy was determined by the Four Ministers Conference, with the Army and Navy Ministers providing liaison with the supreme command. From these conferences, even the Finance Minister was excluded.

August 3, the Japanese Ambassador to the United States protested the U.S. embargo of aviation gasoline. September 4, Hull informed him that any change in the status of French Indochina would have an "unfortunate effect" on American public opinion.

Nevertheless, the Governor General of the now impotent French Indochina agreed to permit Japan to establish three air bases in Tongking, to garrison them with not more than 6,000 troops and to maintain a small force at Hai–phong. Despite this offer, the Japanese crossed the northern border and attacked the French defenders.

These steps led to the alienation of America that culminated with the Japanese signing of the Tripartite Pact Sept. 27, 1940.

Oct. 8, 1940 the U.S. State Department, as we have seen, advised its Far East consuls to encourage all Americans to leave Japan, Manchoukuo, China, Indochina, Korea, Formosa and Hong Kong. When Great Britain reopened the Burma Road, October 17, it advised British citizens to leave Japan and Japan–occupied territory.

158

November 30, Japan signed a treaty in Nanking formally recognizing the puppet government of Wang Ching-Wei. America responded by advancing $100 million to Chiang Kai-shek.

So began the fateful year of 1941 with Nomura, February 14, presenting his credentials to Roosevelt. Besides the strained relationship between his country and America and his inexperience in diplomacy, Nomura was further handicapped by his imperfect English. The situation had also been muddied by two Maryknoll priests who, though well-intentioned, had misrepresented the positions of the two nations to each other.

These two priests, Bishop James E. Walsh and Father James M. Drought, had arrived in Japan in the fall of 1940 with letters of introduction from Lewis. L. Strauss to several Japanese, including Tadao Ikawa, formerly an official in the Ministry of Finance. Strauss was associated with the Wall Street firm of Kuhn, Loeb and Co., well known in Japan because it had helped the Japanese government float a loan during a critical period in the Russo-Japanese War. Since many Japanese believed that Wall Street exerted great influence on American politics, the Japanese concerned assumed that the two priests were acting in some kind of semiofficial capacity.

Drought gave Ikawa a long memorandum indicating that America would give Japan substantially all it asked for and calling for a high-level Japanese-American conference in Tōkyō or possibly Honolulu. The two priests returned to the United States in December 1940 and gained access to Roosevelt through the good offices of Postmaster General Frank Walker. Now Walsh presented a memorandum different from the memorandum Drought had given the Japanese. The Walsh memorandum intimated that Japan was weary of war in China and would accept American settlement there and was willing to alter her commitment to the Axis. The memorandum argued that a "Far Eastern Monroe Doctrine" based on a Japanese–American guarantee of the status quo in the Philippines, Hong Kong, Singapore and Malaya and on the establishment of autonomous governments in Indochina and the Dutch East Indies would restrain the militarists.

Hull warned the President to be wary of the suggestions, but Roosevelt encouraged the priests to keep up their contacts with the Japanese.

Ikawa came to Washington and he and the priests hammered out a long document entitled *Preliminary Draft of Agreement in Principle*. At this point, Col. Hideo Iwakuro, sent by the Army to advise Nomura, arrived; he made changes in the *Preliminary Draft*. The revision made the draft favor the Japanese position and so was less acceptable to the Americans.

Early in April, Hull suggested to Nomura that the *Draft* might be used as a starting point for negotiations with the understanding that both sides would want to propose changes. Nomura responded by cabling the text of the *Draft* to Tōkyō. The cable arrived April 17 when Matsuoka was absent on his trip to Germany, Italy and the Soviet Union

Matsuoka entered into the 20th Liaison Conference of April 22, 1941 looking tired. He seemed to gradually overcome his fatigue and become vigorous.

He said that in Moscow he had told the American Ambassador to Russia that Roosevelt is quite a gambler. American aid had kept the European War and the China Incident going. The peace–loving President of the United States, as Roosevelt styled himself, should work with Japan, which also loved peace. He should urge Chiang to propose peace. As the result of these exhortations, the American ambassador had sent a telegram to Roosevelt; Matsuoka had expected to receive a reply while still in Moscow, but had not.

"After returning to Japan," Matsuoka said, "I learned of the proposal sent by Nomura. Since this proposal

160

includes important matters besides the settlement of the China Incident. I will have to consider it carefully for two weeks or perhaps for one or two months."

Matsuoka was enraged that negotiations were about to begin with America on the basis of a proposal he was learning about for the first time, his rage was the greater that the proposal had originated outside regular diplomatic channels.

Nevertheless, the Japanese decision-makers deliberated and came up with a counterproposal for America, which elicited an American response. Each side seemed to the other to be reneging from what the Maryknoll priests had represented as the original proposals.

In succeeding conferences Matsuoka laid down what were to become known as his three principles for the adjustment of diplomatic relations with America:

1. **Any agreement must contribute to the settlement of the China Incident.**
2. **It must not conflict with the Tripartite Pact.**
3. **Japan must not betray international good faith: that is, Japan must keep its promise to Germany to try to keep America from entering the European War.**

On the other hand, at the Conference of May 8, 1941 he talked provocatively of going to war with America. On one occasion, after listening to Matsuoka, Navy Minister Adm. Koshirō Ōikawa (kō shē lo'   ōe kä'wä) asked, "Is Matsuoka sane?"

The question of his sanity was unpursued but the invasion of Russia by Germany undermined his reputation for competence. The pact he had negotiated with Russia now seemed an encumbrance to those who thought the German invasion presented an opportunity for Japan to attack Russia from the rear. Despite having negotiated the pact, Matsuoka favored such action; the Navy opposed it in favor of striking south to gain the oil and raw materials it needed.

In any case, American neutrality was a desirable prerequisite for further Japanese military action.

At the 38th Japanese Liaison Conference, July 10, Adviser Yoshie Saitō (yō' shē ā sī'tō) complained of Hull's "Oral Statement" made in response to the most recent Japanese proposal. He said:

> Hull's "Oral Statement" contains especially outrageous language. For instance, it says, "We have no intention of considering the stationing of troops a defense against Communism." Or again: "There are differences of opinion within the Japanese Government. I understand that there are Cabinet members who say Japan should ally herself with the Axis and fight side-by-side with Hitler. We cannot make an agreement with a Japanese Government of that kind. If you want to facilitate an improvement in Japanese-American relations, you had better change your Cabinet." His attitude is one of contempt for Japan...This language is not the kind one would use toward a country of equal standing: it expresses an attitude one would take toward a protectorate or possession. These words are inexcusable.

At the meeting of the 12th of July, Minister of Home Affairs Keiichirō Hiranuma spoke against Matsuoka''s proposal to break off negotiations. "If the present Cabinet is bad, wouldn't it be better to change it, if necessary, to avoid getting into the war?"

They drafted a reply to the American proposal of June 21; when they submitted it to Matsuoka, he refused to look at it. July 14, finally pressured into agreeing to revising the earlier draft for eventual transmission to the United States, he insisted that he must first send Hull a note rejecting the Oral Statement.

Konoye and the armed forces agreed that the Oral Statement rejection should be sent together with the Japanese reply.

Disregarding their wishes, Matsuoka wired his rejection before sending the Japanese counterproposal.

As prerequisite to further Japanese military action American neutrality was desirable; the other Conference members concluded that Matsuoka had made himself so odious to America that Japan would benefit by ousting him as Foreign Minister. Konoye feared that if he simply discharged Matsuoka the admirers of the Foreign Minister would charge that the Japanese government had bowed to American pressure. Konoye consulted with the War, Navy and Home Ministers and, July 16, asked for the resignation of the Cabinet.

Two days later the Emperor authorized him to organize a third Konoye Cabinet. Except for Matsuoka, Konoye invited the same persons to join him who had been in the previous Cabinet. He replaced Matsuoka as Foreign Minister with Adm. Teijirō Toyoda (tā ē jē'lō tō yō'dä). The Cabinet believed the United States would trust Toyoda.

As we have seen, despite the elimination of Matsuoka Japanese-American relations went from bad to worse. When the Dutch East Indies, July 28, followed the lead of Great Britain and America in suspending her oil agreement with Japan and freezing all Japanese assets, the Japanese concluded she had done so with the assurance of American military cooperation if Japan attempted to take by force the needed oil. The suspicion was well-founded: before the execution of the embargo the Americans, British and Dutch had consulted on means to counter Japan.

On the 30th, Japanese aircraft attacked and damaged

the American gunboat *Tutuila* as it lay in Chunking. The Japanese settled this incident with a speedy apology.

Welles assailed Vichy's cession of Indochina bases to Japan. Roosevelt set off to confer with Churchill at Argentia, Placentia Bay. The conference more than ever persuaded the Japanese that America was bent on war.

This was the dismal situation that beset Nomura when at precisely 4:30 August 17 he was shown in for his meeting with the President. Roosevelt was his most charming self. As one old salt to another, Roosevelt began by saying he had spent some days enjoying life at sea...the sailing was fine and little fog had been encountered to mar the pleasure of the voyage.

Then he turned to business. "The Secretary of State, you and I are continuing our efforts to bring about peace in the Pacific, but no one else is."

Nomura said, "There are many third powers who desire war in the Pacific."

Roosevelt agreed, but he identified the United States, Great Britain "and probably the Soviet, too" as nations desiring peace. " Neither you, the Secretary, nor I have come up through the diplomatic ranks and, therefore, do not observe diplomatic conventions." The document he was presenting was not a formal note or memory aid "but is merely what we want to say."

He read the statement. The section reviewing Japanese iniquities and America's patient response followed the Welles' draft, but the critical last paragraph of the original draft now emerged as innocuous.

> "This Government," Roosevelt read, "now finds
> it necessary to say to the Government of Japan
> that if the Japanese Government takes any
> further steps in pursuance of a policy or
> program of military aggression by force or
> threat of force of neighboring countries, the

Government of the United States will be
compelled to take immediately any and all steps
which it may deem necessary toward safeguarding
the legitimate rights and interests of the
United States and American nationals and toward
insuring the safety and security of the United
States."

In reply, Nomura read a note that stressed the desire
of Japan for good relations and that revived Konoye's
project of meeting with Roosevelt.

Roosevelt showed interest in the proposed meeting.
Nomura was encouraged by the friendly atmosphere.

Roosevelt said, in oblique reference to the visit of
Perry to Japan 88 years before, "It is not that I welcome
the 'closed door' such as we have today, but since we have
been forced to it by Japan's actions, there is only one
country that can open the door. This time it is Japan's
turn."

He made clear to Nomura that the Presidential request
to see him, upon returning from Argentia, before he saw any
other than Hull, underlined the gravity with which
Roosevelt viewed the strained relations between Japan and
America.

After the interview there remained the need to
communicate the significance of it to Churchill. August
18, Hull drafted and Roosevelt approved the following
message:

"On August 17 I sent for the Japanese
ambassador and the Secretary of State and I
received him. I made to him a
statement...along the lines of the proposed
statement such as you and I had discussed. The
statement I made to him was no less vigorous
than and was substantially similar to the
statement we discussed."

The emasculated statement to Japan and Roosevelt's justification of it may have disheartened Churchill, but he persuaded himself and attempted to persuade his nation that at Argentia he had gained the assurance "more important than any words" that a Japanese move against British or Dutch possessions would bring the U.S. into the fight.

August 24, Churchill broadcast over the BBC a description of the meeting with Roosevelt. He identified it as the first mobilization of the forces of good against the forces of evil. As he often did, he spoke of "the deep underlying unities which stir and at decisive moments rule the English-speaking peoples throughout the world." He denounced Hitler's "methodical, merciless butchery" in Eastern Europe as "a crime without a name." Turning his attention to what he considered Germany's counterpart in the Orient, he added:

> For five long years the Japanese military factions, seeking to emulate the style of Hitler and Mussolini...have been invading and harrying the 500 million inhabitants of China...Now they stretch a grasping hand into the southern seas of China; they snatch Indochina from the wretched Vichy French; they menace ...Siam; menace Singapore, the British link with Australasia; and menace the Philippine Islands under the protection of the United States. It is certain that this has got to stop...The United States are laboring with infinite patience to arrive at a fair and amicable settlement which will give Japan the utmost reassurance for her legitimate interests. We earnestly hope these negotiations will succeed. But this I must say: that if these hopes fail we shall of course range ourselves at the side of the

United States.

The Japanese had arrived at a similar conclusion.

Feb. 15, 1940, Japan called upon Generalissimo Chiang Kai-shek, above, to surrender since the Japanese armies had conquered enough Chinese territory to support the puppet government of Wang Ching-wei. Chiang spurned the demand.

9

THE JAPANESE NAVY GIRDS FOR WAR WITH THE WEST

Both sides conceded that war between Japan and America would be primarily a naval war. Consequently the man to whom the Japanese looked for leadership at this critical juncture was the Commander in Chief of the Combined Imperial Fleet, Adm. Isoroku Yamamoto. Held in high repute by his colleagues, Yamamoto was known to be opposed to pro-Axis leanings and likewise opposed to war with America.

He was also at odds with some naval experts who cherished the belief that the battleship was the decisive weapon in naval warfare. Yamamoto held that the airplane would be the decisive weapon.

They might ask, "How can you destroy a battleship except with another battleship?"

"Torpedo planes can do it." He would quote a proverb: "The fiercest serpent may be overcome by a swarm of ants."

Yamamoto was born April 4, 1884 on the northwest side of Japan's main island of Honshū in the village of Kushigun Sonshomura, Niigata prefecture. The region is noted for its heavy snowfalls. But that year spring had come early. As Isoroku prepared to enter the world, his father, the village schoolmaster, Sadakichi Takano, was engaged in a game of <u>go,</u> a Japanese form of chess. One of his children interrupted the game to inform him that Mrs. Takano was in labor and wanted a midwife.

Takano sent the child for the midwife and continued his game. Siring children was no novelty for him. His

wife, Mineko, was his second, the younger sister of the
first wife whom she had succeeded when he became widowed.
By the two wives he had five boys and one girl. He was 56.

The birth of a seventh child, a boy, failed to
impress him. Though a diligent diarist, he even failed to
note the birth in his diary until three weeks later.

When his wife told him he must think of a name for
his son, he said, "I was 56 when he was born. Call him
Fifty-Six." So the infant became Fifty-Six, Isoroku when
written in Japanese.

The son whose birth had only evoked indifference from
him soon became the father's greatest joy. He told the boy
tales of the former generation when the samurai of the
Echigo clan, of which Sadakichi had been one, had resisted
the efforts of Emperor Meiji to unify Japan under his rule.

The forces of the Emperor defeated the Echigo.
Defeat plundered the samurai of their calling and
livelihood. The Takano family now lived in a wooden house
not much larger than a rabbit hutch.

Soon after the birth of Isoroku, Sadaichi became
headmaster of the primary school in the nearby market town
of Nagaoka. In the winter, icy winds blowing from Siberia
across the Sea of Japan brought snow that piled up to a
depth of 12 to 14 feet. The thatch-roofed houses
disappeared beneath the snow. The outside walls, sheltered
by planks under the eaves made a dim corridor under the
snow through which the residents could move.

Too poor to afford textbooks when he attended school,
Isoroku borrowed them and copied out the contents.

In the 1890's, the students had military training as
early as middle school. Thousands of boys, from several
prefectures, participated in the military maneuvers. The
boys carried real weapons but not live bullets. Army
officers commanded the exercises.

At the turn of the century, Isoroku applied for
admission to the Naval Academy at Etajima. He scored

second highest among 300 applicants.

Naval training was rigid and Spartan. The cadets were forbidden to drink, smoke, eat sweets or go out with girls. They marched everywhere, even from locker rooms to playing fields. They spent the fourth year aboard naval vessels – close to currents, storms and winds.

Isoroku graduated from Etajima, seventh in his class, in 1904, the same year Kimmel graduated from Annapolis. In contrast to Kimmel, Isoroku was five feet three inches tall and weighed about 125 pounds.

The Russo–Japanese War had begun that February. He was ordered to the cruiser *Nisshin*, part of the protective screen for *Mikasa*, flagship of Adm. Heihachirō Togo.

In the Battle of Tsushima Strait, beginning May 27, 1905, the Russians were credited with a direct hit on the *Nisshin*. He wrote of the experience: "With a great roar, a shell scored a direct hit on the forward 8-inch gun that still remained. Billows of acrid smoke covered the forward half of the vessel, and I felt myself almost swept away by a fierce blast. I staggered a few steps — and found that the record charts that had been hanging round my neck had disappeared, and that two fingers of my left hand had been snapped off and were hanging by the skin alone."

Though for many years he evidently believed his wound had been caused by a Russian shell, it appears it had been caused by the bursting of one of the *Nisshin's* own guns. His body would carry other shocking scars caused by the same explosion.

The faster Japanese ships, with more highly trained crews, sailed across the bows of the van of Russians. The fleets engaged early in the afternoon; in a half-hour the Japanese sank one Russian battleship and crippled another.

Their line being broken, the Russians made for the cover of Vladivostok, the Japanese pursuing with destroyers and torpedo boats. During the night the Japanese sank three more Russian ships and continued the destruction the

170

following day until all but 12 of the Russian fleet of 45 ships had been sunk, captured or driven ashore.

The Japanese also captured the wounded Russian commander. All this with the loss of only three torpedo boats.

It was the greatest naval battle since Trafalgar, Oct. 21, 1805, when the British under Adm. Lord Nelson defeated a combined Spanish-French fleet, establishing British naval supremacy for a century. The defeat at Tsushima drove the demoralized Russians to seek peace terms.

Isoroku emerged from the battle with a wound in his right leg and two fingers missing from his left hand. He spent two months in hospital before going home.

In the following decade he followed the usual peacetime naval career. He also read extensively, even books in English, including the Bible. He told his fellow officers that the Japanese could learn much from foreign books. He taught cadets on training cruises to China and Korea. In March 1909 his squadron briefly visited the west-coast ports of the United States. The following year he went on a six-months voyage, calling at every major Australian port.

In 1913, his father, age 85, died. His mother died shortly afterwards. Their deaths led to the Yamamoto family moving to adopt Isoroku.

It was traditional for a prominent Japanese family, lacking a male heir, to adopt a promising young man to perpetuate the family name. Vice Adm. Baron Yamamoto, had been Minister of Marine during the Russo-Japanese war. Isoroku showed promise. The family solemnized the adoption at Nagaoka May 19, 1915.

Isoroku had put off marriage, among other reasons because of his straitened finances, which he made harsher by sending money home to his family as well as paying for the schooling of children of relatives and of his former teacher. The Yamamoto family had an illustrious history within the Nagaoka clan but was desperately poor. Adoption worsened his financial situation.

Just after adoption he was posted to Naval Headquarters. Here he began to work on what was to become his main interest in life – naval aircraft and foreign communications.

Now 33 he felt able to afford seeking a wife. He found a suitable prospect in Reiko Mihashi, daughter of a local dairy farmer.

He wrote her a long letter in which he cataloged his faults and the drawbacks of being the wife of a career naval officer. There followed an interview at her home. Alone together they made judgments. He did not mind her being an inch taller.

They liked each other. Neither considered love necessary.

They were married August 31, 1918 at the Navy Club in Shiba, Tōkyō. She was 22; in his fourth year as lieutenant commander, he was 34. In the next 14 years four children would be born to them – two boys and two girls. He would be dutiful towards the needs of his family, but his relations with his wife would always remain cool.

Once when he learned that one of his officers kept a photo of his wife in his cabin, Yamamoto said to him, "You're lucky to be in love with your wife. I threw in the sponge long ago."

April 5, 1919, only eight months after his marriage, he was ordered to language study in the United States. Largely at his own prodding, he was given the corollary assignment of studying petroleum. Leaving his wife behind, he sailed from Yokohama to San Francisco on a mail steamer.

He pursued his language studies in Boston. In September 1919 he applied for enrollment in Harvard as a "special student in English," but withdrew during the first month of that term.

He learned to play poker, which would thereafter become a passion with him. He diligently studied oil and its relationship to naval policy, reading omnivorously and visiting nearby oil installations and refineries. He became proficient in English and learned a lot about oil. He decided he needed to see the oil fields of the southwest, and he visited them.

While he was in America, the World War was drawing to a close. The war had introduced a new weapon – the airplane. He studied every report on planes in action on the European Western Front. He toured American aircraft factories. He had already decided that air power would be the key to victory in future wars. He was enormously interested when at the end of the war in 1918 the British Royal Navy completed the world's first aircraft carrier.

In early May 1921, he was ordered home; he arrived in Yokohama July 19. After three weeks leave, he returned to the Second Fleet, this time as executive officer of the light cruiser *Kitagami*. In December 1921 he went as instructor to the Naval Staff College.

In June 1923 he embarked on a nine-month trip to Europe and the United States with Adm. Kenji Ide, the naval Vice-Minister. They studied reactions to the Washington Disarmament Conference of 1922. He returned to Yokohama, a captain, March 31, 1924.

He was appointed to the Kasumigaura Aviation Corps effective September 1. The Corps had been founded only in 1921. Though this was his first practical contact with aircraft, and he was beginning on it late in his career, from that time he would be concerned chiefly with aviation.

He became one of the leading theorists of Japan on the military applications of aviation. As commander of the flying school his main preoccupation was night flying. In those days night flying was extremely hazardous, but because he felt that a plane attack at night would have the advantage of surprise, he insisted that every pilot have the maximum night-flying training. He persisted in this course despite high casualties among both pilots and aircraft.

After 18 months at Kasumigaura, he was sent back to America. In Washington he initiated a change in Japanese intelligence methods. His predecessors had concentrated on information of a tactical nature: problems and techniques of gunnery, technological details of American vessels, battle order and detailed data on technical progress of the American Fleet. Yamamoto advanced beyond this into the area of highest strategy. Even at this early stage of sea-air-power development, he recognized the significance of carriers.

The American officers taught him bridge, and he quickly became expert at the game. When he returned to Japan March 5, 1928, he told a correspondent, "The United States Navy is a social organization of golfers and bridge players."

On the other hand he made remarks indicating that he had come away from America with a deep respect for Americans. He derided the charge that the Americans were weak-willed and spoiled by material luxuries. He asserted that they were infused with "a fierce fighting spirit and an adventurous temperament." He cited the legendary frontier spirit of America, the daring exploits of Adm. David G. Farragut who with his "Damn the torpedoes (mines)" defeated the defending Confederate squadron in the Battle of Mobile Bay in August 1864.

Yamamoto also cited the American blockade of Santiago and the advance through the minefield in Manila Bay during the Spanish American War.

Contrasting the vaunted Yamato spirit and the Yankee spirit, he pointed out that the former too often verged on blind daredevilry, whereas the Yankee spirit was soundly grounded on science and technology. To his subordinates he

174

recommended Carl Sandburg's biography of Abraham Lincoln, in the English original, as the best introduction to the American national character.

He returned to sea in August 1928 as captain of the light cruiser *Isuzu*. In December he moved to the aircraft carrier *Akagi*. He returned to shore duty on the Navy General Staff in October 1929, with concurrent duty in the Bureau of Naval Affairs. In these posts he introduced many innovations. He remained in the last until assigned as naval aide to the next London Naval Conference in 1930.

Commissioned rear-admiral before departing from Yokohama in November 1929, he landed at Seattle, went overland to New York City and thence to London. There with his fluent English and detailed knowledge of the American Navy, he was impressive. He contributed to getting agreement to a plan that gave Japan equality in submarines and light cruisers.

He returned to Japan in mid-June and became commander of the First Air Fleet. He immediately stepped up training. Many pilots died trying to land on the new aircraft carriers.

When the pilots complained that the training was over rigorous, he said, "The Japanese Fleet lags a long way behind the West...There is very little time to attain its level. That is why I regard death in training the same as a hero's death in action. The Japanese spirit should not fear death."

Recognizing the sacrifice of those who had been killed, he had his pilots, before take-off, salute a list of pilots who had been killed in training.

The Manchurian Incident, beginning Sept. 18, 1931, brought him assignment to Naval Air Corps headquarters and soon to Chief of the Technical Division. In those days Japan bought most of her military planes from Great Britain and America. The Japanese-manufactured planes were inferior. Yamamoto moved to reverse this situation.

He wanted first-rate Japanese-made torpedo planes and long range bombers, but even more he wanted a fast fighter that could fly off the deck of an aircraft carrier. Mitsubishi would finally produce the plane he desired.

Great Britain requested a 1935 naval conference. Both Great Britain and America sent its high-ranking officers. As an indication of the low esteem in which they held the proposed talks, Japan sent Yamamoto who was only a rear admiral.

When Yamamoto arrived in Seattle October 1, he refused all newspaper interviews. He travelled to New York locked in his compartment. He refused to read the American newspapers, even though they were giving him considerable publicity.

William "Billy" Mitchell was prophesying war with Japan and campaigning for increased air power to cope with it. This circumstance provoked Yamamoto's only public remark while en route to New York.

He said, "I do not look upon relations with the United States and Japan from the same angle as Gen. Mitchell. I have never looked upon the United States as a potential enemy. Japan's naval plans have never included the possibility of an American-Japanese war."

Though for years Japan's navy had been training with the United States as the hypothetical enemy!

In London, December 29, Japan formally denounced the Washington Naval Treaty. The American delegates went home. Yamamoto stayed and tried to win over the British to at least Japan's claim for naval parity. With Yamamoto appearing intransigent, conversations dragged on into 1935.

To a suggestion that the three powers exchange information on their naval building programs, Yamamoto countered, "Such an arrangement would be of no advantage to Japan. We can always find out what other powers are building, but you cannot know what we are doing."

Despite his seeming intransigence, he was presumably seeking a compromise while acting within the lines laid down in his instructions from his government. Having seen the Detroit automobile industry and the oil fields of Texas, he frequently said to his countrymen that Japan would overstrain its resources if it became involved in a shipbuilding race with America.

Many were undeterred by such reasoning. Instead of the 60 percent of the American quota granted by the 1922 Washington Naval Conference, the Japanese hawks insisted upon at least 70 percent. But from the point of view of Yamamoto, this ten percent difference, if granted, might not improve the defensive position of Japan as opposed to America. The greater industrial capacity of America would permit it, in case of war, to build so that the ratio more and more favored America and whittled down the Japanese percentage so that it might vanish. Such being the case, Japan would still need to avoid conflict with America.

Ostensibly hoping for a more favorable treaty, he must have been disappointed that the conference ended with no treaty. He must also have known that had he failed to remove the present ratio that organizations such as the Black Dragon plotted to kill him and his entire delegation.

His handling of the situation apparently found favor at home. While still in London, he was promoted to vice admiral. The talks broke off in mid-January 1935. January 28 the Japanese delegation boarded a train at Victoria Station to begin the trip home.

Since no treaty had been negotiated, the world powers were to embark on unrestricted naval building. Though Yamamoto avoided blaming the British and Americans for the failure of the Conference, they put the blame squarely on him and Japan.

In contrast to the disfavor in which the West regarded him, when he reached Tōkyō a parade of admirals and members of ultranationalistic societies like the Black

Dragon greeted him with <u>banzais</u>, the Japanese cheer of enthusiastic approval. He went to the palace, where the Emperor congratulated him.

By this time Yamamoto had become involved in a love affair with a geisha, Chiyoko Kawai, professionally known as Umeryū. Had he been wealthy, he might have been able to buy her from her employers and establish her as mistress in his own quarters. Or at less cost, but still at great expense, he might have become her patron, she continuing her occupation with the understanding he had priority on her services. He could afford neither method.

He was particularly welcome in the geisha houses because his fame attracted other naval officers to them. So capitalizing on his popularity he continued his relationship with Chiyoko while sharing her with a wealthy real estate man who had become her patron.

The arrangement being satisfactory to both men, he and Chiyoko had frequent liaisons. This contrasted with his relationship with his wife, Reiko, who would later sadly remark, "I never so much as went for a walk with my husband."

In the autumn of 1935 Japan gave the required formal notice that she was withdrawing from the Washington Naval Treaty. She had not built a battleship for 15 years, but even as the notice of withdrawal from the treaty reached Washington and London, Japan was laying the keel of the giant battleship *Yamato*, which with her sister ship *Musashi* would be the largest the world had ever seen. A rough plan for the construction of such ships had been ready in the fall of 1934. The Navy counted on getting a head start on America by at least five years. If the United States were to build such ships they would be too big to navigate the Panama Canal.

Each would be 863 feet long and weigh 73,700 tons. The main gun turrets would weigh as much as a large destroyer. The ships' side armor would be 16 inches thick.

178

Each would carry nine 18-inch guns, which would fire a 3,200 pound projectile — 50 percent heavier than a 16-inch shell.

Yamamoto was the only Japanese admiral unenthusiastic about the building of these and other proposed great warships. Now Vice-Minister of the Navy, he insisted the giants were obsolete before the keels were laid. Not the battleship, but the aircraft carrier would bring supremacy in modern sea battles.

He said, "These ships are like elaborate religious scrolls that old people hang up in their homes. They are of no proven worth. They are purely a matter of faith."

Again he said, "Military people always carry history around with them in the shape of old campaigns. They carry obsolete weapons like swords and it is a long time before they realize they have become purely ornamental. These battleships will be as useful to Japan in modern warfare as a samurai sword."

The battleship admirals, in America as well as Japan, held that carriers should provide an 'air umbrella' for the striking force of battleships. Yamamoto preached that the carriers should project fire power deep into enemy territory.

As we have seen, it was he who in December 1937, as Navy Vice-Minister, had issued the statement thanking the United States for accepting Japanese apologies for the attack on the *Panay*. He pledged the Navy to be more careful in the future.

At his insistence, Japan built the 30,000 ton 34-knot *Shokaku* and *Zuikaku*, both being faster and more modern than Japan's other big carriers, the *Akagi* and *Kaga*. His demand for better Japanese-made planes also began to be realized.

August 14, 1938, 20 Japanese bombers took off from bases at Taipei and Kaohsiung at the northern tip of Formosa, crossed the East China Sea in a storm, made a dusk attack on the Chinese airfields at Kuangte and Hangchow and returned without refueling. With this attack followed by two more in the following two days they dealt the Chinese National Air Force an almost fatal blow.

This first use of the type-96 land-based bombers, each carrying a 2,000 pound bomb load, making a return raid of 1,200 miles across the ocean under extremely unfavorable, low-pressure conditions astonished the Western navies but made no lasting impression on the British or American intelligence services.

Yamamoto regularly read the American aviation magazines, and he realized that he had an unwitting ally in them, for the magazines constantly belittled the Japanese air force. *Aviation* magazine also reported that the Japanese pilots suffered from the world's highest accident rate, which may have been true because of the rigorous, dangerous training to which they were subjected. It also reported the Japanese pilots were definitely inferior to Chinese pilots, which was untrue. According to *Aviation*, Japan trained fewer than 1,000 pilots a year and the Japanese air force would never develop enough air power for large-scale operations. According to *Aviation*, Japan's aviation engineering depended entirely on old-fashioned copies of planes made in the United States, Great Britain, Germany, Italy and the Soviet Union.

"America's aviation experts can say without hesitation that the chief military airplanes of Japan are either outdated or are becoming outdated."

Another magazine assured its readers: "The Japanese navy air force consists of four aircraft carriers with 200 planes."

Such articles persuaded Yamamoto that the Japanese strategy of concealing its increasing strength from foreign observers was successful.

When the government "by assassination" move flared again toward the end of the thirties, the Navy, offered him a bodyguard in recognition that his opposition to war had made enemies for him among the militarist fanatics. He resisted the offer. Aware that he was marked for assassination, he strolled about Tōkyō or rode alone in streetcars in civilian clothes. He walked alone from the Navy Ministry to the book shop district where he browsed through the book stalls.

He continued to feel that Japan should avoid war with America. If asked outright, "Do you think our gallant Navy will win?" he would reply, "I do not."

Such remarks caused the militarists to brand him as a traitor. In July 1939, the navy learned of an ultranationalist plot to kill him. Over Yamamoto's objection, Yonai assigned a special police guard at both his office and official residence. Thereafter a squad of armed plainclothes police surrounded him wherever he went.

Even these precautions seemed insufficient to Yonai. In mid-August he appointed him Commander in Chief of the Combined Fleet with the rank of full admiral and sent him to sea.

Yonai later said of this move, "It was the only way to save his life."

Two weeks after his appointment, Germany invaded Poland. The European war had begun; Yamamoto knew it would spread. Almost as soon as he stepped onto the bridge of the flagship *Nagato* he laid down his fleet policy:

1. Priority must be given to air training.
2. If war breaks out, the American Fleet in
Hawaii must be brought to decisive battle at
the earliest opportunity.

He made training even more rigorous. A Fleet pamphlet read: "With tenacious and timeless spirit we are striving to reach a superhuman degree of skill and fighting efficiency."

His last hope of avoiding war was that the Navy stand firm against entering the Axis pact. About three weeks before the signing of the Tripartite, in early September 1940, Koshirō Oikawa, the new Navy Minister, convoked a conference of naval leaders in Tōkyō. The ostensible object of the meeting was to determine the final attitude of the Navy on the proposed Tripartite Pact, though presumably Oikawa had determined in advance that the Navy would consent.

With a large amount of reference material, Yamamoto came from the Combined Fleet flagship, anchored at Hiroshima in the Inland Sea. He pointed out that a war between Japan and the United States would be a major calamity for the world. For Japan, already at war for several years with China, war with the United States would mean acquiring yet another powerful enemy and imperil the nation.

If after Japan and America had inflicted serious wounds on each other the Soviet Union or Germany should step in with the purpose of achieving world hegemony, what country could deter them? If in its war with Great Britain, Germany should be victorious Japan might look to its goodwill as a friendly nation. But if at the time of German victory Japan were in a wounded state, its advances would carry no weight; a friendly nation can only look for friendly treatment so long as it has powerful forces of its own. Japan was respected and its hand frequently sought in alliance because it had power in its naval and other forces. Japan and America must seek every means to avoid a direct clash. In no circumstances should Japan conclude an alliance with Germany.

Oikawa asserted that if the navy opposed the pact, the second Konoye Cabinet would be obliged to resign. The Navy should not bear the onus of bringing down the government. He asked those present to consent to the treaty. Neither Prince Fushimi, chief of the Naval General

Staff, nor any of the military councilors and commanders of fleets and naval stations had anything to say.

Yamamoto arose. "I accept the Minister's authority implicitly. I haven't the slightest intention of raising any objections to steps on which the Minister has already decided. However, there is one point that worries me greatly and on which I should like to ask your opinion. According to the Cabinet Planning Board's blueprint for the mobilization of material resources – as it was until August last year when I was Vice Minister – 80 percent of all materials were due to be supplied from areas under the control of Britain or America. Signing of the Tripartite Pact will inevitably mean losing these, and I should like you to tell us quite clearly – since I wish to be able to carry out my duties as Commander in Chief of the Combined Fleet with an easy mind – what switches have been made in the materials program in order to make up for the resulting inadequacies."

Oikawa simply repeated, "I'm sure each of you has his own views, but the situation is as I described it. I ask that you give your approval to the Tripartite Pact."

A murmur of assent went round the table.

Yamamoto's pessimism continued. Sept. 18, 1941 at a Tōkyō meeting of his old Nagaoka schoolmates, he said:

> **It is a mistake to regard Americans as luxury loving and weak. I can tell you that they are full of spirit, adventure, fight and justice. Their thinking is scientific and well-advanced. Lindbergh's solo flight across the Atlantic was an act characteristic of Americans – adventuresome but scientifically based. Remember that American industry is much more developed than ours, and – unlike us– they have all the oil they want. Japan cannot beat America; therefore, we should not fight**

America."

The actions of the Imperial Cabinet indicated that his advice would go unheeded.

As we have seen, the Tripartite was signed. Yamamoto identified the signing as "impulsive" and "irrational," and resigned himself to the fear that war with America had become inevitable.

In December 1940 in a letter to Adm. Shigetarō Shimada, Yamamoto wrote:

> **As I see the circumstances surrounding the conclusion of the Tripartite alliance and the subsequent course of the materials mobilization program, the government is putting the cart before the horse in all these matters. To be stunned, enraged and overwhelmed by America's economic pressure at this belated hour is like the response of a schoolboy who has unthinkingly acted on the impulse of the moment.**

Konoye was eager to meet with Yamamoto. On two or three occasions Yamamoto begged off from meeting with the Prime Minister. Konoye persisted and Yamamoto, with the approval of Oikawa, met with Konoye.

Konoye wanted to know the prospects of Japan if it became involved in war with America.

Yamamoto said: "If we are ordered to do it, I can guarantee to put up a tough fight for the first six months, but I have absolutely no confidence in what would happen if it went on for two or three years. It's too late to do anything about the Tripartite Pact now, but I hope at least you'll make every effort to avoid war with America."

Because fuel was limited he restricted the training area of the fleet almost entirely to the waters off the

Pacific shores of Japan. The Fleet practiced gunnery off Sukumo or Cape Ashizuri and other types of training from the Kii Channel to Ise Bay. Winter torpedo training was done at Hashirajima in the Inland Sea.

To conserve fuel, the Fleet on the voyage from Beppu Bay in Kyūshū to Yokosuka practiced daylight training, twilight training, night training and dawn training to where the vessels actually entered harbor.

A bright spot in the gathering gloom was the stream of fighter planes coming off the production lines from 1940.

The American aviation experts bragged about the Brewster Buffalo: "It is the most powerful fighter in the Orient, far superior to anything the Japanese air force has." Actually it was far inferior to the Japanese Zero fighter now appearing.

The Zero, A6M, was a low-wing monoplane fighter designed primarily for agility. Designed by Jirō Horikoshi, it had been used in China as early as mid-1940. The first production Zero was the A6M2, a carrier plane with folding wing tips.

At that time Japanese naval planes were identified by the year in which they came into operation. The year was reckoned according to the nationalistic calendar, which dated from the supposed year of the accession of Japan's first emperor: 660 B.C. Since the Zero came into operation in the Japanese year of 2600 (1940 by the Christian calendar) it was officially named the "type-0 carrier fighter," from the final two digits of the year; hence Zero – in Japanese, *reisen*: Zero fighter.

In China the Zeros with their two machine guns and two 20-mm cannon outgunned every airplane that opposed them. Their 300 mile per hour speed enabled them to pursue and to catch all enemy aircraft within their range. Combining the advantages of speed, rapid climb, excellent maneuverability and heavy firepower they shattered enemy

opposition. Their missions also established a new world
record for combat flights of fighter planes: they flew a
round trip of more than 1,000 miles.

The American Gen. Clair Chennault, who had been
training fighter pilots for the Chinese government, made a
full report of this new menace, but it made little
impression on those who received it.

During the basic maneuvers of the Japanese Combined
Fleet between April and May 1940 a mock air attack had
been a feature of the exercises. The Fleet skillfully
eluded the first and second assault waves of the imaginary
torpedo bombers. But when the "enemy" launched aerial
torpedoes from both flanks it inflicted heavy damage,
reducing the Fleet strength by one-half.

Rear Adm. Shigeru Fukudome (shē gā'lōo   fōo'kōo dō
mā), Chief of Staff, said to Yamamoto: "There is no way
for a surface fleet to elude aerial torpedoes launched
simultaneously from both sides. It seems to me that the
time is ripe for a decisive fleet engagement with aerial
torpedo attacks as the main striking force."

"Well," said Yamamoto, "it appears that a crushing
blow could be struck on an enemy surface force by mass
aerial torpedo attacks executed jointly with shore-based
air forces."

Fukudome later interpreted this remark as indicating
that even at this early date Yamamoto was mulling over the
possibility of a successful attack on Pearl Harbor. Such
an achievement would plunder the American Fleet of the
initiative and put the Japanese Fleet into at least a
temporarily impregnable position. The idea of a surprise
attack on the enemy was not new. In November 1936 the
Navy War College had produced a "Study of Strategy and
Tactics in Operations Against the United States," which
contained the declaration: "In case the enemy's main fleet
is berthed at Pearl Harbor, the idea should be to open
hostilities by surprise attacks from the air."

186

Lieut. Comdr. Minoru Genda. He processed reports of the attack on Taranto where British planes crippled the Italian fleet in waters more shallow than those of Pearl Harbor.

But Fukudome was speaking of torpedo attacks, and to this there was the usual objection that Pearl Harbor was supposed to be only 45 feet deep – considered too shallow for the successful use of torpedoes.

As we have seen, not long after the Japanese signing of the Tripartite Pact the British crippled the Italian Fleet at Taranto. Lieut. Takeshi Naitō, serving as ass't naval attache in Berlin at the time, flew to Taranto to investigate. In London, Naval Attache Lieut. Comdr. Minoru Genda (mē nō'lōō Gen'dä) processed the reports of the attack and forwarded them to Japan.

As the Taranto attack had given the American Naval General Staff cause for reflection, likewise did it do so for the high-ranking Japanese military officers. Soon it began to appear that Yamamoto was thinking along lines similar to the view Knox had expressed in his letter to Kimmel about the attack.

The Japanese knew the waters to be more shallow than those of Pearl Harbor. The British had prevented the torpedoes from diving into the bottom of the harbor by fitting them with wooden fins.

10

THE JAPANESE ARMY DECIDES ON WAR

Had Yamamoto been a participant in the Imperial Conferences, he would have known even better the need for haste in preparing his command. At the 50th Liaisaon Conference Sept. 3, 1941, the conferees discussed a policy document entitled *The Essentials for Carrying Out the Empire's Policies*, which hinged on simultaneously negotiating with the United States and preparing for war. If negotiations failed to succeed by October 10, Japan would go to war.

Konoye and Foreign Minister Toyoda, both opposed to war with the United States, may still have hoped that a meeting with Roosevelt might avert war. In general, the Army planners felt that a war with the United States would primarily be the responsibility of the Navy. Apparently the Army had not seriously weighed the prospects of winning such a war, feeling that the task fell to the Navy Ministry and the Naval General Staff. Adm. Osami Nagano, Navy chief of staff had made bellicose statements in previous Liaison Conference; in general, his group favored war.

As presented in this Conference, Nagano's reasons for action was that the Empire was losing materials and growing weaker while the enemy was growing stronger. If action were avoided Japan in time would grow too weak to survive.

Diplomatic negotiations should continue. "But when ultimately there is no hope for diplomacy, and war cannot be avoided, it is essential that we make up our minds

quickly. Although I am confident that at present we have
a chance to win a war, I fear this opportunity will
disappear with the passage of time...In short, our armed
forces have no alternative but to try to avoid being
pushed into a corner, to keep in our hands the power to
decide when to begin hostilities and thus seize the
initiative..."

Gen. Gen Sugiyama, Army chief of staff said the Army
needed until the last ten days of October to mobilize and
to arm and assemble ships. "It is necessary to move as
quickly as possible."

The Conference entered into the document the decision
that "In the event there is no prospect of our demands
being met through diplomatic negotiations by the first
ten days in October, as mentioned above, we will
immediately decide to commence hostilities against the
United States, Britain and the Netherlands."

War Minister Hideki Tōjō moved for the following
reading concerning the Tripartite Pact: "The above does
not alter our obligations under the Tripartite Pact."

Sugiyama strongly concurred in urging this wording,
and it was adopted.

The document was submitted to the Cabinet September 5
and to the Emperor at the Imperial Conference September 6.
In the meantime, Konoye had gone to the Emperor to report
this development. The Emperor was concerned that the
policy statement emphasized war rather then diplomacy.
When Konoye denied that it did, the Emperor said he wanted
to speak with the Army and Navy chiefs of staff about
military matters.

When they appeared the Emperor asked Sugiyama how
long it would take the Army to finish the job in the
event of war with the United States. Sugiyama replied
that operations in the South Pacific would end in three
months.

The Emperor reminded Sugiyama that when the China

Incident had broken out that Sugiyama, then the War
Minister, had said the war would end in a month, but four
years had passed and the war had still not ended.
Sugiyama replied that the interior of China was huge.

In rage, the Emperor asked, "If the interior of China
is huge, isn't the Pacific Ocean even bigger? How can you
be sure that war will end in three months?"

He then asked if the Supreme Command meant to put the
emphasis on diplomacy. Nagano came to the rescue of
Sugiyama by assuring the Emperor that such was the case.

Later the Emperor told his adviser, Lord Keeper of the
Privy Seal Marquis Kōichi Kido (kō'ē'chē kē'dō), that he
was dissatisfied with the lack of real debate on the
issues in Imperial Conferences. Again, 20 minutes before
the opening of the Imperial Conference he suggested
personally asking questions.

Kido disapproved. He persuaded the Emperor that
President of the Privy Council Yoshimichi Hara (yō shē
mē'chē hä'lä), as customary, should ask questions on
behalf of the Emperor.

The Conference began at 10 a.m. Among other things
Konoye brought up the dismal prospect "that the United
States and the Soviet Union will form a united front
against Japan as the war between Germany and the Soviet
Union becomes prolonged."

Nagano summed up his reasons for war that, contrary to
his wish, might be prolonged: "...the outcome of a
prolonged war is closely related to the success or failure
of the first stage in our operations. The essential
conditions that give a chance of success in the first
stage of operations are: first, to decide quickly to
commence hostilities in view of the realities of our
fighting capacity and theirs; second, to take the
initiative rather than to allow them to do so; third to
consider the meterological conditions in the operational
areas in order to make operations easier. It was in view

190

of these considerations that the time when the crucial decision must be made ...was set..."

Sugiyama agreed with Oikawa, including Oikawa's view that war should be avoided if possible. He also pointed out that in the present situation Japan was growing weaker while Great Britain and America were growing stronger. Japan should capitalize on the winter conditions that decreased the menace of a Soviet attack and quickly finish military operations in the South. Thus by spring Japan would be ready to deal with any menace in the North. If Japan found it necessary to go to war it should disclose its intention to Germany and Italy in achieving the aims of the war and not permit them to "conclude a unilateral peace with the United States and Great Britain..."

Toyoda gave the position of the Foreign Ministry and Director of the Planning Board Teiichi Suzuki analyzed the national power.

Speaking for the Emperor, Hara complained that the draft proposal indicated that war came first and diplomacy second, with a determination to begin hostilities seemingly implied. But based on what had been said at the Conference he understood that while preparing for war every effort would be made to break the deadlock through diplomacy. He identified as fifth columnists the ultranationalist terrorists who were actively promoting expansionist policies and war with the United States, who had shot former Prime Minister Hiranuma and were plotting to kill Konoye.

The proposal was approved. But the Conference ended on a sour note when the Emperor read a poem composed by his grandfather, the Emperor Meiji:

> **"All the seas in every quarter are as brothers to one another. Why, then, do the winds and waves of strife rage so turbulently throughout the world?"**

Acknowledging the sentiment expressed by the poem as Imperial censure, Nagano and Sugiyama indicated they would stress diplomacy.

Alarmed by the imminence of war, Konoye secretly met with Grew to urge him to arrange a meeting between the Japanese Prime Minister and Roosevelt. Grew was skeptical about the Japanese proposals for a Roosevelt–Konoye meeting. America insisted on an independent Chinese government under Chiang Kai–shek, but there were three governments in China: the Nationalist Government under Chiang, with its temporary capital in Chunking in southwestern China; the Chinese Communist regime in the north and northwest; and a Japanese–sponsored puppet regime in the north and along the eastern seaboard. Japan was unwilling to withdraw its troops from Inner Mongolia and northern China, where the Communists were strong.

Things were going badly for Konoye. As he was entering his car September 18th, on the way from his official residence to the office, four extremists armed with daggers and swords rushed to assassinate him. The armed guards who constantly attended him thwarted the attempt. Yet he was shaken at this dramatic evidence of the distaste with which many viewed his efforts to achieve peace, the more so because his efforts were viewed with disfavor by members of his own Cabinet.

On the 25th the Armed Forces chiefs of staff informed him that October 15 must be the final deadline for a peaceable settlement with America. October 2, Hull gave Nomura a note, ostensibly the American reply to the Japanese note of September 6, which, among other things, expressed doubt that a meeting of the heads of state would contribute to peace, given the apparent divergences of views on fundamental questions.

Toyoda talked with Grew and urged a quick reply to the proposal of a meeting between Roosevelt and Konoye. Grew urged the State Department to risk the meeting. September

29, in Washington Nomura suggested to Hull that if the proposed meeting were not held, the Konoye government was likely to fall and be succeeded by a less moderate one.

Shocked by the October 15 deadline, which the Armed Forces insisted upon, Konoye threatened to resign. He retired to his home in Kamakura and refused to come to Tōkyō.

Alarmed by the imminence of the decision for war, Konoye summoned the Foreign, War and Navy Ministers to his residence in the Ogikubo section of Tōkyō for a meeting to be held October 12. On the day before the proposed conference Takasumi Oka, chief of the Naval Affairs Bureau of the Navy Ministry called. Oka stated that with the exception of the Naval General Staff, the brains of the Navy opposed a Japanese-American war. But having approved the decision of the Imperial Headquarters, the Navy was unable to say she is unable to do it.

Such being the case, in the conference next day the Navy Minister would propose to leave the decision to the Prime Minister. The Navy would ask him to decide whether to continue diplomatic negotiations.

With this understanding the crucial meeting began at 2 P.M. the following day.

Speaking for the Army, Tōjō said, "There is absolutely no hope for a successful conclusion of the diplomatic negotiation."

Oikawa countered, "Let's leave in the hands of the Prime Minister and the Foreign Minister whether there is any hope for a successful conclusion of the diplomatic negotiation...If there is any hope for a successful conclusion of the diplomatic negotiation, we want the negotiation to be continued..."

Tōjō replied, "...I believe there is no hope for a successful conclusion of the diplomatic negotiation, but if the Foreign Minister is fully confident of success, it may be given further consideration. Does the Foreign Minister have a confidence of success?"

Toyoda answered, "Since there is the second party, I can't say that I'm confident of success, but generally speaking, the important points in the negotiation with America are:

1. **The Tripartite Alliance**
2. **The economic problem in China**
3. **The question of keeping our troops in China**

These three items are the obstacles. Of these, some sort of agreement can be reached in regard to item 1 and 2, but the third item, pertaining to the question of keeping our troops in China, is the most difficult one. Since America is emphatically demanding the complete withdrawal of troops, I believe a compromise may be reached if we agree to a complete withdrawal of troops as a principle and station troops according to the time and place as specifically designated by an agreement or something between Japan and China, but I believe this will be considerably difficult."

Tōjō said emphatically, "We can't yield on the question of withdrawal of troops..."

Konoye said, "If the War Minister insists, as he does, it is not a question of whether there is any hope for a successful conclusion of the diplomatic negotiation. There definitely is no hope..."

Yet he thought another attempt to soften Tōjō was justified. Early on the morning of October 14 he phoned him and arranged to talk to him before the ten o'clock Cabinet meeting. There he suggested caution, considering the great superiority of America's material resources.

Tōjō said, "There are times when we must have the courage to do extraordinary things – like jumping from the platform of Kiyomizu." Kiyomizu is a Buddhist temple located on a hill at the edge of a ravine in Kyotō. The

194

At a Liaison Conference, which preceded the Imperial Conferences (top), Adm. Osami Nagano, Naval chief of staff (above, left) said: "our armed forces have no alternative but to try to avoid being pushed into a corner..."

War Minister Hideki Tōjō (above, right, in a later photo) declared: "...we must have the courage to do extraordinary things - like leaping from the platform of Kiyomizu..."

platform is a favorite suicide spot, and leaping from it symbolizes daring to the Japanese, who often use the expression.

"Persons in responsible positions should not think that way."

"There is a difference in our characters."

Tōjō was dominating the meetings. When the Cabinet met he flicked a paper and said, "The Army will continue its preparations. I don't mean this will necessarily interfere with the negotiations, but I will not consider another day's delay."

To Toyoda's mention of the American demand that Japanese troops withdraw from China, Tōjō shouted, "I make no concession regarding withdrawal. It would mean the defeat of Japan by the United States – a stain on the history of the Japanese Empire!"

He turned his wrath on the Navy, Oikawa in particular, for failing to openly declare if the Navy could beat America.

Konoye and the Cabinet listened in stunned silence. Communication between Tōjō and the Prime Minister had become impossible, with Tōjō later quoted as saying, "If I see him, I may not be able to control myself."

He was soon to learn that he had been relieved of the need of such a meeting. Several hours after the meeting, Gen. Teiichi Suzuki, head of the Planning Board, called on behalf of Konoye. Since the War Minister had expressed such a forceful opinion, Konoye was unable to continue as Prime Minister.

11

TŌJŌ TAKES COMMAND

Tōjō's intransigence had precipitated a crisis. Unwilling to lead the nation into war with the Allies, Konoye resigned. To the surprise of Tōjō, the fall of the Cabinet caused his own preferment. Among the reasons for his preferment was the belief of the Emperor's advisers that Tōjō would be able to control the Army. His career testified to his ability.

He was born Eiki Tōjō in Tōkyō in December 1884 into a family that would ultimately include seven boys, of which he was the third, and three girls. Of humble feudal stock, the father, Hidenori, after the abolition of the privileges of the samurai caste, had enlisted in the new national army as a noncommissioned cadet.

In 1887, Hidenori took the field against the Satsuma rebels. Later he excelled at the Army War College where he studied under the influential Prussian instructor Meckel. Hidenori spent three years in Germany and served in the Sino–Japanese conflict of 1894–1895. As brigade commander he fought in the Russo–Japanese War of 1904–5. Like thousands of other Japanese soldiers serving in Manchuria, he contracted beri–beri, a disease caused in large part from a dietary deficiency of thiamine (vitamin B). The diet of polished rice afflicted the Japanese soldiers with beri–beri when the eating of brown rice might have preserved them.

Hidenori never fully recovered from the disease; he died at age 59. In the meantime his two older sons had died. Hideki (hē dā'kē), as he was later to be known, now being the eldest son, was expected to assume responsibility for the family.

Recognizing that he lacked his father's brilliance, Hideki sought compensation through superior diligence and dedication. He graduated from military preparatory school and entered the military academy. He clawed his way upward to tenth place among a graduating class of 353.

By this time the Russo-Japanese War was nearing an end, so the 21-year-old 2nd lieutenant, on reaching Manchuria, was unable to participate. In 1907 he was promoted to 1st lieutenant, a rank he would hold for seven years.

As a 1st lieutenant of 25, he said, "I'm not intelligent, so unless I study hard I shall not become a great man." Later in life he would tell a group of Japanese youths, "Endeavor and hard work have been my friends throughout life, as I am just an ordinary man, possessing no brilliant talents."

While still a 1st lieutenant, he married the well-educated Katsuko Ito, who would bear him three boys and four girls.

In December 1915, now a captain, he graduated with honors in the 27th class of the prestigious and difficult War College. His classmates included Hiroshi Ōshima, future Germanophile ambassador to Hitler's Third Reich, and Masaru Honma of whom more will be heard later. As an outstanding graduate conversant with the elite military language, German, Tōjō, like his father, would ordinarily have been able to look forward to a leisurely trip to Berlin to collect information and to study politics, economics, culture and language.

The outbreak of the World War, however, had transformed Germany into Japan's official enemy. Delayed in going to Germany, he used the interim to acquire experience. In the office of the war ministry's adjutant general, particularly under Wada and Tatekawa, he evinced dedication, speed and efficiency.

In August 1919, the war over, he was ordered to Europe. For two years he served as assistant military attache in Switzerland. In July 1921 he proceeded to Germany. This European interlude was to be his only sustained exposure to a non-Asian milieu. The rest of his life would be spent in Asia.

Though promoted to major in 1920 his salary was inadequate to permit his family to accompany him. He is said to have consoled himself with a German mistress.

Speaking and understanding German, he must have heard the bitterness the Germans felt for the British, French and Americans who had thwarted the ambition of Germany. Again he must have learned of their outrage at the humiliating peace terms the Allies had imposed on her when she in good faith had asked for an armistice to enter the family of nations under the 14 points President Wilson had dangled before her.

In Europe, Tōjō rubbed elbows with Japanese military men who would go on to become famous: Tomoyuki Yamashita, Yoshijirō Umezu and Tetsuzan Nagata. He also associated with the able diplomats Naotake Satō and Shigenori Tōgō.

When ordered back to Japan in late 1921, Tōjō travelled by way of the United States to observe the Washington Conference, which was then considering naval limitation and Far Eastern affairs. Unfamiliar with the English language and eager to return to Tōkyō, he soon abandoned the Conference and boarded a train to San Francisco. America impressed him unfavorably; he considered the Americans undisciplined, unmilitary and preoccupied with the pursuit of pleasure.

At home a lectureship in military science awaited him at the Army War College. In 1924 he became a lieutenant colonel. In 1926 he became a member of the senior staff in the military affairs bureau of the war ministry. In 1928 he headed the mobilization section; in the same year he became a full colonel.

Now 44, he had been on active duty 23 years. He had impressed the War Minister as a reliable office manager. From about this time he became known as "The Razor", because of his quick mind and sharp mannerisms.

In August 1929 he was given command of the 1st Infantry Regiment of the 1st Division in Tōkyō under Gen. Jinzaburō Mazaki and so favorably impressed him that Mazaki called him a "ball of fire". When Mazaki was sent off to Formosa to command the garrison army, Tōjō became chief of the organization and mobilization section of the Army General Staff in Tōkyō.

In March 1933, Tōjō became a major general. As chief of the military research committee in the war ministry, he generated publicity to foster public appreciation of the importance of national security. In this post, where it was necessary to articulate his views, it became apparent that he had discerned an "international conspiracy" against Japan, not only by the League of Nations but by the Soviet Union, America, Great Britain and China.

He also considered the post a dead end, detrimental to the advancement of his career. So in March 1934 he was pleased to become the deputy commandant of the military academy. Despite his great executive skills, he found a situation in the academy that was to compromise his career.

Mazaki had become one of the catalysts of the Imperial Way faction. Tōjō shared the hawkish aspirations of the plotters' cabals but was not a member of any of them. He would have avoided excesses and wild adventures and sought to reform the system from within.

In November 1934 the plot for a violent change in government came to the attention of Capt. Masanobu Tsuji whom Tōjō had chosen for company commander at the academy. Tsuji had the military police arrest the conspirators.

Sympathizers of the cabal accused Tōjō of planting Tsuji as an informer and setting a trap for the accused.

Thus falling from favor, Tōjō was hustled off to be 24th Infantry Brigade commander at Kurumae in Kyūshū, far from the center of national activity. He was attached to the 12th Division when Lt. Col. Saburō Aizawa cut down Gen. Tetsuzan Nagata, as previously related.

When Tōjō learned of the assassination of Nagata he wept openly. He promised to take good care of Nagata's disciples, such as Akira Muto, to clean up Japanese military politics and to avenge Nagata.

Gen. Jirō Minami, commander of the powerful Kwantung Army, and disfavored by the Imperial Way, invited Tōjō to become his military police (Kempei) commander in Manchuria.

At first Tōjō was displeased with his Manchurian assignment. He considered it a suitable post for a mediocre officer but unsuitable for a star War College graduate such as he. But as time went on he began to see the job as a mighty weapon with which to crush the members of the Imperial Way. He expected help from Minami, he being on the Imperial Way black list.

Besides managing such Army sidelines as the narcotic and prostitution monopolies, Tōjō was said to have kept under surveillance some 30 million civilians. He deployed agents from the farthest frontiers to hotels in the cities and compiled dossiers on every Kwantung Army officer.

When the 2-26 Incident broke out in 1936, Tōjō declared that the Army was under the direct command of the Emperor; anyone who manipulated it without Imperial permission, or who directed subordinates to do so, was an outlaw. He acted accordingly.

He declared a state of emergency, suppressed communications and moved against anyone known or suspected to be encouraging or sympathizing with the revolt in Japan. He also moved against any others on his black list. He arrested between 500 and 600 persons – 20 percent of them being military personnel, the remainder South Manchurian Railway employees

He was to send only 20 or 30 to Tōkyō under arrest. He pressed no serious charges. But though there had been rumors of a projected violent government overthrow in Manchuria to parallel that in Tōkyō, no guidance came to it from higher authority. Tōjō kept order in Manchuria.

In Tōkyō, the knowledge that the Kwantung Army recommended stern punitive action enheartened the loyalists and disheartened the rebels. Defeat of the insurgency ruined the Imperial Way faction. Through good judgment and good luck, Tōjō emerged on the winning side.

In December 1936, presumably as a reward for his successful handling of the situation, he was promoted to lieutenant general.

He said, "Now I can face my father without shame."

When the Sino-Japanese War broke out early in July 1937, Tōjō, believing in solutions by force, cheerfully rushed reinforcements into North China. To those who viewed the war prospect with trepidation, he said there was nothing to fear from the Soviet where Stalin's purge of the Red Army was in full swing. The Russians had responded feebly only a month before when an affray between them and the Japanese occurred on the Amur river boundary between Manchoukuo and Siberia. Except in numbers, the Chinese forces were inconsequential. Hostilities should end in an early Japanese victory.

With the enlisted men he was the traditionally paternal commander, attending to the smallest details to promote the morale and welfare of his troops. He ate the same food as they. When a cold wave struck, he saw to it that quilted clothing was purchased for them.

He had heard that his father was a fine strategist but no combat commander. At 53, Hideki had had no experience in combat command. He decided to secure some.

To join Japanese forces in Tientsin and to control the adjacent Inner Mongolia through a separatist government confronting the Mongolian People's Republic and the Soviet

Union, he planned to clear the Chahar province of Chinese resistance. Despite his eagerness and his badgering to commence the action, the High Command in Tōkyō procrastinated.

In August 1937, he set up a combat headquarters, left his office building in Hsinking and personally conducted blitzkreig operations by three brigades – the Tōjō Corps– against a reputed force of 100,000 Chinese. With deep raids, relentless pursuit and a policy of *fait accompli* he achieved extensive military successes in Chahar–Inner Mongolia within two weeks.

Then he flew back to Army headquarters. He glossed over his expedition having been several times on the point of disaster, making it appear that only success could have attended his finely developed offensive ardor. He said little about his fine commanders Honda and Togawa but directed malicious remarks at several officers who had encountered difficulties.

His exploit was only one of the many military successes the Japanese were achieving. But though the Japanese won victory after victory and penetrated deeper and deeper into China, it had become apparent to many that the conquest of China was a will-o'-the wisp. In mid-January, the exasperated Konoye, then Prime Minister, issued a policy statement:

> **Even after the capture of Nanking, the Japanese government has continued to be patient..However, the Chinese (Nationalist) Government persists in its opposition without appreciating the true intentions of Japan and without consideration internally for the miserable plight of the people or externally for the peace and tranquility of East Asia. Accordingly the Japanese government will henceforth cease to deal with that government,**

> but will look forward to the establishment and
> growth of a new Chinese regime...With such a
> regime Japan will fully cooperate to adjust Sino-
> Japanese relations and to build a rejuvenated
> China.

Konoye called upon the Japanese to exert "still greater efforts toward the accomplishment of this important task."

In March 1938 the Diet enacted a national general mobilization law.

Such pronouncements and actions improved rather than undermined the position of Chiang Kai-shek.

Near despair, Konoye thought of resigning, then made a further attempt to break the deadlock by revamping his Cabinet. He replaced Koki Hirota as Foreign Minister with Gen. Kazushige Ugaki, the first non-career diplomat to hold the post. To placate Imperial Way feeling, he made Gen. Sadao Araki Education Minister. He replaced Gen. Gen Sugiyama as War Minister with Gen. Seishirō Itagaki, a Chinese expert who was not committed to any military faction and was believed to want to localize and quickly end the fighting in China.

In May 1938, Tōjō was called from Manchuria to replace Yoshirō Umezu as deputy to Itagaki. Tōjō and Itagaki had been in accord on such hawkish ideologies as the seizure of Shansi and the creation of a separatist North China movement. Now Itagaki, Minister of War, and Tōjō, Vice Minister, spoke as one in opposition to Konoye.

Among Tōjō's potential rivals was then Vice Adm. Isoroku Yamamoto, Tōjō's Navy counterpart, with whom Tōjō dealt with extreme caution. As revealed in a speech he made before the Veteran's Association in Tōkyō in the autumn of 1938, Tōjō was less cautious with the doves in general.

Tōjō declared that a solution to the Chinese problem

had been delayed because of Soviet, British and American assistance to China. Japan must therefore make resolute preparations against the Reds in the north and the Anglo-Saxon powers in the south.

The press gave banner headlines to these declarations: Vice Minister Tōjō emphasized the need to prepare for a two-front war. This to a public not only beginning to weary of the stalemate in China but concerned over the military conflagration made imminent by Hitler's claim to a substantial part of Czechoslovakia.

Troubles multiplied: Japanese and Russian troops had fought a bloody undeclared war to seize Changkufeng Hill on the Manchuria-Siberian border. Japan and Great Britain were at loggerheads at Tientsin in North China.

Tōjō gave daily press conferences in which he talked belligerently, his bellicose statements being publicized. Becoming involved in factional disputes, he was demoted to Inspector-General of Army aviation – a new post – and Chief of Air Headquarters. As Vice Minister of War he had lasted little more than six months.

He is said to have contributed significantly to Army aviation in his new post. Having more time on his hands than ever before, he moped about hoping to be recalled to a position of greater importance.

He had reason to regret his exile from the center of activity: events were occurring in Europe and Asia that would vitally affect his future and the future of Japan.

Germany occupied the remnants of Czechoslovakia; the Fascist rebels triumphed in the Spanish Civil War; the Russians defeated the Japanese at Nomonhan; Germany and Russia concluded the nonaggression pact. Germany invaded Poland and overran Denmark, Norway, the Netherlands and France. Russia subdued Finland. Italy entered the war on the side of Germany. Japan set up a puppet regime in Nanking.

It was during this period of crisis in July 1940, with

Great Britain exposed to mortal peril in Europe, with the
United States isolated geopolitically, with the rich
empires of the Dutch and French in the East Indies and
Indochina denuded of military protection, that Tōjō was
recalled from exile to become War Minister.

Throughout the period when he was War Minister,
Japanese-American relations continued to deteriorate.
Sept. 7, 1941, the day after the Imperial Conference where
the Cabinet had set a deadline for further negotiations
with America, Prince Naruhiko Higashikuni, uncle of the
Emperor, told him of an ominous prediction made while he
had been a student in France.

Georges Clemenceau, wartime Premier of France, and
Marshal Philippe Petain, wartime hero, had privately
warned him that the Americans had utilized the World War
to eliminate Germany as a hindrance to them in Europe.
Japan posed a similar obstacle to America in the Far East.
Since Tōkyō's diplomacy was notably unskilled, the
Americans would provoke Japan to war. Then the vast,
hidden power of America would overpower Japan.

Tōjō replied that America was oppressing Japan through
an envelopment engineered among the American, British,
Chinese, Dutch (ABCD) countries. Though war offered only
an even chance of victory, peace on American terms meant
the gradual impoverishment of Japan.

"I know it's risky," Tōjō said of the proposed war,
"but it's better than to be ground down without doing
anything."

This was the situation when the Emperor summoned Tōjō
and said: "We direct you to form a Cabinet and to abide by
the provisions of the Constitution. We believe that an
exceedingly grave situation confronts the nation. Bear in
mind, at this time, that cooperation between the Army and
Navy should be closer than ever before."

This new responsibility sobered and humbled Tōjō. He
asked permission to withdraw to an anteroom to reflect on

whether he was worthy of the proffered honor. The
indulgence granted, he withdrew. After a suitable time he
returned to say, with great humility, that he was prepared
to accept the Prime Ministership.

After receiving his mandate, he went from the palace
to offer homage at the Tōkyō shrine to Emperor Meiji. He
then paid his respects at the memorial to the Russo-
Japanese war hero Adm. Heihachirō Tōgō. From there he
went to the great Yasukuni shrine dedicated to Gen.
Maresuke Nogi.

When he returned to the War Ministry, a group of
officers clustered about the entrance and offered him
congratulations. They found him considerably sobered.

In his mind echoed the words of Kido, expressed on
behalf of the Emperor, that Tōjō should not feel shackled
by the decision of September 6 in carrying out the basic
principles of national policy. Instead he should accord
profound and cautious consideration to the entire domestic
and external situation confronting Japan – he must start
from scratch to form his policy.

Next day, to give him all the authority possible, the
Army promoted him to full general. He stayed on active
Army duty, holding the post of War Minister as well as
Prime Minister. He also assumed the post of Home Minister
in charge of domestic security. In these two lesser posts
he held the reins of both military and civil police.

October 18 he announced his new government. The navy
ministry went to Adm. Shigetarō Shimada who had commanded
the China Fleet in 1940. Gen. Teiichi Suzuki retained his
post of planning chief. Shigenori Tōgō became Foreign
Minister.

Japanese Prime Minister Hideki Tōjō

Admiral Isoroku Yamamoto, Commander in Chief, Japanese Combined Fleet.

12

YAMAMOTO AIMS AT PEARL HARBOR

At mess the day after Tōjō became Prime Minister,
Yamamoto offered his opinion of the appointment:

**In this critical period Tōjō has become
Prime Minister. This is unsatisfactory. Though
he is bold, he doesn't know the background of the
situation. He will be unable to improve matters.**

The appointment made little difference in the Fleet
training. Though Yamamoto had hoped for improvement in the
situation, he had prepared for the worst. Though he still
held a faint glimmer of hope that war with America might be
avoided, he felt war was imminent. When it came he planned
to strike a crushing blow at America's most vital spot in
the Pacific.

The idea of a surprise attack on the enemy was not new.
In November 1936 the Navy War College had produced a "Study
of Strategy and Tactics in Operations against the United
States," which contained the declaration: "In case the
enemy's main fleet is berthed at Pearl Harbor, the idea
should be to open hostilities by surprise attacks from the
air."

Yamamoto ridiculed the American belief that the
assembling of a great fleet at Pearl Harbor deterred Japan.
He contended that it had the opposite effect.

He said, "...the other side has brought a great fleet
to show us it's in striking distance of Japan, but it shows
we are in striking distance too. In trying to intimidate
us, America has put itself in a vulnerable position."

Then had come the successful British attack on the Italian fleet at Taranto, with reports of the action sent by Genda sent from London. The depth of Taranto Harbor was 42 feet or less as compared with Pearl Harbor's 45.

Toward the end of December 1940, Fukudome and Yamamoto were pacing the deck discussing the British attack when Yamamoto suddenly turned to the other and said, "An air attack on Pearl Harbor might be possible now, especially as our air training has turned out so successfully."

This was the first time he had specifically mentioned a surprise attack on the American fleet. He added, "Get me a senior flying officer whose past career has not influenced him in favor of conventional operations. Keep this matter a secret from all other fleet staff officers."

Yamamoto then secretly summoned Rear Adm. Takijirō Ōnishi (tä kē jē'lō Ō'nē shē) and entrusted him with working out the plan.

In contrast to Yamamoto whose main experience had been in naval organization and administration, Ōnishi ranked first in the field of practical aviation. Ōnishi turned to his friend and subordinate Genda who had been recalled to Japan and promoted to commander.

Before being posted to London, Genda had been a fighter pilot whose skill and daring in China had won his unit the nickname Genda Circus. Then as air operations officer in the Shanghai area in 1937 he had introduced new methods of mass long-range operations by fighter aircraft.

For ten days Genda studied the prospect of attacking Pearl Harbor. Then he reported it would be difficult to mount and risky but had "a reasonable chance of success."

Toward the end of April 1941 Ōnishi completed the general plan for a Pearl Harbor attack and submitted it to Fukudome at his office in the Naval General Staff, to which Fukudome had recently been transferred.

Said Ōnishi, "This operation involves two difficult problems. One is the technical difficulty of launching

aerial torpedo attacks in Pearl Harbor, which is so shallow
that aerial torpedoes launched by ordinary methods would
strike the bottom. The other is the tactical problem of
whether a surprise attack can be made. Apparently this
operation can't succeed without the element of surprise."

Yet even though he pointed out various difficulties,
Ōnishi estimated that the plan had a 60 percent chance of
succeeding. Taking the difficulties more seriously than
Ōnishi, Fukudome concluded the chance of success was no
better than 40 percent.

In the early part of September 1941, Ōnishi again
called on Fukudome at the Naval General Staff. This time
Ōnishi reported that the Hawaiian operation seemed too
risky; he recommended that it be abandoned. Later he
called on Yamamoto aboard the flagship *Nagato* accompanied
by Rear Adm. Ryūnosuke Kusaka (ryū nō sōō'kā kōō sä'kä).
Kusaka, 48, was the son of a business executive, but the
boy had been called to the sea. He graduated from the
Naval Academy in 1913, in the same class with Fukudome. He
had spent most of his career in naval aviation, once even
crossing the Pacific as an observer in the *Graf Zeppelin*.
He had captained two carriers, the *Hosho* and *Akagi*; he had
recently commanded the 24th Air Squadron in Palau.

Fukudome had chosen Kusaka as one of the first to be
informed of the proposal to attack Pearl Harbor. The more
Kusaka studied the plan the more impracticable it had
seemed: too risky. If the attack ended in a Japanese
defeat, the defeat would mean that Japan had lost the war.

Both Ōnishi and Kusaka advised abandonment of the plan.
Despite their opinion, Yamamoto continued perfecting the
project.

In the meantime the naval drilling, always strenuous,
had so increased in severity that the men in the lower
ranks began to suspect that a test of their training might
be imminent. Lieut. Cmdr. Mitsuo Fuchida (mē tsōō'ō fōō
chē'dä), in particular, had reason to suspect something

unusual was brewing.

Fuchida found himself transferred from the staff of the Third Carrier Division to aircraft carrier *Akagi*, which he had left a year earlier. When he had received the order, it had seemed like a demotion. But after reaching the *Akagi* he was made commander of all air groups of the First Air Fleet.

The father of Fuchida was a farmer in the vicinity of Kashiwahara, about 35 miles from Kyotō in southern Kyūshū. His mother's father had been a samurai.

Before Mitsuo had become four-years old, Tōgō had defeated the Russian fleet at Tsushima. The joy and admiration that feat inspired in those around him inspired the child to want to grow up to be an admiral.

On his first cruise as an officer, after graduating from the Naval Academy in 1924, he visited Hawaii. In January 1925, he visited San Francisco.

The U.S. battleship *Maryland* happened to be docked at San Francisco and Fuchida and some of his fellow officers were invited aboard. Above the deck of the *Maryland*, Fuchida saw three scout planes poised on catapults. At that moment he decided to become an aviator.

When he returned to Japan, he enrolled as a student pilot at the Kasumigaura Naval Air Base.

When he was made commander of all air groups, he was a veteran of the China war and had spent 25 of his 39 years in the Imperial Navy. He had logged 3,000 hours in the air.

One day, at the air base at Kagoshima, at the tip of Japan's southernmost main island, Kyūshū, Fuchida received a visit from his old friend, Genda.

Though a few problems remained unsolved, Genda had worked out his plan for the Pearl Harbor attack in meticulous detail.

Genda said, "Now don't be alarmed, Fuchida, but in the event we attack Pearl Harbor we want you to lead our force."

Thereupon, Genda took the dumfounded Fuchida to a conference on the *Akagi*, which was anchored in Ariake Bay. Aboard the *Akagi*, the two conferred with Vice Adm. Chūichi Nagumo (chū ē'chē   nä gōo' mō) and his staff, which included Kusaka. Nagumo's long and honorable career had had no connection with air power. Born in Yamagata prefecture in northern Honshū March 25, 1887, Nagumo graduated from Etajima, the Japanese Naval Academy, in the top ten of his class. He embarked upon a varied service aboard battleships, cruisers and destroyers. In the mid-1920s he travelled in Europe and the United States. Returning to Japan, he went to sea once more, then taught at the Naval Staff College, where he was promoted to captain. Then he was back at sea as commander first of the light cruiser *Naka*, next of the 11th Destroyer Division. He served on the Naval General Staff for two years.

After shore duty, he always returned to sea with joy and relief. Nov. 15, 1934, he boarded the battleship *Yamashiro* as her skipper. Exactly one year later, at the age of 48, he became a rear admiral. When the European war broke out he was commander of the Third Battleship Division. November 15, 1939 he was promoted to vice admiral. A year later he came ashore again as president of the Naval Staff College in Tōkyō. He was serving there when ordered to command the First Air Fleet.

Nagumo was an old-line officer, a specialist in torpedo attack and large-scale maneuvers. Neither background, training, experience nor interest in giving Japan's naval air arm a major role fitted him for his new post. Against this was his demonstrated competence in the posts he had already filled.

Physically he was husky; in character generous, outgoing and kindhearted. He showed keen interest in his officers and men.

Those assembled for the conference with Fuchida were

remarkably well-informed of the movements of ships in Pearl Harbor. According to Genda's plan, the primary target was Battleship Row, the two lines of battleships expected to be moored off Ford Island in the middle of Pearl Harbor. The primary prey, if available, would be the American carriers. Genda believed that aircraft carriers would be the decisive weapon in war between the two countries.

Surprise was essential. Torpedo planes would first swoop down and launch their torpedoes at the outside row of ships. Fuchida pointed out that considering the width of the harbor, not more than 547 yards and the depth, less then 40 feet, such a plan was almost impossible of execution. Genda insisted that because of the difficulty the Americans would also consider it impossible, so executing it would add to the surprise of the attack and multiply its effectiveness.

Next, according to Genda, dive bombers and high-level (horizontal) bombers would attack the inner row. Among other objections, Kusaka insisted that the second attack, to be successful, must use bombs capable of piercing a battleship's thick armor without detonating. This was a problem for which a solution must be sought.

Won over, Fuchida switched his men from ordinary fleet practice to training for the specific mission, though for security reasons he was unable to tell them of the exact mission. Kagoshima Bay had been selected for the training because of its resemblance to Pearl Harbor. Conscious of the need for haste, Fuchida drove the men relentlessly.

In the meantime, others worked on technical problems. Genda, Fuchida and the engineers hit on a solution for suitable bombs by reconstructing battleship shells into bombs, with their outer faces so reinforced they would not explode on impact. A torpedo expert at Yokosuka solved the problem of making the torpedoes run true in shallow water by fitting them with wooden fins made from aerial stabilizers.

212

A fleet of submarines would support the aerial attack on Pearl Harbor. To be known as the Advance Expeditionary Force, the submarines would sail from Kure by a southern route a week before the sailing of Nagumo's fleet. Some of the giant submarines, known as "I" class because a character from the Japanese alphabet resembling a small "i" preceded its identifying number, carried a seaplane for extra reconnaissance. In a large tube on each deck, five would carry a midget submarine.

The midgets were supposed to steal into Pearl Harbor before the planned attack and launch their torpedoes after the attack began. The "I" submarines were to lurk outside Pearl Harbor and torpedo any ship escaping after the attack began. They were also to sink supporting shipping from the mainland.

The plan still had to win official approval. From about the middle of September the Combined Fleet headquarters engaged in serious discussions with the Naval General Staff about the general operational plan to be carried out in the event of war. In these discussions, the Hawaii operation came to the fore.

In early October, staff officers of the Combined Fleet went up to Tōkyō and reported to the General Staff that Yamamoto desired to launch an attack on Hawaii at the outset of war. The General Staff disapproved.

Comdr. Tatsukichi Miyo (tä tsoō kē'chē mē'yō), Navy General Staff aviation operations officer, was one of the few members of the Operations Division of the Navy General Staff who had been closely connected with naval aviation. In late 1941, from the division and section chiefs on down, the overwhelming majority adhered to the old precept of "huge battleships and big guns."

Despite his belief in aircraft as the decisive weapon in modern naval warfare, and his knowledge of the readiness of the Japanese naval airmen, he was doubtful of victory for Japan in a war with America. In August, when Capt.

(Baron) Sadatoshi Tomioka had instructed members of his section to prepare for hostilities, Miyo had mentioned his lack of confidence in the anticipated war.

"Nonsense!" exclaimed Tomioka in anger, "One doesn't go to war because one has or doesn't have confidence. The decision is for the government to make. What kind of navy would we be if the government said, "It's war!" and we replied, 'Sorry, but we didn't have confidence so we haven't made any preparations.'?"

Beginning October 9, five days of map maneuvers were held on board the *Nagato*, which was once again the Combined Fleet flagship. The fleets had completed preparations for war and assembled in the west of the Inland Sea. Yamamoto sought to bring together commanding officers at various levels and thoroughly acquaint them with the plan of operations. Some were hearing about the planned attack on Hawaii for the first time.

"Some of you may have objections," said Yamamoto, "but as long as I'm C-n-C I'm intent on going through with the raid on Hawaii."

Nevertheless many on the General Staff felt the proposed attack on Pearl Harbor unwise and spelled out their objections. The Staff held that since preparatory initiation of the operation would be necessary, it might be noted and so unfavorably affect the negotiations being conducted in Washington. The attack could succeed only if it achieved surprise, and the only hope of avoiding detection would be to take the northern route. Almost all naval vessels participating in the attack would have to be refueled at sea; destroyers at least twice. Meteorological statistics showed that on the northern route only seven days in a month were favorable for refueling.

Even if the task force took the northern route it would likely be detected en route, especially at the point where the attacking planes would be launched. The operation was unnecessary to success in the war; if it failed much would be lost.

After receiving his staff's report of the disapproval of the Naval General Staff, Yamamoto elaborated on the plan and sent Rear Adm. Matome Ugaki, chief of staff Combined Fleet, and other staff officers to Tōkyō to submit his recommendation. Though acknowledging the difficulties, Yamamoto insisted that the attack was essential to the successful prosecution of the war. Again the Naval General Staff disapproved.

Yamamoto's letter to the Naval General Staff read:

> The presence of the U.S. fleet in Hawaii is a dagger pointed at our throats. Should war be declared, the length and breadth of our southern operations would immediately be exposed to a serious threat on its flank.
>
> The Hawaii operation is absolutely indispensable. Unless it is carried out Adm. Yamamoto has no confidence that he can fulfill his assigned responsibility. The numerous difficulties of this operation do not make it impossible. Weather conditions worry us most but as there are seven days in a month when refuelling at sea is possible the chance of success is by no means small. If good fortune is bestowed upon us we will be assured of success.
>
> Should the Hawaii operation end in failure, that would imply that fortune is not on our side. That should also be the time for halting all operations.
>
> If this plan fails it will mean defeat in war.

Yamamoto had warned his messenger not to return without obtaining permission. The senior admirals were disturbed by the last sentence of the letter, but they tended to feel that Yamamoto would be unwilling to take the risk of attacking Pearl Harbor if he were unsure of success. Nevertheless they still stopped short of granting permission to proceed.

Capt. Kameto Kuroshima, senior staff officer of the Combined Fleet telephoned Yamamoto of the stalemate.

Yamamoto replied, "Tell them I will step down as C-n-C and personally take over the carriers to direct the attack."

When Kuroshima delivered this message, the staff officers, though visibly shaken, remained intransigent. After another hour of argument, Kuroshima went into another room and again phoned Yamamoto.

White-faced, Kuroshima returned from the telephone and addressed the half-dozen admirals sitting around the table.

"I have the authority of the C-n-C to tell you that if you do not agree to his plan he must resign from his position and retire to civilian life."

With tears in his eyes, an admiral said, "This situation must be made known at once to Nagano, the Chief of Staff."

They took Kuroshima to the office of Vice Adm. Seiichi Ito, vice chief of the Naval General Staff. Ito listened to what had occurred. Then, without comment, he entered Nagano's office.

After a while, Nagano came out and put his arm around Kuroshima. "I fully understand how Yamamoto feels. If he has that much confidence he must be allowed to carry on. I will approve his plan."

Few wanted to go to war without Yamamoto at the helm.

It was November 3.

Before this, Fuchida had asked Comdr. Akira Sasaki, staff officer for air, Combined Fleet, whether Yamamoto was satisfied with the results of training.

"No," said Sasaki, "he's still worried, judging from the way he talks. Only the other day he said that the attacks were still being made from too far away. I was to

216

Lieut. Comdr. Mitsuo Fuchida: chosen to lead the Japanese attack on Pearl Harbor.

tell them to get closer."

Fuchida sought an interview with Yamamoto and told him, "I hear you're not completely happy about the attack force, sir. If so, I'd like you to put out another fleet order for maneuvers. Please put all six carriers on the job. We'll assume that Saeki Bay is Pearl Harbor and make contact with the enemy somewhere around Cape Ashizuri and finish by bombing Saeki itself."

After midnight, November 3, Yamamoto's order for these final special exercises went out. On the morning of the fourth, half an hour before sunrise, the first attack force took off from the carriers. In four groups – horizontal bombers, dive-bombers, torpedo bombers and escort fighters, it converged on Saeki Bay, carried out the prescribed operations and returned to the carriers. Spanning three days, the exercises were for the most part successful.

When the exercise was finished, Fuchida again confronted Yamamoto. "Well, sir, were you satisfied?"

"Yes, I'm sure you can do it."

13

THE DRAWN SWORD POINTS AT WASHINGTON

The Imperial Conferences were now being held almost daily. On that of October 27 it was decided not to entertain great expectations from Italy and Germany in the event of war, but to get them to agree to declare war on the United States, to make no separate peace, to act in concert with Japan through increased operations in the Near East and to cooperate to destroy enemy commerce.

The 66th Liaison Conference, November 1, was held to discuss whether negotiations with America should be continued. What would happen to Japan if the American proposals were accepted in their entirety? All except Foreign Minister Tōgō judged that the Empire would become a third-rate country. Tōgō contended that if the American conditions were softened and accepted everything would turn out for the better.

Born to a samurai family in Kagoshima in 1882, Tōgō attended Tōkyō Imperial University where he specialized in law. He entered the foreign service in 1912. He served in minor diplomatic posts in Europe, where he married a German, and in Asia until 1921 when he was made chief of the first section of the European and American Bureau. He headed the European and American Bureau in 1933, the Asiatic Bureau in 1934. He became ambassador to Berlin in 1939.

In his dispatches as ambassador to Berlin, Tōgō wrote that forming a military alliance with Germany would endanger Japan and involve her in war against the West. So the Army tended to bypass him in its efforts in favor of

218

Marquis Koichi Kido (above,right), Japanese Lord Privy Seal.   As adviser to the Emperor, he recommended the promotion of Tōjō to the Prime Ministership as a means of keeping the Army under control.

Shigenori Tōgō (left).   Long pessimistic about the prospect of Axis victory, as Japanese Foreign Minister he cautioned moderation in dealing with America.   He hoped American terms might be softened and war with America avoided.

the alliance and to rely on its attache, Lt. Gen. Hiroshi Ōshima, who favored the pact, was on close terms with Nazi officialdom and reported neither to the ambassador nor the Foreign Office but directly to the Army. Because of the opposition of Tōgō, the government transferred him to Moscow, appointing Ōshima to replace him as ambassador to Berlin.

As ambassador to Moscow Tōgō participated in agreements that ended the dangerous Russian–Manchoukuoan border incidents.

Now, basing his opinion on an October 3 cable from Nomura, Tōgō felt an understanding had almost been reached on the Tripartite and nondiscriminatory trade treatment, leaving unresolved only the stationing of troops in China. Tōgō felt that a compromise might be reached if a definite time limit were set for the withdrawal of Japanese forces— a position the Army General Staff sharply opposed. At last an agreement emerged: all Japanese forces were to be withdrawn from China within 25 years after a peace settlement.

The Conference also decided to make a final attempt to reach an understanding with America through two proposals known as A and B. A modified version of former Japanese offers, Proposal A would have the Japanese Army agree to withdraw all troops from China by 1966, including those used as a defense against Communism.

Proposal B would be used as a last resort if the Americans rejected Proposal A. Proposal B would be a temporary working agreement or compromise pending a settlement of the differences (modus vivendi) by which Japan promised not to make any more aggressive moves south and that once peace was restored with China or a general peace in the Pacific established, all troops would be pulled out of Indochina. In the meantime, Japan would at once move all groups in south Indochina to the north of that country. In return, America was to sell Japan one million tons of aviation gasoline.

Tōgō felt that in the little time left for negotiating there was no hope for American acceptance of Proposal A. He was so insistent the others began to fear he might resign and thus cause the Cabinet to fall. Except for him and Finance Minister Okinori Kaya all felt that war was being forced on Japan and that it should be fought at once, before the nation became further debilitated. Finally, to avoid delay and the fall of the Cabinet, they reluctantly softened the conditions for diplomatic negotiations.

Negotiations might continue until five days prior to the outbreak of war. Sugiyama decided "it would be all right to negotiate until midnight November 30 (Tōkyō time). If diplomacy succeeded by that time, the war would be called off.

After 17 hours of discussion, the conference adjourned.

At the Imperial Conference of November 5, the Cabinet adopted a policy entitled "Essentials for Carrying Out the Empire's Policies," which differed from the September 6 document with the same title. The new document set the opening of war for the beginning of December. An addendum stated: *If negotiations with the United States are successful by midnight of December 1, the use of force will be suspended.*

Tōjō opened the meeting "With His Majesty's permission." Foreign Minister Tōgō attributed the continued resistance of the Chiang Kai-shek regime "after four and a half years ofour holy war depends a great deal, it is clear, on aid from the United States and Great Britain.

He ticked off the grievances of Japan against the United States and Great Britain. The "United States has taken steps to encircle Japan by persuading Great Britain and the Netherlands to join her and by cooperating with the Chiang regime.   ...by supplying oil and other war materials to the Soviet Union through the Far East, despite warnings from our Government... by using the economically superior position of the United States, (Roosevelt) has continued to aid Great Britain, which is almost tantamount to entering the war...(The United States) has taken many measures to tighten the encirclement of Japan— strengthening of military faciliities in the South; encouragement to Chiang through economic assistance, supplying arms, and sending military missions; meetings with military leaders in Singapore and Manila; and holding frequent military and economic conferences in Batavia, Hong Kong and so forth..."

Sugiyama reported that the enemy army strength in the several countries in the south was gradually being increased. Malaya has an army of about 60,000 to 70,000 and about 320 planes; the Philippines 42,000 and 170 planes; the Netherland East Indies aabout 85,000 and 300 planes; Burma about 35,000 and 60 planes. Compared to the strength before the outbreak of war in Europe, enemy strength has been increased about eight times in Malaya, four times in the Philippines, two and one-half times in the Netherland East Indies and five times in Burma." He rated the enemy aircraft as excellent and the pilots as comparatively skilled.

On the other hand there had been a relaxation of pressure by the Russians, desperately trying to stem the German tide in Europe. Russia had sent westward to the European theater forces equal to 13 infantry divisions, about 1,300 tanks and at least 1,300 planes. There was little probability of the Soviet taking the offensive against Japan in the Far East.

Nagano said, "The ratio of our fleet to that of the United States is 7.5 to 10; but 40 percent of the American fleet is in the Atlantic and 60 percent in the Pacific."

Speaking for the Emperor, Hara spoke some words of caution:

Statesmen must give serious consideration to
the wisdom of waging war against a great power
like the United States without the prospect of the
China Incident being settled quickly.

...Although the China Incident is one cause for
war between Japan and the United States and Great
Britain, another is the German-British war. ...We
have come to where we are because of the war
between Germany and Great Britain.

What we should always keep in mind here is what
would happen to relations between Germany and
Great Britain and Germany and the United States,
all of them being countries whose population
belongs to the white race, if Japan should enter
the war. Hitler has said that the Japanese are a
second-class race and Germany has not declared war
against the United States. Japan will take
positive action against the United States.

In that event, will the American people adopt
the same attitude toward us psychologically that
they do toward the Germans? Their indignation
against the Japanese will be stronger than their
hatred of Hitler. The Germans in the United
States are considering ways of bringing about
peace between the United States and Germany. I
fear, therefore, that if Japan begins a war
against the United States, Germany and Great
Britain and Germany and the United States will
come to terms, leaving Japan by herself.

That is, we must be prepared for the
possibility that hatred of the yellow race might
shift hatred now being directed against Germany to
Japan, thus resulting in the German-British war
being turned against Japan...we must give serious
consideration to race relations...don't let hatred

of Japan become stronger than hatred of Hitler, so that everybody will in name and in fact gang up on Japan...

Tōjō replied, "...I fear that we would become a third-class nation after two or three years if we just sat tight ...I intend to take measures to prevent a racial war once war is started...As to what our moral basis for going to war should be, there is some merit in making it clear that Great Britain and the United States represent a strong threat to Japan's self-preservation. Also, if we are fair in governing the occupied areas, attitudes toward us would probably relax. America may be enraged for a while, but later she will come to understand. In any case I will be careful to avoid the war's becoming a racial war."

Foreign Minister Tōgō had sent the text of Proposals A and B to Nomura the preceding day. Immediately after this Imperial Conference he instructed Nomura to proceed with the negotiations on the basis of Proposal A.

Along with the proposals, Tōgō sent a long cable, which included the observation: "We have endured what is difficult to endure for more than half a year...there is a limit to our patience...the United States should seriously reflect on whether it is wise to continue to ignore Japan's demands...the present situation cannot be overlooked even for a day."

Meanwhile, pressed for time, Tōgō negotiated in Tōkyō with Grew, British Ambassador Robert Craigie and German Ambassador Maj. Gen. Eugen Ott. Tōgō told Grew that economic pressure might be more of a menace than force to the national existence of Japan. "...we must find a solution quickly and should not call the present talks 'preliminary discussions.' ...For the United States to insist that Japan disregard the sacrifices she is making in China is tantamount to telling us to commit suicide. Please convey this to your Government."

Obviously dispirited by this blunt warning, Grew replied, "I understand. I will convey it to my Government. I am most anxious to find a solution."

Tōgō talked to Craigie because if an accord with America materialized he wanted a simultaneous agreement with Great Britain. Because he doubted negotiations with America would succeed, Tōgō also talked with Ott in order to strengthen ties with Germany. The prestige of Germany was still high because, among other things, the Japanese military still expected Germany to invade Great Britain, clinging to this conviction despite the Japanese naval attache in Berlin reporting as early as April and May that such an invasion seemed unlikely.

Ott said, "I hear that in the negotiations between Japan and the United States the two sides are far apart. Is this so?"

Tōgō said, "That is so. There may be developments, Mr. Ambassador that I will need to tell you about."

But in the 69th Liaison Conference, November 15, Tōgō, though stressing the need to strengthen the alliance with Germany, pointed out that it was awkward for him to attempt to do so while negotiating with the United States. Accordingly he arranged for Maj. Gen. Kiyofuku Okamoto, Chief of the Intelligence Section, Army General Staff, to undertake this task.

Puzzled over what the developments in Tōkyō might be, Nomura, on the evening of November 7, paid his first call on Hull since the establishment of the Tōjō Cabinet. Nomura had become more and more unhappy with his role in Washington. In a series of cables to the Foreign Minister and to the Minister of the Navy he had reported that he was not only puzzled but at the end of his rope.

The Navy was not supporting the Foreign Office as it had promised to do before he left for Washington. Contrary to his hopes, the American government was unconciliatory. The Japanese Cabinet had changed and now he was ignorant of what the government wanted him to do. He asked permission to resign.

"I do not want to continue this hypocritical existence, deceiving myself and other people."

The new Cabinet asked him to remain and urged him to make a greater effort to save Japan. November 4, Tōgō cabled: "In view of the gravity of the present negotiations...Ambassador Kurusu is leaving – by Clipper on the 7th to assist you."

Nomura had requested this assistance months before. When approached by Tōgō, Kurusu had been hesitant about accepting the assignment but finally consented.

To avoid exposing him to assassination by war-minded staff officers or ultranationalists, his mission and destination was kept secret. Kurusu called on Grew and told him that he was surprised and consternated at being ordered to proceed immediately to Washington to assist Nomura.

Kurusu's knowledge of the details of the American-Japanese conversations was limited to what he had been able to pick up that afternoon from reading the Foreign Office files. Aghast at the difficulties of the task he had been ordered to undertake, he nevertheless resolved to bring the conversations to a successful conclusion.

Grew was well-acquainted with Kurusu and impressed with his sincerity. To help get him to Washington as soon as possible, Grew arranged to have the American Clipper held over in Hong Kong for 48 hours.

On the afternoon of November 4, Kurusu bade farewell to Tōjō, who said, "The American people are against war and their supply of rubber and tin is dwindling." He had thought the chances of Kurusu succeeding were 30 percent, but two days of reflection had persuaded him to reduce this figure to 10 percent.

Nevertheless, Tōjō said, "Please do your best to reach an agreement."

Late that night Kurusu tiptoed into the bedroom and sat on his wife's bed.

She asked, "Where are you going?"

"Probably to the United States."

She wrapped a steamer blanket around him and made coffee for him. Since she too feared he might otherwise be assassinated, she suggested that their 22-year-old son accompany him on the first leg of the journey from Tōkyō Station to Yokosuka. The son was an Army aviation engineer. Seeing the two together, reporters would assume that Kurusu was simply seeing his son off on an assignment.

Kurusu agreed. As he left, he said, "I may never return."

In Washington, Nomura presented Proposal A to Hull. As if he were being informed of the proposal for the first time, Hull glanced over the papers that had been presented to him. He observed that Japan had a wonderful chance to launch forth on a real new order that would secure moral leadership for it in the Far East.

November 10, Nomura conferred with Roosevelt. Roosevelt well knew the perilous position in which he had precipitated Japanese American relations by his imposition of the oil embargo. July 24, a week before he had invoked the embargo, he had made a careful statement to that effect.

That morning New York Mayor Fiorello LaGuardia had brought a home defense group, the Volunteer Participation Committee to the White House. The President chose to speak to them on a subject probing reporters had been unable to get him to comment on – oil for Japan. As he often did in addressing the public, Roosevelt used simple, conversational language, though he well knew that his words would be proclaimed throughout the world. He said:

> **Here on the east coast, you have been reading
> that the Secretary of the Interior, as Oil**

226

Administrator, is faced with the problem of not having enough gasoline to go around in the east coast, and how he is asking everybody to curtail their consumption of gasoline.

All right. Now, I am – I might be called an American citizen, living in Hyde Park, N.Y. And I say, "That's a funny thing. Why am I asked to curtail my consumption of gasoline when I read in the papers that thousands of tons of gasoline are going out from Los Angeles – west coast – to Japan; and we are helping Japan in what looks like an act of aggression.

All right. Now the answer is a very simple one. There is a world war going on, and has been for some time – nearly two years. One of our efforts, from the very beginning, was to prevent the spread of that world war in certain areas where it hadn't started. One of those areas is a place called the Pacific Ocean – one of the largest areas of the earth. There happened to be a place in the South Pacific where we had to get a lot of things—rubber, tin and so forth and so on – down in the Dutch Indies, the Straits Settlements and Indochina. And we had to help get the Australian surplus of meat and corn for England.

It was very essential from our own selfish point of view of defense to prevent a war from starting in the South Pacific. So our foreign policy was – trying to stop a war from breaking out down there. At the same time, from the point of view of even France at that time – of course France still had her head above water – we wanted to keep that line of supplies from Australia and New Zealand going to the Near East – all their troops, all their supplies that they have maintained in Syria, North Africa and Palestine. So it was essential for Great Britain that we try to keep the peace down there in the South Pacific.

All right. And now here is a nation called Japan. Whether they had at that time aggressive purposes to enlarge their empire southward, they didn't have any oil of their own up in the north. Now, if we cut the oil off, they probably would have gone down to the Dutch East Indies a year ago, and you would have had war.

Therefore, there was – you might call – a method in letting this oil go to Japan, with the hope – and it has worked for two years – of keeping war out of the South Pacific for our own good, for the good of the defense of Great Britain and the freedom of the seas.

His military advisers had shared this view of the perverse effect an embargo on oil would have on Japanese policy. In a report dated July 19, the War Plans Division of the Navy had submitted the results of "Study of the effect of an embargo of trade between the United States and Japan." In one section the report said: "An embargo would probably result in a fairly early attack by Japan on Malaya and the Netherlands East Indies, and possibly would involve the United States in early war in the Pacific..."

Recognizing its weakness in the Pacific, the Navy recommended against an embargo. The Army was equally averse to becoming involved at present in a Pacific War.

November 5, Stark and Marshall submitted a memorandum to Roosevelt that concluded with "That no ultimatum be delivered to Japan."

November 7, Roosevelt asked the Cabinet for advice. All agreed that the situation was so serious that Japan might attack at any time. He asked if those present believed that the American public would back the government if it struck at Japan because Japan had attacked British or

Dutch territories in the Pacific. All agreed that the public would, but that speeches should be made to acquaint the country with the situation.

Welles and Knox would deliver these proposed speeches.

This was the situation November 10 when Nomura, having failed to persuade Hull, took Proposal A to Roosevelt. Roosevelt responded to the proposal by replying that Japan should prove its intentions by beginning to move its troops out of China and Indochina.

Thus Proposal A died. Kurusu arrived in Washington 1:30 P.M., November 15, the ill-odor of his association with the Tripartite Pact clinging to his garments. At 10:30 A.M., November 17, Nomura presented Kurusu to Hull.

Kurusu failed to make the favorable impression on Hull that he had on Grew. Hull later said of Kurusu: "Kurusu seemed to me the antithesis of Nomura. Neither his appearance nor his attitude commanded confidence or respect. I felt from the start that he was deceitful. His only recommendation in my eyes was that he spoke excellent English..."

The three left for the White House for their appointment with the President, all dressed for the November chill. Hull, in the center, towered over the Japanese. At his left was Kurusu, wearing a homburg and double-breasted overcoat and jauntily swinging a cane.

Just before the meeting another cable had come from Grew. Japan would probably exploit every possible advantage, such as surprise and initiative; the cable warned against sudden naval and military action.

Though gracious as usual, Roosevelt was cooler to Kurusu than he had been to Nomura. The only indication of progress that came from the interview occurred when the President quoted from former Secretary of State William Jennings Bryan: "There is no last word between friends."

Besides the ominous cable from Grew, there was a reason for the coolness of the President. Besides the other portents, there was available to him a channel of information so secret and awesome it was known as Magic. Magic was bringing him news of the drawn Japanese sword poised to strike.

U.S. Secretary of State Cordell Hull, center, escorts Japanese Ambassador Kichisaburō Nomura (left) and newly arrived envoy Saburō Kurusu to an interview with President Roosevelt.

14

HULL ABANDONS DIPLOMACY

May 5, 1941 Tōkyō had sent to the Embassy in Washington the message: "According to a fairly reliable source of information, it appears almost certain that the United States government is reading your code messages. Please let me know whether you have any suspicion of above."

The source of information was German; it had notified Ōshima in Berlin that German agents had made the discovery. Nomura investigated. May 20 he informed Tōkyō the Americans were breaking some of the Japanese codes. Perhaps the Tōkyō Foreign Office felt the codes in question were not top-secret ones. March 20, the Foreign Office signaled Ōshima: "I feel that we need not worry about our code messages being deciphered." Even after the confirmation from Nomura it did nothing to increase security in the handling of codes.

In 1929, Secretary of State Stimson had curtailed the existing, moderate operation in cryptology because, as he said, " Gentlemen do not read each other's mail." By the time the American policy changed, the Japanese had built a cipher machine, known as the Red machine, for the transmission of their diplomatic messages by automated ciphers. Rear Adm. Walter S. Anderson, director of the Office of Naval Intelligence identified decrypted Japanese code messages as Magic. Operation Magic was the complete program of breaking the Japanese codes.

Through intrigue and analysis, the Office of Naval Intelligence (ONI), in 1935, reconstructed the Red machine.

By 1937 the Japanese had reason to believe that American intelligence experts might have compromised or broken some of their code systems. Capt. Jinsaburō Ito of the Imperial Japanese Navy invented a new cipher machine consisting of a battery of standard, six-level, 25-point relays (electrically controlled switches), working on the principle of a telephone switchboard. American cryptologists later identified this innovation as the Purple machine.

Col. William Friedman, a U.S. intelligence officer, and his team finally cracked Purple. They achieved this triumph though neither Friedman nor his associates had ever seen the Japanese machine and were unaware of its components and principle of operation. By means of the code machine they had designed for the purpose, the Americans, Sept. 25, 1940, recovered the first fully intelligible, ungarbled text.

His 19-month effort to crack the Purple code brought a nervous breakdown upon Friedman. In these critical months he was unavailable for work on the Japanese codes. Nevertheless, by this time the Purple code, the highest priority Japanese diplomatic code, was being competently processed by arms of the Army and Navy intelligence sections.

The Navy called its section the Communications Security Unit (Op-20-G). It had a staff of about 300 under the supervision of Comdr. Laurence F. Safford. After his unit decrypted a message, it sent it to a special section of ONI headed by Lieut. Comdr. Alvin D. Kramer. A skilled Japanese-language linguist with a staff of six translators, Kramer had them render the message into English. ONI then determined which Purple messages should be routed to civilian and military leaders.

Purple was considered of such value that secrecy surrounded its operation; only the top brass in Washington was kept informed of its decoded, translated messages.

These persons included Knox, Stark or his flag secretary Comdr. Charles Wellborn Jr.; Director of Naval Intelligence, Capt. Theodore S. Wilkinson; the head of the Far East section of the Division of Naval Intelligence, Comdr. Arthur H. McCollum; the director of the War Plans Division, Rear Adm. Richmond Kelly Turner; and either Roosevelt or his naval aide, Capt. John R. Beardall.

The Army Signal Intelligence Section (SIS) of the Signal Corps also intercepted, decrypted and translated Japanese coded messages. SIS had a staff of 224 in Washington and 150 persons working on Magic in the field. The Army head of Far Eastern intelligence selected the persons to whom decrypted Purple messages were distributed. Army Capt. Harold Doud, Section B (Code and Cipher Solutions), automatically distributed all messages typed by the Navy section to the parallel sections of the Army Signal Intelligence Section.

Since the Japanese used a variety of codes, some of which the cryptologists had never broken, there was always a backlog of undecoded and untranslated messages. The Navy had particularly encountered difficulty when the Japanese changed their top-secret Flag Officers' code in November 1940. Navy Intelligence had broken the former code in 1926, but a year after the change it was still unbroken.

The United States Army never broke the Japanese Army code. Consequently American intelligence lacked specific insight into Japanese military plans.

After the intercept was given a rough translation, it was evaluated to ascertain if it had sufficient political or military value to merit the precious time needed for a smooth translation. Both Army and Navy units were so understaffed most worked overtime. Kramer put in a 16-hour day translating, evaluating and hand-delivering intercepts.

No intercepts of military significance were sent to the State Department. Nevertheless, clues of particular significance were constantly being gleaned from Magic by those few in the top echelon to which it was available.

The intercepts brought the conclusion that Japan would
not support Germany by attacking Russia; instead Japan
would strike south.

Hull and Roosevelt often received the diplomatic
messages the Tōkyō Foreign Office sent to its Washington
Embassy before they were put into the hands of Nomura.
Thus Hull had read Proposal A before Nomura handed it to
him, though he had then made a pretense of reading it as if
for the first time, and was prepared to reject it though a
communication from Grew had warned:

> ...facts have failed to support the view that
> the Far East conflict can best be avoided by the
> continued imposition of embargoes on trade and, as
> has been suggested, by blockading Japan...(if the
> efforts of Japan to achieve a satisfactory
> adjustment of relations with the United States
> fail) in all probability Japan will revert once
> again to her previous position or go even
> further...even to the point of risking national
> suicide rather than yield to pressure from
> abroad...
>
> My only purpose is to make sure that my country
> does not become involved in war with Japan as a
> result of any possible misunderstanding of the
> ability or readiness of this country to plunge into
> a suicidal war with the United States...
> Action by Japan which might render unavoidable an
> armed conflict with the United States may come with
> dangerous and dramatic suddenness.

Hull also knew of the urgency with which Tōkyō regarded
the need of acceptance of the proposals, for an intercept
of November 5 read:

Because of various circumstances, it is
absolutely necessary that all arrangements for the
signing of this agreement be completed by the 25th
of this month...Please understand this and tackle
the problem of saving the Japanese-U.S. relations
from falling into a chaotic condition...

Another message, intercepted November 11, and
translated November 12, emphasized the need for haste and
repeated that November 25 was an "absolutely immovable"
deadline. A message intercepted and translated November 15
again made this point.

Nomura pleaded that Japan be patient for one or two
months. November 16, Tōkyō rejected his plea:

I have read your #1090, and you may be sure
that you have all my gratitude for the efforts you
have put forth, but the fate of our Empire hangs by
the slender thread of a few days, so please fight
harder than you ever did before.

What you say in the last paragraph of your
message is, of course, so and I have given it
already the fullest consideration, but I have only
to refer you to the fundamental policy laid down in
my #725. Will you please try to realize what that
means. In your opinion we ought to wait and see
what turn the war takes and remain patient.
However, I am awfully sorry to say that the
situation renders this out of the question.

I set the deadline for the solution of
these negotiations in my #736, and there will be no
change. Please try to understand that. You see
how short the time is, therefore, do not allow the
United States to sidetrack us and delay the
negotiations any further. Press them for a
solution on the basis of our proposals, and do your

best to bring about an immediate solution.

On the 15th, the same day that Kurusu arrived, an intercept the Japanese Ministry sent to Washington, as well as to several other Japanese diplomatic missions, not including Berlin or Rome, gave instructions for destroying the code machines in the event of emergency.   An intercept received November 18 stated that a new code was being sent to Nomura. Signals would be given in the daily Japanese-language shortwave newscasts. Comments upon the direction of the wind would inform whether diplomatic relations were about to be broken with the United States, Great Britain or Russia or all of them. Magic posted listeners to catch the described signals, which they believed would indicate Japan was about to begin hostilities against the nation or nations indicated.

The Navy officers responsible for monitoring were furnished with cards that read:

East wind rain: Japan-United States
North wind cloudy: Japan-USSR
West wind clear: Japan-British

According to the intercept, the key word would be repeated five times and included at the end of the broadcast. If any of these three signals were identified, the listeners were to telephone headquarters immediately, avoiding slower channels of communication.

November 19, in instructing the ambassador to present Proposal B, Tōkyō added: "If the U.S. consent to this cannot be secured, the negotiations will have to be broken off; therefore, with the above well in mind put forth your very best effort."

November 20 Nomura presented Proposal B to Hull. The text had been intercepted and read some days before. Hull knew it was the last offer. He glanced over the text and

ascertained that it was the same with which he had already
familiarized himself. From his point of view the situation
had too far deteriorated to be healed by the patchwork
formula of Proposal B.

The ambassadors again pleaded with Tōkyō for more time.
They were pressing the United States for a reply within 10
days. They asked permission not to announce they were
"having ships, with all the accompanying dark implications,
leave on or about the 25th or 26th." (The ships were to
evacuate Japanese nationals from the United States and
Panama.)

Tōkyō replied November 22:

> ...There are reasons beyond your ability to
> guess why we wanted to settle Japanese-American
> relations by the 25th, but if within the next three
> or four days you can finish your conversations with
> the Americans; if the signing can be completed by
> the 29th, (let me write it out for you – twenty-
> ninth); if the pertinent notes can be exchanged; if
> we can get an understanding with Great Britain and
> the Netherlands; and in short if everything can be
> finished, we have decided to wait until that date.
> This time we mean it, that the deadline absolutely
> cannot be changed. After that things are
> automatically going to happen. Please take this
> into your careful consideration and work harder
> than you ever have before. This, for the present,
> is for the information of you two Ambassadors
> alone.

Hull set to work on a counterproposal though news of
Japanese activities discouraged optimism. Large Japanese
forces were moving into their bases in Southern Indochina;
Japanese transports were gathering at the point in the
Japanese mandated islands nearest the Indies.

On the evening of the 24th, Roosevelt sent a message to Churchill outlining the terms of the proposed counterproposal. In return primarily for a Japanese promise not to advance north or south, the American and other concerned governments would permit Japan to obtain a monthly quota of oil for civilian needs and limited amounts of foodstuffs, drugs, cotton, ship bunkers and supplies.

"I am not very hopeful," he concluded, "and we must be prepared for real trouble, possibly soon."

At noon the next day Hull, Stimson and Knox went to the White House where they were joined by Stark and Marshall.

According to Stimson's notes,, Roosevelt "brought up the event that we were likely to be attacked perhaps (as soon as) next Monday (December 1), for the Japanese are notorious for making an attack without warning, and the question was what we should do. The question was how we should maneuver them into the position of firing the first shot without allowing too much danger to ourselves."

Back in his office Stimson learned that the Japanese were embarking a large force – from 30 to 50 ships – at Shanghai and the first elements of this expedition had been sighted proceeding south of Formosa along the Chinese coast. He telephoned this information to Roosevelt and Hull. They interpreted the news as evidence of Japanese duplicity.

Then Stimson met again with Stark and Marshall. They drafted warnings to be sent to the American commanders in the Pacific.

On the 26th Hull gave the Japanese ambassadors his "comprehensive basic proposal," which the President had approved. It was a proposal he knew that the Japanese could not accept. Japan and America were to mutually promise to abide by the principles for which America stood; they were to sponsor a nonaggression peace among all countries concerned in the Far East – in effect a revalidation of the Nine-Power Treaty. Japan was to withdraw all military, naval, air and police forces from China and Indochina.

When Stimson inquired about the situation on the 27th, Hull indicated the effect his counterproposal would have.

He said, "I have washed my hands of it, and it (the situation) is now in the hands of you and Knox, the Army and Navy."

The Communications Security Unit had a staff of about 300 under the supervision of Comdr. Laurence F. Safford (above, right). After his unit decrypted a message, it sent it to a special section of ONI headed by Lieut. Comdr. Alvin D. Kramer (left). A skilled Japanese-language linguist with a staff of six translators, Kramer had them render the message into English.

15

THE ARROW LEAVES THE BOW

In Tōkyō the Liaison Conference of November 27 considered the American response to Proposal B, which was a blunt reaffirmation of the original American position expressed in nondiplomatic language. Though the American response specified no deadline for acceptance, the Japanese considered it an ultimatum.

Among the reasons the Japanese found it unacceptable was the demand that all Japanese troops be withdrawn from China: the Japanese suspected that this included a demand that all Japanese troops be withdrawn from Manchoukuo.

The Japanese decision-makers concluded that negotiations had reached an impasse. Henceforth their attention would be primarily directed to the prosecution of the coming war.

November 29 the agenda for the Imperial Conference formally sanctioned war. Foreign Minister Tōgō wanted to know when war would begin and how to deal with the British and Americans in the meantime.

Someone said, "I should like to see diplomacy carried out in such a way it will enable us to win the war."

Tōgō asked, "Is there enough time left for us to carry on diplomacy?"

Nagano answered, "We do have enough time."

"Tell me what the zero hour is. Otherwise I can't carry on diplomacy."

"Well then," Nagano said, "I'll tell you. The zero hour," he lowered his voice, "is December 8." (December 7, American time). "There's still time, so you had better resort to the kind of diplomacy that will be helpful in winning the war."

Nagano, Shimada, Oka and others from the Navy strongly urged that "diplomacy should be sacrificed in order to win the war."

Tōgō replied, "We can't continue to keep our diplomats in the dark, can we?"

"Our diplomats will have to be sacrificed. What we want is to carry on diplomacy in such a way that until the very last minute the United States will continue to think about the problem. We will ask questions, and our (real) plans will be kept secret."

"...I will tell our representatives to exert their efforts in diplomacy so that the United States will continue to consider the problem, and we will continue to ask questions."

The decisions made required formalization at an Imperial Conference, which was held December 1. The agenda was: Failure of Negotiations with the United States Based on the "Essentials for Carrying out the Empire's Policies" approved on November 5; Declaration of War on the United States, Great Britain and the Netherlands.

Tōjō opened the meeting. Then Foreign Minister Tōgō gave a long review of his negotiations with America that had ended in failure.

Then as Minister for Home Affairs, one of the three posts he held, Tōjō again spoke.

He said, "When we take an overall view of popular opinion relating to Japanese-American problems, we conclude that the people in general are aware that our nation, in view of the present world situation, stands at a crossroad, one road leading to glory and the other to decline."

Speaking for the Emperor, Hara questioned the various ministers, ending with a question to Teiichi Suzuki, head of the Planning Board, Hara said:

"...There is one thing I don't understand, and that is what will happen in the event of air raids.It's admirable that you are providing a good deal of training for emergencies, such as air-raid drills, in order to avoid damage as much as possible. But in the event of conflagration, can we bring it under control, given the kind of buildings in Tōkyō, even though we may try to prevent it from spreading? What are we going to do if a large fire should break out in Tōkyō? Do we have a plan to cope with it?"

Suzuki answered, "First, we have enough food stored. Next, we hope that some of the people whose homes are burned can seek refuge elsewhere. As for those who must remain, we are planning to put up simple shelters."

Hara said, "It's not enough merely to have given some thought to the matter. Your plans are inadequate. I hope you will be fully prepared."

Hara then began to give his own views: "In negotiating with the United States, our Empire hoped to maintain peace by making one concession after another. But to our surprise, the American position from beginning to end was to say what Chiang Kai-shek wanted her to say and to emphasize those ideals she had stated in the past. The United States is being utterly conceited, obstinate and disrespectful...We simply cannot tolerate such an attitude..."

Tōjō replied: "We are fully prepared for a long war. We would also like to do everything we can in the future to bring the war to an early conclusion...At the moment our Empire stands at the threshold of glory or oblivion. We tremble with fear in the presence of His Majesty...Once His Majesty reaches a decision to commence hostilities, we will all strive to repay our obligations to him, bring the government and the military ever closer together, resolve

that the nation united will go on to victory, make an all-
out effort to achieve our war aims and set His Majesty's
mind at ease..."

The Emperor had showed no uneasiness during the
conference. He seemed in an excellent mood and nodded
agreement to the statements made.

December 4, when the 75th Liaison Conference was held,
Tōgō brought up the final communication to the United
States.

He said: "I should like to include the following in the
final diplomatic communication we shall send to the United
States Government: the American position, Japan's response
to it and the contents of the Imperial Rescript announcing
the declaration of war. In this way we will bring things
to an end and sever diplomatic relations."

Someone said, "State it in such a way that it will not
be the final word, but there will be some room for
negotiations."

Nagano interposed, "There's no time for that."

Tōgō continued, "We have time to send one last
statement but no more. If we rework this draft
communication to sever diplomatic relations, send it by
wire tomorrow afternoon, the 5th, and allow the 6th for
translation, it will be delivered on the right day."

Someone said, "The Foreign Minister can word the text
on the basis of the draft. As for the time when it should
be delivered to them: if it is too early, it will allow
them time to get ready; on the other hand, if it is too
late, there will be no point in delivering the note. At
any rate, the most important thing now is to win the war.
So the time of delivery must be coordinated with the
requirements of the Supreme Command."

In this way it was decided that the text would be left
to Tōgō and that the times when the telegram should be sent
and the note delivered would be determined by conferences
between him and the Supreme Command. Early that afternoon

the Liaison Conference convened to discuss the delivery date of the final note to Hull.

Both Tōjō and Tōgō wanted the note delivered before hostilities began. Though Tōgō wanted a simple declaration of war, the final decision was for a notice terminating negotiations. Vice Adm. Seiichirō Ito had no objection to it being delivered to Hull at 12:30 P.M., December 7, Washington time.

In the meantime the Armed Forces had been busily engaged in preparing the thunderbolt for hurling at the specified hour. As chief of staff, Sugiyama had seen his army grow to 51 divisions. Most were deployed for garrison duty in China, Manchoukuo, Korea, Formosa, Indochina and the home islands of Japan.

By the target date, the Army would have grown to 2.4 million trained men and 3 million partially trained reserves. The air fleet of 7,500 planes, including 2,675 first-line planes, would be divided equally with the Navy.

As Minister of War, before becoming Prime Minister, Tōjō had ordered the drafting of plans for war with the United States, Great Britain and the Netherlands. In May the strategy had begun to take shape; in November it was completed.

The Japanese Army offensive would begin with a two-pronged thrust, one prong directed against Malaya, the other against the Philippines. The whole Southern Operation was to be under the command of Gen. Count Hisaichi Terauchi.

Born in Yamaguchi province in 1879, he was the son of Count Masakata Terauchi, Army field marshal, Prime Minister of Japan and Governor-General of Korea. The younger Terauchi had held various high positions, including Chief of Staff of the Korean Army; Commander Independent Garrison Manchuria; Commander Fourth and Fifth Divisions, 1930; Commander Formosan Army 1932; member of the Supreme War Council, 1935; War Minister in the Hirota Cabinet, 1936–

1937; Inspector-General military training, 1937; C-n-C Japanese troops in North China beginning September 1937.

After the Army revolt of Feb. 26, 1936, Terauchi had been regarded as the man best fitted to restore harmony in Army circles. As War Minister he administered severe punishment to the leaders of the revolt. At that time he successfully pressed for a greatly enlarged Army appropriation in the national budget.

Under him in the Southern Operation would be three senior generals, each considered outstanding in ability. They were Tomoyuki Yamashita (tō mō yōō'kē yä mä shē' tä), Hitoshi Imamura (hē tō' shē ē mä mōō' lä) and Masaharu Honma (mä sä hä' lōō hōn' mä).

November 2, Sugiyama summoned these three to his office and informed them that in a few weeks Japan would be at war with the United States and Great Britain. In order to gain the oil and raw materials needed to continue the war, the immediate objective was to capture the Southeast Asian possessions of the British and Dutch.

Under the overall command of Terauchi, Yamashita would command the 25th Army, which would attack Malaya and Singapore; Imamura would command the 16th to conquer the Dutch East Indies and Honma the 14th to conquer the Philippines.

Immediately after the neutralization of the United States Fleet at Pearl Harbor, the Japanese would make simultaneous air attacks against the Philippines and Malaya to destroy Allied air power in the Far East. While Japanese troops were landing in the Philippines and Malaya, other Japanese troops were to occupy Guam, Wake, Hong Kong, British Borneo and Thailand. They would establish advance bases in the Bismarks, Dutch Borneo, the Celebes, Molucca and Timor.

After they had completely controlled Malaya and the Philippines, Japanese forces would be partly released to concentrate on the occupation of Java and Burma, thus completing the first phase of the war plan.

The Japanese attack plans were enormously complex. They required meticulous coordination and precise timing. In the first few hours of the war the Japanese would strike at some 29 different targets, targets widely scattered across the Pacific and along the Asian coast. Though such a plan violated the military taboo against dividing one's forces, they considered it justified on the basis of their shrewd estimate of the strength of the enemy forces.

There had never been anything comparable to such widespread dispersion and boldness in execution of attacking forces. When informed of the part he was to play, Honma pointed out what appeared to be a flaw.

Both Honma and Yamashita were known to have opposed war with the Allies.

Honma was born Nov. 27, 1887 on Sado Island off the northwest coast of Japan. His father, a wealthy landowner, died while Masaharu was still a boy. His mother never fully recovered from the shock of her husband's passing. Dwelling on her bereavement, she neglected her son.

At 15, Honma turned his back on his luxurious but lonely environment and took the examinations for the military academy. He scored high and was accepted. At the academy his brilliance and leadership abilities became apparent. At the critical examinations he finished the tests and walked out of the examination room before anyone else. He graduated at the head of his class.

When in 1918 he was sent to London as a military student, he began a lifelong connection with England. In September of that year he was assigned as a Japanese observer of the British Expeditionary Force on the Western Front. He served as resident officer in India in 1922–25, after which he became the United States–Europe Desk Chief of the Japanese Army General Staff.

Despite his outstanding qualities as soldier, he was unusual in that he had a deep interest in the arts and a

246

Field Marshal Hisaichi Terauchi (above) became Supreme Commander of the Japanese Southern Army Nov. 6, 1941 with instructions to seize all American, Dutch and British possessions in the southern area beginning December 8 (Tōkyō time).

Under Terauchi was Lieut. Gen. Tomoyuki Yamashita (right), Commander of the 25th Army.

weakness with women. He idealized women. He had had many
unfortunate love affairs and one disastrous marriage when,
at 36, he met Fujiko Takata, 21. From a respected family,
gentle and cultured, she had been married and divorced from
a college professor, had travelled widely and had spent
long periods in the United States.

She won the love of Honma. They wed, and the marriage
steadied him. Thereafter he directed his energies to his
military career with salutary results.

The plan calling for his conquest of the Philippines
was based on a detailed knowledge of the country and a
fairly accurate analysis of the military forces and
fortifications there. Japanese headquarters predicted that
on the day of the attack the Philippine army would number
125,000. But the Japanese rated the Filipino soldier as
lacking in endurance and responsibility. They were more
concerned about the American troops, believed to number
about 20,000, including the Philippine Scouts. But even on
this score they were enheartened by the opinion that in a
tropical climate American troops tended to decline
physically and mentally.

Imperial Headquarters believed that the 14th Army of
43,000 proven and well-led troops would be sufficient to
defeat the three times larger enemy force. It was to
conclude the conquest of the Philippines within 50 days of
the beginning of the offensive.

Honma asked, "This figure of 50 days – how has it been
arrived at?"

"By the General Staff."

"But on what information? Has there been a complete
intelligence study of enemy forces, dispositions and
equipment? Have you taken into account American troop
movements in progress now? Also, I would like to ask, why
is the 14th Army being allotted only two divisions? Who,
exactly, decided that such a force would be sufficient?"

Surprised by these objections, Sugiyama began to reply,

"The General Staff, after a detailed review of the situation..."

"The fact is," said Honma, "we don't really know the probably strength of the enemy. So isn't quite unreasonable to ask me to take Manila with two divisions in 50 days?"

Besides having openly opposed the impending war, Honma had been opposed to Tōjō personally. Now he was angering the Chief of Staff who was sure to report these new objections to the Prime Minister.

"Whatever your opinions may be, the 50-day period is an integral part of the strategic pattern for the Pacific campaign...You will have to accept it."

This statement silenced any objections that might have been forthcoming from Imamura and Yamashita. Yamashita was in disfavor with Tōjō for reasons similar to those that alienated Tōjō from Honma.

Yamashita was born Nov. 8, 1885 in a small village on the Island of Shikoku, which faces the Japan Sea. His father was a simple country doctor. The reasons for Yamashita becoming a soldier were so obscure he was later to reminisce:

"My father suggested the idea because I was big and healthy. My mother, bless her soul, did not seriously object because she believed that I would never pass the highly competitive entrance examinations."

Yet Yamashita passed the examinations and was sent to Cadet's Academy, Japan's equivalent of West Point. He graduated with high honors. He quickly established a reputation as a hard-working officer and gifted leader. In three years he was named to the staff of the infantry school and in 1914 appointed to the Army Staff College.

As a member of the War Ministry's War Affairs Section, he drafted a radical plan of disarmament, proposing the reduction of men and weapons within the Army. The plan angered the General Staff, particularly Tōjō who was advocating the opposite policy.

When Tōjō, as lieutenant general, came into control of the Army, he turned his attention on this man who had balked him. In 1936 he transferred Maj. Gen. Yamashita from his influential position in the War Ministry to the command of an infantry brigade in Korea, isolating him further from the seat of power by sending him to remote sections of North China and Manchoukuo. Then he ordered Yamashita, as member of a small military group, to tour Europe for six months to inspect German and Italian armament.

The group was homeward bound from this trip when it learned that Germany had invaded Russia. All but Yamashita argued that there would be a quick German victory. He argued that the front was too large for the German drive to be successful; the campaign would become prolonged; Russia would hold out and, in the end, triumph.

He also made another unpopular prediction: War with America would end in Japanese defeat. He insisted that the China Incident should be brought to an immediate close and relations with America and Great Britain put on a peaceful basis.

Consequently he and his unpopular views again suffered isolation. In September 1941 he was again transferred to Manchoukuo to assume the relatively unimportant command of the Kwantung Army.

But when the General Staff decided on war with the ABD powers, they felt the talents of Yamashita, brilliant leader and strategist, too valuable to forego.

They gave him command of the 25th Army, 30,000 men, with which to invade Malaya, which would be defended by 100,000 British troops. The British fortress of Singapore there was generally considered to be impregnable, so he was not required to take it. Instead he was to fight his way toward it down the Malayan peninsula, holding as much of the mineral rich land as possible while diverting Allied strength from other theaters.

The 25th Army planned to land at Kota Bharu to begin operations 7/8 December. Believing that the success or failure of all the operations in the Southern Regions depended on the success of the Malaya landings, the Army sought to ensure success by beginning to disembark its troops halfway through the night of 7/8 December, and to have completed the operation by day on the 8th, which would be the 7th American time.

The Navy opposed operations beginning before the attack on Pearl Harbor, scheduled for December 7 American time. From the point of view of Yamamoto, success in the Pearl Harbor attack depended upon surprise, and success there was essential for success in the war.

To reconcile these divergent views on the proper time for the beginning of Army action, Yamamoto, Ugaki and the C-n-C of the Second Fleet, Vice Adm. Nobutake Kondo met with Army representatives at the Military Academy in Tōkyō November 8. Terauchi and his Chief of Staff Lieut. Gen Ko Tsukada represented the Army.

The conference, which extended three days, seemed deadlocked until the Navy, for the first time, revealed to the Southern Army leaders the plan for the attack on Pearl Harbor. Then the Army conceded: to coincide with the 6 A.M. (Pearl Harbor time) attack, it set the Kota Bharu landings to begin at 1:30 A.M., December 8 Japan time.

November 5, the second day of the Combined Fleet's special exercises, Nagano, in the name of the Emperor, had issued "Imperial Headquarters Navy Section Order No. 1". It read:

> **To Commander in Chief Yamamoto of the Combined Fleet:**
>
> **1. In the interest of self-defense and survival, the Empire is due to open hostilities**

with the United States, Britain and Holland in the first ten days of December. Preparations are to be completed for the various operations involved.

2. The Commander in Chief of the Combined Fleet is to carry out preparations for the operations under his command.

3. Details will be laid down by the Chief of the Naval General Staff.

Accordingly Yamamoto had issued a Combined Fleet Secret Operations Order No. 1, which began: "The Combined Fleet's operations in the war against the United States, Britain and Holland will be put into effect as detailed in the accompanying booklet."

November 11, having finished his business in Tōkyō, which not only included signing an operations agreement with the Army but also issuing Combined Fleet Operational Order No. 2, he enplaned back to Iwakuni.

November 10, Vice Adm. Mitsumi Shimizu, commander in chief of the Sixth Fleet (submarines), summoned all division, squadron and individual submarine commanders aboard the *Katori* in Saeki Bay. There Comdr. Midori Matsumura delivered the first official briefing, informing them that their objective was Pearl Harbor.

At 11 the next morning, the Third Submarine Squadron, under command of Rear Adm. Shigeyoshi Miwa (shē gä yō' shē mē' wä), slipped out of Saeki Bay for Pearl Harbor via Kwajalein. The squadron of nine submarines left at this early date because they would have to refuel in the Marshalls.

After refueling, the subs would follow a route between Johnston and Palmyra Islands. Once in the Hawaiian archipelago, Miwa's *I-72* and *I-73* were to reconnoiter Lahaina Roads off the Island of Maui. No later than

December 6, Hawaiian time, they were to report all information on the anchorage of the west coast of Maui and the east coast of the Island of Lanai. If this information revealed substantial American naval forces at anchor in Lahaina, it would give Nagumo time to shift his attack plan to that area.

On the day of the attack, *I-74* would crawl close to the Island of Niihau, a small island at the northeast of the chain, which the Japanese mistakenly believed to be uninhabited, to pick up any fliers who might have been shot up and forced to land there or at sea. The remaining subs had the mission of sinking any American ship within range after the air strike.

November 13, Yamamoto summoned to the Iwakuni Naval Air Base for explanation of the operational order, the commanders in chief, chiefs of staff and senior officers of all the fleets except the Hawaii-bound fleet. He informed them that the tentative date for the opening of hostilities was December 7, Hawaii time. The main task force would assemble in Hitokappu Bay off Etorofu in the Kuriles; from there, in late November, it would take the northern route to Hawaii.

He added: "However, should the negotiations now in progress in Washington with the United States be successful, we shall order our forces to withdraw. If such an order is received, you are to turn about and come back to base, even if the attack force has already taken off from the carriers."

Objections began.

Nagumo arose. "Turn back once we'd started out! It couldn't be done. It would damage morale and just wouldn't be practicable."

Several other commanders were equally urgent in disapproval.

Yamamoto arose and said grimly, "Just why do you think we spend so much time training military men? If there's a commander here who thinks he could not come back if ordered I here and now forbid him to go. He can hand in his resignation forthwith."

His statement ended the objections. No one rose to the challenge.

The meeting ended with drinking of toasts and the taking of a commemorative photograph. Later Rear Adm. Shigeyoshi Inouye, who had been named commander in chief of the 4th Fleet, found Yamamoto musing alone on a sofa in the office of the Iwakuni command.

"Yamamoto," said Inouye, "this is one hell of a mess, isn't it? (Kiyoshi) Hasegawa was saying we'd suffer for this – their industrial capacity is ten times ours. As for the Minister (War Minister Shigetarō Shimada), I just can't make him out. Before I left, I went to say goodbye and to tell him I was going to Iwakuni. I found him all smiles, as if everything in the world were wonderful."

"I'm sure you did. Shimada lives in a fool's paradise."

This may have been the last time Yamamoto indicated he was opposed to the war.

Nov. 16, the Second Submarine Squadron, under command of Rear Adm. Shigeki Yamasaki (shē gā' kē yä mä sä' kē), slipped from its base at Yokosuka and headed northeasterly. Its route would take it far beyond Midway as it scouted for the enemy. It would approach the Island of Oahu from the north. Once in the Hawaiian archipelago, the submarines were to deploy between Oahu and the Island of Kauai and between Oahu and the Island of Molokai. There they would look for the U.S. Pacific Fleet and torpedo any ships sighted after the aerial attack.

On the same day, Comdr. Yasuchika Kayahara's submarine, *I-10*, left Yokosuka to proceed on a long sweep southeast to the Fiji Islands to observe Suva Harbor. Then it was to sail northeast to Samoa, Christmas Island and east of the Hawaiian archipelago to about 900 nautical miles southwest of San Francisco. He was to check everywhere for possible U.S. Fleet movements. If he saw an American warship he was to track it, but was to withhold fire until after the air raid on Pearl Harbor began.

After the attack he was to lurk between Hawaii and the West Coast to finish off any crippled American ship sighted.

The other vessels that were to participate in the Pearl Harbor attack had already put ashore inflammables, personal possessions and all unneeded articles. They were taking on weapons, ammunition and foodstuffs.

The air squadrons had all gone aboard. They had treated the flaps and rudders of the planes with antifreeze grease. To disguise the mission, the command had issued both winter woolies and tropical wear.

November 17, the *Nagato*, bearing Yamamoto, diverted to Saeki. There on the task force flagship *Akagi*, he participated in a farewell party for Nagumo and his men.

About 100 officers assembled on the flight deck: Nagumo and his staff, all commanders, their staffs and the flight officers. Though their expressions were grim, the general atmosphere was that of calm confidence. Yamamoto told them:

> In this operation, though we hope to achieve surprise, everyone should be prepared for terrific American resistance. In her glorious history, Japan has faced many worthy opponents – Mongols, Chinese, Russians – but in this operation we shall meet the strongest and most resourceful opponent of all.
>
> The American commander is no ordinary or average man. Such a relatively junior admiral would not have been given the important position of Commander in Chief, Pacific unless he were able, gallant and brave. We can expect him to put up a

courageous fight. Moreover, he is said to be
farsighted and cautious, so it is quite possible
that he has instituted very close measures to
cope with any emergency. Therefore, you must
take into careful consideration the possibility
that the attack may not be a surprise. You may
have to fight your way to the target.

It is the custom of bushidō to select an
equal or stronger opponent. On this score you
have nothing to complain about – the American
Navy is a good match for the Japanese Navy.

Having thus exhorted them to avoid overconfidence, he
strode to Fuchida and grasped his hand. All then adjourned
to the wardroom for the farewell party.

At about 4 P.M. that day, November 17, the carriers
Sōryū and *Hiryū*, with a four-destroyer escort, sailed
from Saeki Bay for the rendezvous in the Kuriles. Then the
other ships glided out of the harbor one by one. Some
sailed along the coastline, others sailed as far away from
the coast as 100 miles.

As the *Hiryū* rounded Okinoshima, near the eastern
entrance to the Bungo Channel, a sailor casting trash
overboard fell to his death in the sea. This accident
seemed an ill omen to the man's chief, Lieut. Heita
Matsumura.

As darkness settled over Saeki Bay, the *Akagi* blacked
out, weighed anchor and slipped out to sea accompanied by
two destroyers. The *Akagi* sailed south to the Nanpo
Islands, then turned north.

While the *Akigumo* with a formation of seven destroyers
and the tanker *Nippon Maru* moved out of Saeki Bay in the
small hours of November 18, workmen at Sasebo loaded the
final batch of modified torpedoes aboard the *Kaga*. Having
just arrived from Nagasaki, the torpedoes delayed the
departure of the *Kaga* a full day behind the other ships of

the First Air Fleet.

To avert any last-minute trouble with the new torpedoes, Comdr. Hisao Tsuchita, Chief of the Water Torpedo Department at Yokosuka, was to sail with the *Kaga*.

The release equipment of the dive bombers had been accommodated to the new bombs before the dive bombers had left their home bases for Saeki Bay. Aboard ship and ignorant of their destination, non-crew members worked to adjust the bomb releases of high-level bombers to the unusually long and thin new bombs. In effect they would be held prisoner at Hitokappu Bay until news was received of the Pearl Harbor attack.

The gunboat *Kunajiri* sped to instruct the Yona post office on Etorofu to suspend all communications. The *Kunajiri* would bring to a halt telephone, telegraph, postal service and private travel to the 2,587 square mile island. In effect, the crew would also be held prisoner until news was received of the Pearl Harbor attack.

The task force ships also took extraordinary precautions against communication leaks. As a precaution against inadvertently touching them off, some operators even sealed key points on their radio transmitters.

The Kuriles to which they were headed stretch like a string of irregularly shaped beads between Hokkaidō, at the north of Japan, to the Siberian peninsula Kamchatka. The Kuriles bound the Sea of Okhotsk to the west from the Pacific to the east. Etorofu, near the southern end of the string of beads, is a 140 mile sliver of an island of 2,587 square miles. Hitokappu Bay, on the Pacific side, is six miles wide and six miles deep.

On the eastern shore of Hitokappu Bay, high, steep bluffs overlook a narrow, boulder beach. The only buildings were a small cluster of shabby houses at Toshimoi, a dismal fishing village on the northern edge of the bay, and at Uembetsu on the south.

Heavy mists shrouded the waters as the task force began

256

to arrive. Intermittently falling snow covered hills and beaches with a thick white blanket. Last ship to enter was the *Kaga*, which arrived November 22 with its modified torpedoes.

On that day, Nagumo summoned his staff, as well as Fuchida, to an intelligence briefing conducted by Lieut. Comdr. Suguru Suzuki (sōō' gōō lōō sōō zōō' kē). In midsummer, Suzuki had been involved in a complicated intelligence mission. At that time the United States had frozen Japanese assets and Japan had been negotiating for the release of immobilized Japanese ships.

After several weeks of discussion, Hull and Nomura had agreed that three Japanese passenger vessels might make one voyage each from Japan to the United States provided they carried no commercial cargo. One, the *Taiyō Maru*, was to leave Yokohama October 22 and arrive in Honolulu November 1.

The Third Bureau (Intelligence) of the Naval General Staff saw the voyage of the *Taiyō Maru* as a means of expanding its intelligence research in Hawaii. Japanese Consul General Nagao Kita (nä gä' ō kē' tä) had been sending helpful information by way of the Foreign Office. The *Taiyō Maru* voyage provided a chance to verify the information.

Two of the naval officers selected for the task were to concentrate on the possibilities of submarine attack in Hawaii. The third, Suzuki, an aviation officer and friend of Genda, was given a more general mission.

Suzuki had served 13 months in the Intelligence Section of the Naval General Staff with the specific duty of studying U.S. air power and carrier warfare. Although not officially informed of the Pearl Harbor attack plan until early September, he had attended the war games in Tōkyō that month, including the closely guarded discussions in the Secret Room.

At a final briefing on his Honolulu mission at the

Naval General Staff, Suzuki received an extensive questionnaire with orders to guard it with his life. The three assigned to the voyage were to be alert for all ship movements in the northern Pacific sea lanes, for the *Taiyō Maru* would be making a trial run of the course to be taken by Nagumo's task force.

The *Taiyō Maru* sailed from Yokohama October 22, observing strict radio silence and operating directly under the Japanese government for the trip. Suzuki served as assistant purser. Daily he prepared a report on visibility, direction and velocity of the wind, pitch and roll of the ship and sea conditions.

The *Taiyō Maru* changed course and approached Oahu from the north. The sea grew calm, the weather warm. Before dawn November 1, the ship reached the area 200 miles north of Oahu, the point where the Task Force planned to launch its planes.

Here, for the first time during the voyage, a U.S. patrol plane detected the *Taiyō Maru*. Suzuki made a note: "Reconnaissance line – 200 miles."

One hundred miles north of Oahu, he saw a formation of U.S. planes. To him it appeared they simulated an attack on the ship. He wrote: "Attack line 100 miles."

At 8:30 A.M., Saturday, November 1, the *Taiyō Maru* entered Honolulu Harbor. On the bridge, with binoculars, he was able to observe what might be the conditions around Oahu at the approximate time of the planned attack. So that the intelligence officers could survey the scene, the Naval General Staff had planned that the *Taiyō Maru* would be in port on a Sunday, the day chosen for the attack.

Suzuki remained aboard. Fearing the American authorities might suddenly arrive to inspect the ship, he took no notes. Thus he could not be surprised with notes on his person.

Consul General Kita came aboard the first day. He was to call three or four times, usually accompanied by two members of the consulate who could help in carrying materials. Suzuki revealed his identity only to Kita, not to the others. The organization delivered newspapers to the ship every day; enclosed in the bundles were slips of paper conveying military information.

At the first meeting, Suzuki gave Kita the questionnaire with the 100 items of interest to the Naval Staff. Kita had his own Naval spy lodged at the Consulate, but to minimize the risk of exposing this agent, Kita himself briefed the visitors. But when he returned from the first meeting, Kita turned over the questionnaire to the spy lodged at the Consulate, Takeo Yoshikawa.

Yoshikawa, 29, had arrived in Honolulu March 27, 1941 on the liner *Nitta Maru*. He was listed as Tadashi Morimura, and he was to bear this name during his stay in Hawaii.

A stomach ailment had forced the retirement of Yoshikawa from the Navy, though he was a graduate of Etajima. The Navy recruited him into Intelligence from this retirement.

His first assignment was to improve his English and to become an expert on the U.S. Pacific Fleet and the American bases at Guam, Manila and Pearl Harbor. After four years of intensive study, he took the Foreign Ministry's English-language examination, passed and became a junior diplomat. His chief, Capt. Masao Nishida, informed him he was to go to Honolulu as diplomat and report by diplomatic code on the daily status of the U.S. Fleet and its bases.

Yoshikawa was to play a role similar to that of Comdr. Gitarō Mori, who had arrived in Port Arthur Feb. 8, 1904 listed as the valet of the Japanese consul. His actual mission was to scout the Russian naval squadron there so that the Japanese Navy could launch a surprise attack upon it while the two nations were still technically at peace.

As a cover for the spy activities, Kita gave Yoshikawa the title of Chancellor. Much of his activity would be strictly legal. Fleet movements were reported in the local newspapers; he needed only to follow the reports carefully.

Pearl Harbor is only seven miles from the Japanese Consulate on Nuuanu Avenue, Honolulu. Near the consulate were vantage points from which he could easily observe the ship movements – Aiea Heights, and a teahouse on Alewa Heights from which he could use the teahouse telescope to view Pearl Harbor.

Seen from above, Pearl Harbor resembles a clover with Ford Island as its center. Ford Island was the site of a hospital and Naval Air Station. Both sides of the island were lined with mooring quays, the ones on the southeast side being known as "Battleship Row." The three leaves of the clover were known as East, Middle and West lochs.

The stem from which the clover seemed to draw its sustenance from the sea is a narrow channel through which large ships could enter or leave only one at a time. Consequently there was always the danger that one large ship sinking there could bottle up the harbor, preventing access and egress.

Thus Yoshikawa found it easy to observe the movements of ships in Pearl Harbor. He also found a spot on Kamehameha Highway, between Aiea and Makalapa, where he could observe the submarine base, though with less favorable results.

To check air patrols, he left the consulate very early. He observed the number of planes, their general direction of flight and times of departure and return. He discovered that the Americans conducted almost no patrols north of Oahu.

The Fleet left Pearl Harbor on either Mondays or Tuesdays and returned on Saturdays or Sundays. By monitoring radio traffic of American ships and shipborne planes, Japanese Naval intelligence had concluded that the American Fleet customarily practiced in an area about 45 minutes flight from Pearl Harbor.

Consul General Nagao Kita (above, right) used his Honolulu Consulate to carry on espionage against the American Fleet stationed at nearby Pearl Harbor.

Working out of the consulate on a full time basis was Takeo Yoshikawa (above. left). Yoshikawa was a graduate of Etajima, the Japanese Naval Academy. For cover, he renamed himself Tadashi Morimura; Kita gave him the title of Chancellor.

September 24, at the behest of Naval Intelligence, the Foreign Ministry sent "Strictly secret" Message No. 83.

Henceforth, we would like to have you make reports concerning vessels along the following lines insofar as possible:
1.   The waters (of Pearl Harbor) are to be divided roughly into five subareas. (We have no objection to your abbreviating as much as you like.)
Area A.   Waters between Ford Island and the Arsenal.
Area B.   Waters adjacent to the Island south and west of Ford Island.   (This area is on the opposite side of the Island from Area A.)
Area C. East Loch
Area D. Middle Loch
Area E. West Loch and the communicating water routes.

2. With regard to warships and aircraft carriers, we would like to have you report on those at anchor (these are not so important), tied up at wharves, buoys and in docks. (Designate types and classes briefly. If possible we would like to have you mention the fact when there are two or more vessels alongside the same wharf.)

Picked up by Magic, this directive became known to American Intelligence as the "bomb plot" message. Seen in retrospect, it is significant in indicating a broadening of the Japanese Navy's inquisitiveness to include the desire for precise information on the location of vessels in Pearl Harbor, where it had previously been restricted to a preoccupation with U.S. Fleet movements.

Yoshikawa had interpreted the arrival of the *Taiyo Maru*

as evidence that a crisis was imminent. Evidently arriving
at a similar conclusion, Kita instructed him to facilitate
smuggling information aboard the *Taiyō Maru* by writing his
answers to the questionnaire as small as possible.

Yoshikawa worked day and night on the questionnaire.
He prepared maps . One showed the Fleet dispositions at
Pearl Harbor. Another showed all airports and reserve
fields, even golf courses that the Americans might use as
emergency landing fields.

The Naval General Staff wanted to know if the Americans
could be surprised. Yoshikawa suggested they could.
Suzuki was able to confirm the impression. Suzuki saw
trainer and bomber flights on weekdays but none on the
Sunday morning when the liner was in port.

Kita smuggled Yoshikawa's report aboard under the eyes
of the American counterintelligence. They were preoccupied
with the disembarking and embarking passengers, in whose
baggage they found nothing of interest from a military or
naval viewpoint.

On the evening of November 5, the *Taiyō Maru* moved away
from Pier 8, where it had been moored, and slipped out to
sea. Aboard were the three Japanese intelligence officers,
happy in the knowledge that they had successfully completed
their mission.

Homeward bound, the *Taiyō Maru* traversed the
approximate route Nagumo intended to use after the attack
on Pearl Harbor. It arrived in Japan on the same day the
Task Force sailed for Hitokappu Bay.

On landing, the three intelligence officers went to the
Navy Ministry and reported their findings. Suzuki then
returned to his home in Tōkyō.

Next day he went to the Naval General Staff. There he
worked with various members of the Intelligence Section,
organizing and collating the information gathered on Pearl
Harbor. That evening he boarded the flagship *Hiei* at
Yokosuka and sailed for Hitokappu.

Aboard the *Akagi* in Hitokappu Bay, Suzuki repeated in substance what he had told the Naval General Staff. During the round trip he had seen no vessel of any type. He stressed that many ships of all shapes and size had been anchored in Pearl Harbor on Sunday, November 2. He estimated the strength of the American Army and Naval air arms.

The Americans no longer used the anchorage at Lahaina, Maui.

On one important point - the whereabouts of the American carriers - he was unable to give information. Though three were supposed to be in the area, he had not even seen one, though he had seen a number of carrier planes.

On weekdays Oahu hummed with work groups and training maneuvers. Judging by the Sunday he had spent in Honolulu, Pearl Harbor awoke late on Sundays; there were few planes in the sky; officers and men received the usual weekend liberties; all activity slowed. Kita had assured him that this had been standard procedure all summer and autumn.

He badly overestimated the number of American planes on Oahu but said, correctly: "United States air patrols are very inadequate to the north of the island," adding, "...I feel reasonably sure that the United States scouting planes do not begin their patrols before sunrise nor do they continue such activity after sunset."

During this summation, Nagumo had sat motionless, gaze fixed on the speaker. Nagumo had been opposed to the Pearl Harbor attack from the start: one well-placed bomb could sink a carrier. Now he was haunted by the ignorance concerning the whereabouts of the American carriers. They might be lying in wait to drop bombs on his carriers.

On the morning of November 23, in the wardroom of the *Akagi*, he made an announcement. Addressing the assembled captains and staffs of the carriers, battleships, cruisers and destroyers, Capt. Ijirō Imaizumi and the skippers of

Imaizumi's three submarines and the commanding officer of the *Kyokutō Maru*, flagship of the tankers, he said, "Our mission is to attack Pearl Harbor."

Though many there had known of the mission for months, this was the first time he had openly revealed the objective to all his commanding officers and staffs. He explained that if negotiations between the United States and Japan proved successful, the Task Force would be ordered to return.

After lunch, Nagumo held another meeting in the wardroom attended by his staff, those of Rear Adm. Tamon Yamaguchi (tä' mōn yä mä gōō' chē) and Rear Adm. Chūichi Hara (chū' ē chē hä' lä) and all the flying officers. He told the flying officers they were to attack Pearl Harbor.

On this day, Yamamoto dispatched sortie orders: **The Task Force will move out of Hitokappu Bay on 26 November and proceed, without being detected, to the evening rendezvous point (Lat. 40* N. Long. 179* W) set for 3 December.**

On the appointed day a cold, sullen dawn stole over Hitokappu Bay. Snow spilled from the leaden sky, swirling over the surface of the water and rendering each ship a gray blur to its neighbors.

Blinker signals stabbed the gloom. At the stroke of 6 A.M. (10:30 of November 25 in Hawaii and 4 P.M. in Washington), decks and ladders echoed to the steps of men speeding to stations. There came the shout of orders, the rattle of giant chains, the droning of huge turbines.

The *Akagi's* anchor chain stuck, delaying the sailing a half hour. Then like a train of ghosts the Task Force of six carriers, two battleships, two heavy cruisers, nine destroyers, seven tankers and one light cruiser, 30 vessels all told, glided from the bay and plunged into the Pacific.

16

LIGHTNING LACES THE STORM CLOUDS

On the morning of November 26 news was still arriving in Washington of a large Japanese expeditionary force moving south from Shanghai. Stimson thought it probable that the force intended to move into Thailand where it would be in a position to attack Singapore. Roosevelt pointed out the movement might turn into an attack on Rangoon, thus cutting off the Burma Road at its initial stage.

The top military and naval advisers continued to feel that a confrontation with Japan should be delayed if possible, but that if Japan attacked American, British or Dutch territory or moved her forces in Indo-China west of 100 degrees east, or south of 10 degrees north, America must take military action.

Knox, Stark and Brig. Gen. Leonard T. Gerow , chief of the War Plans Division, conferred with Stimson. Marshall was attending Army maneuvers. They sent a warning message to Short, Hawaiian Department, and to the three other commanding officers in Panama, the Philippines and the West Coast of America, which included Alaska.

The message to Short read:

Commanding General, Hawaiian Department, Fort Shafter, T.H.

Negotiations with Japan appear to be terminated to all practical purposes with only the barest possibilities that the Japanese Government might

come back and offer to continue. Japanese future action unpredictable but hostile action possible at any moment...Prior to hostile Japanese action you are directed to undertake such reconnaissance and other measures as you deem necessary but these measures should be carried out so as not, repeat not, to alarm civil population. Report measures taken. Should hostilities occur you will carry out the tasks assigned in Rainbow Five so far as they pertain to Japan. Limit dissemination this highly secret information to minimum essential officers.

MARSHALL

The special warning against alarming the civilian population was considered especially appropriate for Short because of the large Japanese population the senders believed to reside there. They feared that alarm might precipitate an incident that might afford an excuse to Japan to claim that America had precipitated the first overt act from which war would follow.

At noon, Friday, November 28, Stimson met with the so-called War Cabinet, Marshall having returned. They decided that though expecting a surprise attack, America could not attack without warning. Roosevelt suggested he would send a special telegram to the Japanese Emperor, without making it public. At the same time he would deliver a special message to Congress, reporting the danger and what must be done to counter it.

After the meeting, Roosevelt left to keep his engagement at Warm Springs, where he was to have Thanksgiving with the children. Stimson spent most of the rest of the weekend with Knox, Hull and Hull's associates in the State Department, preparing a draft of the message Roosevelt was to deliver to Congress. Then Stimson and Knox flew to Philadelphia to attend the Army–Navy football game.

Late in the afternoon, Hull received some inflammatory extracts of a speech Tōjō was supposed to have delivered that day. After consulting his Far East experts, Hull phoned Roosevelt.

In buoyant spirits, Roosevelt had sat down with the patients in Warm Springs for a belated Thanksgiving dinner. But in the midst of it, his physical therapist, Lieut. Comdr. George Fox, had to wheel him out to answer Hull's call.

Hull told him that Tōjō in a "bellicose speech" had proclaimed that Japan was "morally bound for the honor and pride of mankind" to "purge" Great Britain and the United States "from all of East Asia with a vengeance." Hull construed the statement as "a last straw". He urged the President to return to Washington immediately as a Japanese attack seemed imminent. The President agreed to return December 1.

The President returned to Washington as agreed on Monday, December 1. In the meantime, Washington had received evidence that the Japanese expedition was landing in Indochina, in the neighborhood of Saigon, instead of rounding the peninsula and entering the Gulf of Siam.

American Intelligence had failed to translate the Japanese bomb plot message of September 24 until October 9. Then when the document reached Col. Rufus S. Bratton in G-2 it invited his wholehearted interest. It was the first time the Japanese had set up a grid system for reporting the presence and position of ships in harbor.

A graduate of both the U.S. Military Academy and the Imperial Japanese Army Staff College, Bratton, 48, had helped break the Japanese code.

He interpreted the Japanese intercept promising things would automatically happen after November 29 as meaning that Japan intended to attack on that date, a Saturday. When the day came and went without the anticipated attack, his credibility as forecaster diminished.

Nevertheless, the lack of action, the uncertainty, if anything contributed to the feeling of heightening crisis. So it may have been with a feeling almost of relief that Safford, December 4, received what he interpreted to be the Winds Execute message from Kramer.

Unlike Bratton, Kramer, 38, and most of his colleagues did not expect Japan to attack America. He later said of the message that the only nation mentioned in it was England; he did not regard it as a Winds Execute message. Indeed there is no evidence that Japan ever sent such a message.

Nevertheless, matters were now approaching a climax, one clue to which was a message from Tōgō to Nomura intercepted at 6:56 a.m., December 6, and which became known as the Pilot Message. The message read:

1. The Government has deliberated deeply on the American proposal of the 26th of November, and as a result we have drawn up a memorandum for the United States contained in my separate message #902 (in English).

2. This separate message is a very long one. I will send it in fourteen parts, and I imagine you will receive it tomorrow. However, I am not sure. The situation is extremely delicate, and when you receive it I want you to please keep it secret for the time being.

3. Concerning the time of presenting this memorandum to the United States, I will wire you in a separate message. However, I want you in the meantime to put it in nicely drafted form and make every preparation to present it to the Americans just as soon as you receive my instructions.

Another dispatch added:

**There is really no need to tell you this, but in
the preparation of the aide memoire be absolutely
sure not to use a typist or any other person.**

Be most extremely cautious in preserving secrecy.

The message confronted Nomura with a formidable task.
How, without a typist, was he to prepare the memorandum in
form suitable for presentation to the Secretary of State?
In anticipation of the important memorandum, Nomura
directed the five cipher clerks under Telegraph Official
Masara Horiuchi to stand by. Of the diplomatic staff only
First Secretary Katsuzō Okumura could type, and he only by
the two finger method. For lack of a better qualified
typist, Nomura directed Okumura to type out the memorandum
as it arrived.
The Americans were equally on the alert for messages
from the Japanese Foreign Ministry. At 6:56 A.M., December
6, Magic interpreted the Pilot Message. At 3 P.M., Kramer
made a final check of the teletype to see if anything were
coming in on the Tōkyō-to-Washington circuit, such as
dispatches that might be a reply to Hull's note of November
26 or that might bear on these negotiations. He found such
a message.
He had previously asked certain of the translators to
remain past the regular quitting time of about 12:45 to put
matters in order. They were still on hand. Now he asked
them to remain to help decipher the message coming in.
Within a half-hour they had determined that the message
coming in was Part 8 of the 14-part message mentioned by
the Pilot Message. The message had an ominous ring. In
part, it read:

The American proposal contains a stipulation which

states: "Both governments will agree that no agreement, which either has concluded with any third powers, shall be interpreted by it in such a way as to conflict with the fundamental purpose of this agreement, the establishment and preservation of peace throughout the Pacific Area." It is presumed that the above provision has been proposed with a view to restrain Japan from fulfilling its obligations under the Tripartite Pact when the United States participates in the war in Europe, and, as such, it cannot be accepted by the Japanese Government.

At this critical moment, Roosevelt was working on his own final measure to avert the crisis – the message to the Japanese Emperor he had been mulling over. At 5:30 P.M. he recalled his secretary, Grace Tully, from a cocktail party at the Mayflower Hotel and dictated the message:

Almost a century ago the President of the United States addressed to the Emperor of Japan a message extending an offer of friendship...

...None of the peoples I have spoken of above can sit either indefinitely or permanently on a keg of dynamite.

There is absolutely no thought on the part of the United States of invading Indochina if every Japanese soldier or sailor were to be withdrawn therefrom.

I think that we can obtain the same assurance from the Governments of Malaya and the Government of Thailand. I would even undertake to ask for the same assurance on the part of the Government of China. Thus a withdrawal of the Japanese forces from Indo-China would result in the assurance of peace throughout the whole of the South Pacific area.

I address myself to Your Majesty at this moment in the fervent hope that Your Majesty may, as I am doing, give thought in this definite emergency to ways of dispelling the dark clouds. I am confident that both of us, for the sake of the peoples not only of our own great countries but for the sake of humanity in neighboring territories, have a sacred duty to restore traditional amity and prevent further death and destruction in the world.

He signed the letter "Franklin D. Roosevelt" and sent it to Hull along with a handwritten note:

Dear Cordell: Shoot this to Grew — I think can go in gray code — saves time — I don't mind if it gets picked up.

By 7:40 P.M. the White House had informed the Washington press corps of the President's appeal. At 8 P.M. Hull cabled Grew that a message from Roosevelt to the Emperor was on its way. At 9 P.M. the message was sent, triple priority.

Concomitant with this action memorable activity was taking place in the office of Navy Intelligence. By 7:30 P.M. the last of the first 13-parts of the anticipated message had come in.

The memorandum stressed the purity of the motives behind the actions of Japan in the Far East, protested that America and Great Britain had assisted the Chungking regime of China to obstruct the establishment of peace, had pressured the Netherlands East Indies and menaced French Indochina to frustrate Japan; had severed economic relations with Japan and increased preparations to militarily encircle Japan; had rejected the proposal for a meeting between the President and the Prime Minister of

Japan; had rejected Proposals A and B and on November 26 had made a proposal that totally ignored Japanese claims.

> The American Government, obsessed with its own views and opinions, may be said to be scheming for the extension of the war. While it seeks, on the one hand, to secure its rear by stabilizing the Pacific area, it is engaged, on the other hand, in aiding Great Britain and preparing to attack, in the name of self-defense, Germany and Italy...
> ...The American government...objects to settling international issues through military pressure, it is exercising in conjunction with Great Britain and other nations pressure by economic power...more inhuman than military pressure.

Kramer was impressed that this message employed far stronger language than the earlier notes and indicated that Japan was concluding negotiations.

Between 8:30 and 8:45 that evening, he had the folders containing the message ready for delivery to the usual recipients. According to his usual practice, about 8:45 he began phoning the probable locations of the proposed recipients - to Knox and so forth.

The Army would distribute the intercepts to the Army counterparts.

Kramer phoned Stark but could not reach him - he apparently being absent from home. Then he phoned Rear Adm. Richard Kelly, Chief of the War Plans Division of the Navy; then Turner; then the situation room at the White House.

Beardall had set up the White House situation room a month or two previously - on the ground floor, south side, center of the White House. Equipped with maps through which the personnel could follow the war in Europe, it was a center through which to route any messages or traffic of Intelligence to the Navy Department.

Beardall had left at 5:30 to attend the party at the Wilkensons', but he had been alerted to the forthcoming intercepts. He recognized their importance and carefully impressed this upon his assistant there, Lieut. Lester Robert Schulz.

From Iowa, Annapolis class of 1934, Schulz had been sent to the White House to assist Beardall the preceding week. Schulz had gone to Warm Springs the preceding weekend; he had returned to Washington December 2. He was acquainted with the President.

This afternoon, Beardall had instructed him to remain in the small office assigned him in the corner of the mail room in the office building to receive Magic intercepts from Kramer that would be important. Immediately upon receiving the intercepts, Schulz was to take them to the President. Beardall gave Schulz the key to the locked pouch that would contain the intercepts.

Kramer, who had impressed his wife into chauffering for him, came with the pouch about 9:30 P.M. He handed the pouch to Schulz with the admonition, "There is something in this folder that the President should see as quickly as possible."

Schulz took the pouch from the mail room to the White House proper. There he obtained permission to go up to the President's study, the Oval Room on the second floor.

An usher accompanied him, announced him and admitted him to the study.

Schulz found Roosevelt seated at his desk. Hopkins, whom Schulz had met the preceding day, was on a sofa near the President. Roosevelt was toying with his stamp collection. He had been talking to Hopkins about a plan they both cherished of someday retiring to the Florida Keys to find a life of ease.

To the President, Schulz announced he had the material

brought by Kramer. Schulz unlocked the pouch and took out the papers. He saw them for the first time – a sheaf of about 15 typewritten pages fastened together. He handed the papers to the President.

Roosevelt read the papers to himself, taking about 10 minutes to do so. As the President read, Schulz stood by; Hopkins paced slowly up and down the room.

Roosevelt handed the papers to Hopkins. Hopkins read them and returned them to the President.

"This means war," said Roosevelt.

Hopkins mentioned that the Japanese would strike when their forces were most properly deployed for their advantage – in Indochina, for example. Roosevelt mentioned the message he had sent to the Emperor, in effect requesting the withdrawal of Japanese troops from Indochina.

Hopkins opined that since war was undoubtedly to come at the convenience of the Japanese, it was too bad that America could not strike the first blow and prevent any sort of surprise.

By a nod the President conceded the need for such forbearance was regrettable, but said, "No, we can't do that. We are a democracy and a peaceful people." He raised his voice, "But we have a good record."

The President said he would talk to Stark. When he tried to get Stark on the phone, the operator said that Stark could be reached at the National Theater, where he was viewing a performance of *The Student Prince*.

The President put down the phone and said he could get in touch with Stark in a half-hour anyway. He wished to avoid having Stark paged or observed suddenly leaving the theater as it might cause alarm.

The President returned the papers. Schulz took them and left.

17

THE CALM THAT PRESAGES STORM

Stimson was later to describe the duties of Short as commanding general of the Hawaiian Department in these words:

> The outpost commander is like a sentinel on duty in the face of the enemy...He must assume that the enemy will attack at his particular post; and that the enemy will attack at the time and in the way in which it will be most difficult to defeat him. It is not the duty of the outpost commander to speculate or rely on the possibilities of the enemy attacking at some other outpost instead of his own. It is his duty to meet him at his post at any time and to make the best possible fight that can be made against him with the weapons with which he has been supplied.

Neither Short nor Kimmel had the use of Purple. They were even ignorant of its existence. In common with Intelligence at Washington there were some other Japanese codes they had been unable to crack, but from a message leaving an enemy ship Navy Intelligence in Hawaii could identify the ship and its approximate location.

In addition, they had the assistance of the local branch of the Federal Bureau of Investigation, which had direct radio communication with the mainland.

Upon assuming command of the Hawaiian Department, Short had found the defense prepared for submarine danger, espionage and sabotage, but inadequately prepared for defense against air attack. Consequently, in cooperation with the Navy, he worked to improve the defense.

In accordance with his instructions from Marshall, he also fostered relations with Kimmel.

With large numbers of officers and men being detached from time to time to meet the demands of expanding procurement and training agencies ashore and the supply of trained personnel to man new ships, Kimmel was conscious of the shortcomings of his defense. He considered the U.S. Pacific Fleet inferior to that of the Japanese in every category of fighting ship.

He said, "No one in authority expected that the Pacific Fleet could meet the Japanese head on."

Accordingly, early in 1941 he reorganized his vessels into three task forces, including one fast carrier task force, one amphibious task force and one battleship task force. He had them operate at sea under wartime conditions, stressing fueling at sea.

He arranged to have one of these task forces always at sea, usually two. During Fleet maneuvers he frequently had the entire Fleet at sea. Periods in port were necessary for all ships, but at no time did he have all the ships at Pearl Harbor at the same time.

Like his predecessor, Richardson, he considered aerial torpedo attack a negligible danger at Pearl Harbor where the water depth was less than 40 feet.

Sometimes it was necessary for the battleships to be at sea without carrier protection. In such situations he calculated they would be more subject to damage from air attack than if they remained in port.

He was the more persuaded to this conclusion because the Bomb Plot, and other signficant Japanese messages, had been withheld from him. Nor did he know that from September 24 the dispatches from Tōkyō acquired a significant increase in interest in Pearl Harbor.

276

He was uninformed that Japanese dispatch No. 736 set November 26 as the deadline for bringing diplomatic negotiations to fruition, nor did he know of subsequent messages referring to this deadline. He was uninformed that the Japanese found the American proposal of November 26 unsatisfactory and that they consequently considered the negotiations at an end. Nor did he know that Tōkyō stressed continuing the appearance of negotiations even though they considered them at an end.

Nevertheless, though Washington kept Kimmel in the dark about the diplomatic intercepts, Stark warned him of the seriousness of the situation as early as October 16. He wrote:

> The resignation of the Japanese (Konoye) cabinet has created a grave situation. If a new cabinet is formed it will probably be strongly nationalistic and anti-American. If the Konoye cabinet remains...it will operate under a new mandate which will not include rapprochement with the United States. In either case hostilities between Japan and the United States are a strong possibility. Since the United States and Britain are held responsible by Japan for her present desperate situation there is also a possibility that Japan may attack these two powers.
>
> In view of all these possibilities you will take due precautions, including such preparatory deployments as will not disclose strategic intention or constitute provocative actions against Japan...

The message asked Kimmel to notify the appropriate Army authorities in his Naval District.

November 7 Stark wrote to Kimmel: "Things seem to be moving steadily toward a crisis in the Pacific...A month may see, literally, most anything..."

November 24 Stark wrote to Kimmel:

> Chances of favorable outcome of negotiations with Japan very doubtful. This situation coupled with statements of Japanese Government and movements their naval and military forces indicate in our opinion that a surprise aggressive movement in any direction including attack on Philippines or Guam is a possibility. Chief of Staff has seen this dispatch concurs and requests addressees to inform section Army officers their areas. Utmost secrecy necessary in order not to complicate an already tense situation or precipitate Japanese action.

November 27 Kimmel received this message:

> This dispatch is to be considered a war warning. Negotiations with Japan looking toward stabilization of conditions in the Pacific have ceased and an aggressive move by Japan is expected within the next few days. The number and equipment of Japanese troops and the organization of the naval task forces indicates an amphibious expedition against either the Philippines, Thai or the Kra Peninsula or possibly Borneo. Execute an appropriate defensive deployment preparatory to carrying out the tasks assigned in WPL 46 (the Navy's basic war plan). Inform district and army authorities. A similar warning is being sent by War Department...

Kimmel responded by issuing orders to the Fleet to exercise extreme vigilance against submarines in operating areas and to depth bomb all contacts expected to be hostile in the Fleet operating areas.

There had been reports of submarines in the operating areas around Hawaii. November 3 a patrol plane observed an oil slick area in latitude 20-10, longitude 157-41. November 28, the day Kimmel issued this order, the *U.S.S. Helena* reported that a radar operator, without knowledge of the just-issued order, was positive that a submarine was in the restricted area. During the night of December 2, the *U.S.S. Gamble* would report a clear metallic echo in latitude 20-30, longitude 158-23. Searches, however, produced negative results.

When Short had received his war warning message of November 26, a copy of which he had forwarded to Kimmel, he was persuaded that Marshall had not written it. Marshall had personally approved Short's long-range aerial reconnaissance arrangement with Rear Adm. Claude C. Bloch, commandant 14th Naval District. Marshall knew that the Navy had assumed the function of long-range aerial reconnaissance.

Short later explained that it appeared that "this message was written basically for MacArthur in the Philippines" where no such arrangement with the Navy for reconnaissance had been made.

Therefore Short issued the first of the three Alerts he had prepared for emergencies: Alert No. 1, which was a defense against sabotage, espionage and subversive activities without any threat from the outside.

He informed Washington: "Reurad (abbreviation for "reference your radio") 472 27th Report Department alerted to prevent sabotage. Liaison with the Navy."

Instead of arming and dispersing his planes to repel an aerial attack, he disarmed them and concentrated them in the open, wing tip to wing tip, where they could be guarded against potential saboteurs.

He also ordered the aircraft control and warning system to operate from 4 A.M. until 7 A.M. daily as well as during regular hours.   His six mobile stations had been operating daily except Sundays from 7:00 A.M. to 11 A.M. for routine training.   They operated daily except Saturday and Sunday from noon to 4 P.M. for training and maintenance.   His radarmen had been working Sundays on their own initiative.

Short expected little from this system, he used them primarily for training.

As for Kimmel, the same day the War Warning message arrived, November 27, he received another message from the Navy Department suggesting that Kimmel send from the immediate vicinity of Pearl Harbor the carriers of the Fleet.   On the same day the War and Navy Departments suggested that 50 percent of the Army's resources in pursuit planes be sent from Oahu.

These suggestions encouraged Kimmel in the conviction there was little likelihood of a Japanese attack on Hawaii.

November 27, Kimmel called a conference concerning the defenses of the American 'picket-line islands', which included Midway, Wake, Johnston and Palmyra.   All were undersupplied with men and arms.   Adm. William F. Halsey Jr., commander of the aircraft battle force, who participated in the conference, urged ferrying a dozen marine F4Fs (Grumman Wildcats) to Wake.

Kimmel entrusted Halsey with the mission and advised him of the gravity of the situation – America was on the verge of war with Japan.   Halsey wondered what action he should take if his force had to cope with Japanese submarines in a situation that might precipitate war.

"How far do you want me to go?" asked Halsey

"Use your common sense."

Halsey interpreted the answer to mean that he had been given full authority to act to protect the secrecy of his mission.   His task force departed from Pearl Harbor at 7 A.M., November 28, comprised of his flagship, the carrier *Enterprise*, three heavy cruisers and nine destroyers.   His would be the only American force in the area towards which he was heading.

He informed all hands that they were "now operating under war conditions." He directed that aircraft and destroyer torpedoes carry warheads, bombers live weapons and pilots were to sink "any shipping sighted and shoot down any planes encountered."

Halsey knew the American ships to be outnumbered in the Pacific. Only three American carriers – the *Enterprise*, the *Lexington*, which was returning from Midway, and the *Saratoga*, being repaired and overhauled at San Diego, faced ten Japanese carriers.

Meanwhile at Pearl Harbor there may have been a slight relaxation of tension because the daily newspapers indicated that negotiations with Japan, after having been terminated, had been resumed. For though Washington knew the Japanese negotiations were not being carried on in good faith it did not impart this information to its military commanders in Hawaii.

The night of November 30 – December 1 brought a significant development to Kimmel's Intelligence, as revealed in its "Communications Intelligence Summary" for December 1. It read:

All service radio calls of (Japanese) forces afloat changed promptly at 0000, 1 December. Previously, service calls changed after a period of six months or more. Calls were last changed on 1 November, 1941. The fact that service calls lasted only one month indicate an additional progressive step in preparing for active operations on a large scale...It appears that the Japanese Navy is adopting more and more security provisions...prior to 0000, 1 December...an effort was made to deliver all dispatches using old calls so that promptly with the change of calls, there would be a minimum of undelivered dispatches and consequent confusions

and compromises. Either that or the large number
of old messages may have been to pad the total
volume and make it appear as if nothing unusual
was pending...

When he received the Summary, Kimmel underlined the
part announcing the lack of traffic. He asked Lieut.
Comdr. Edwin T. Layton, Intelligence Officer, Pacific
Fleet, to prepare a paper showing the approximate locations
of Japanese Fleet units. Principally depending on
Communications Intelligence for the information, Layton
delivered it to Kimmel December 2.

Layton had listed neither Carrier Division One nor Two
"because neither one of these commands had appeared in
traffic for fully 15 and possibly 25 days..."

"What!" exclaimed Kimmel, "You don't know where Carrier
Division One and Carrier Division Two are?"

"No, sir," said Layton, "I think they are in home
waters, but I do not know where they are..."

"Do you mean to say that they could be rounding Diamond
Head and you wouldn't know it?"

"I hope they would be sighted before now."

This, of course, was not the first time the Japanese
carriers had disappeared beyond the American ability to
locate them. But since the Japanese Navy now seemed poised
for a major offensive, the intelligence officers were
particularly perturbed. They had only been able to locate
Carrier Division Three (*Hōshō* and *Zuihō*), which was with
Yamamoto's main body in the Inland Sea, and Carrier
Division Four (*Ryūjō*) with Takagi's Southern Philippine
Support Force, then en route to Palau.

December 5, Kimmel sent another task force under Rear
Adm. John Henry Newton, aboard the heavy cruiser *Chicago* to
transport Marine planes to Midway. Newton's task force was
built around the carrier *Lexington*. Unaware that he might
encounter war, Newton did feel there was danger from enemy

submarines so kept to a speed of 17 knots by day, zigzagged
and sent out scout planes to cover his advance.

Newton's immediate superior, Vice Adm. Wilson Brown,
commander scouting force, left Pearl Harbor the same day
with Task Force Three, headed for Johnston Island. His
group consisted of the heavy cruiser *Indianapolis* and five
old destroyers that had been converted into minesweepers.

Eighty-four warships were based in Pearl Harbor.

Between 2:30 and 3:30 P.M. December 5, the destroyer
Selfridge made an underwater contact and lost it. About
five miles off Pearl Harbor the destroyer *Ralph Talbot*
picked up the contact and reported it as a submarine. The
Talbot asked permission to depth charge. Informing the
Talbot that the contact was a blackfish, the *Selfridge*,
which was the squadron leader, refused permission.

The *Talbot* skipper declared, "If this is a blackfish,
it has a motorboat up its stern."

December 6, Kimmel arrived early at his office. At
8:15 he listened to an intelligence report from Layton.
There had been "no positive indications of the location of
the Japanese carriers except for Carrier Division 3, which
was associated with the Southern movement for some time."

Kimmel believed the Japanese capable of sending
submarines into the area but unaable to send them into
Pearl Harbor itself. For this reason the entrance net was
not a true antisubmarine net but an antitorpedo net
designed to prevent an enemy torpedo being fired up the
channel. He knew of no type of submarine capable of
submerging completely in the shallow waters of the
anchorage.

Some time that morning Layton informed Kimmel that the
Japanese consulate had been burning papers outdoors.
Kimmel attached no particular significance to this
information – the consulate had done likewise several times
during the year.

At about 2 P.M. the FBI's Japanese translator in

Honolulu completed the English transcript of a lengthy telephone conversation of December 3 between a Japanese newspaperman in Tōkyō and Motokazu Mori, husband of Ishiko Mori, the local correspondent for the Tōkyō *Yomiuri Shimbun*. Both Moris were physicians.

Motokazu was the son of Dr. Iga Mori. Iga's brother, Kosaburō Oguri, was an admiral in the Japanese Imperial Navy, though in his eighties at this time. Motokazu had first married Misao Harada, who died in 1927. He expressed his grief in a 296-page memoir of her.

Misao's brother, Ken Harada, had been Japanese ambassador to the Vatican and was now chamberlain in the Japanese Imperial Court.

Ishiko, an alien, met Motokazu while doing her internship at the Japanese Hospital in Honolulu. The two married in 1930.

The immigration law of the time required that she must return to Japan every other year and remain there a year before returning to America. In compliance, she made four round trips.

In the meantime she had learned that permanent residence might be hers as a diplomat, missionary, international merchant or newspaper correspondent. She chose to be a correspondent and, in 1934, went to work for the Tōkyō newspaper as its Honolulu correspondent.

She said, "Very little happened...and I sent mostly society stories to the paper."

Wednesday, December 3, she received a radiogram from the *Yomiuri* informing her that a representative would telephone Friday with the hope of talking to influential members of the Japanese community. He would ask, "How are things in Hawaii?"

To cover the assignment, she first went to Consul General Kita. He declined to be interviewed. Presumably because of the tense international situation the others she consulted also declined. Unable to find anyone else for interview, she shifted the burden to her husband.

The *Yomiuri* reporter, Ogawa, phoned Friday, December 5. Though the Moris were unaware of the significance of the call, it appears that the newspaper was laying the groundwork for a big feature story on Hawaii.

Ogawa said, "I received your telegram and was able to grasp the essential points. I would like to have your impressions on the conditions you are observing at present. Are airplanes flying daily?"

"Yes, lots of them fly around."

Chitchat continued. How many sailors in the Islands? Not so many as at the beginning of the year. What about Japanese-American relations on the Island? They were "getting along harmoniously." What about the U.S. Pacific Fleet? "We try to avoid talking about such matters." "What kind of flowers are in bloom in Hawaii at present?"

"Presently the flowers in bloom are fewest of the whole year. However, the hibiscus and poinsettia are in bloom now."

When Robert L. Shivers, special agent in charge FBI, Honolulu, read the transcript of this conversation he became concerned. By evening he had the transcript in the hands of Lieut. Col. George W. Bicknell, Assistant, G-2 (Intelligence Section), Hawaiian Department. Bicknell took the transcript to Lieut. Col. Kendall J. Fielder, G-2. The two then took it to Short, who lived next door to Fielder.

Both Fielder and Short were on their way to "Ann Etzler's Cabaret" – an annual charity dinner-dance at the Schofield Barracks Officers' Club. Their wives were waiting in the car for them. The three men sat down on Short's porch and mulled over the message. They considered it suspicious but were unable to pinpoint what rendered it suspect.

Short said "the message was a very true picture of what was going on in Hawaii." After 45 minutes discussion they concluded that the message was in order, that it described

the situation in Hawaii and that there was no need to be
disturbed about it. Short suggested that Bicknell was
"perhaps too intelligence conscious."

Bicknell parted from them feeling frustrated.

At 8 P.M. the signal officer of the Hawaiian Air Force
phoned, "We have a flight of B-17s coming in from the
mainland. (The B-17 was a multi-engined bomber, publicized
as Flying Fortress). Will you put Station KGMB on the air
all night so planes can home in on the signal."

It was common knowledge that when KGMB played music all
night aircraft would be flying in.

Displeased at this broadcast of American aerial
activity, Bicknell snapped, "Why don't you have KGMB on the
air every night and not just the night we have airplanes
flying? You folks have the money to do it."

Nevertheless, he made the request. The station knew
that when it granted such requests the Air Force paid. The
station complied.

Kimmel spent that Saturday night at a dinner at the
Halekulani Hotel in Waikiki.

Short and Fielder discussed the Mori phone call all the
way to Schofield, which is on a plateau above Pearl Harbor,
between the Waianae and Koolau Mountains. They left at
10:30 heading straight for home and resuming the discussion
of the phone call.

Below they could see Pearl Harbor ablaze with lights,
occasional searchlight beams probing the sky.

"Isn't that a beautiful sight!" exclaimed Short.

Then the aesthete reverting to the soldier, he added,
"And what a target they would make!"

18

THE THUNDERBOLT COILS TO STRIKE

The bulk of the Japanese Army — 38 divisions — was deployed in China and Manchuria. Gen. Count Juichi Terauchi had taken command of the remainder, the Southern Army, November 6. He gave the forces available for attack the following assignments: 23d Army — Hong Kong; 14th—Philippines; 15th — Thailand and Burma; 16th — Dutch East Indies; 25th — Malaya as well as Sumatra and North Borneo.

The Japanese Navy was composed of seven basic fleets: the 1st — Battle; 2d — Scouting Force; 3d — Blockade and Transport; 4th — Mandates; 5th — Northern; 6th — Submarine; 7th — Air Carrier. In addition to her ten aircraft carriers — four of them light carriers — she had ten battleships, 18 heavy cruisers, 20 light cruisers, 112 destroyers and 65 submarines.

The Japanese had made some experiments with radar but had not developed an operational system. The excellent vision developed by the lookouts of the Combined Fleet – by night and day – plus air reconnaissance, served in place of radar.

Army and Navy were superbly trained.

With the main body of the Combined Fleet — six battleships, two light carriers, two light cruisers and 13 destroyers anchored in the Inland Sea ready to sortie to protect the homeland — Yamamoto planned to sit out the first hours of the assault aboard the Flag Ship *Nagato*.

He had assigned the Southern attack to Vice Adm. Nobutake Kondo. Kondo's force included the battleships Kongo and Haruna (3d Battle Squadron, 2d Division); the light carrier *Zuiho* – soon to be joined by *Shoho* to form the 4th Carriers Squadron; three cruiser squadrons (4th, 5th and 7th) made up of ten 8-inch gun cruisers; a light cruiser squadron, the 16th, with one 8-inch, and three light cruisers; four destroyer flotillas, the 2d, 3d, 4th and 5th; 52 destroyers – each flotilla being commanded by a light cruiser – and the 18 submarines of the 4th, 5th and 6th Submarine flotillas.

Among other problems, Kondo had the task of synchronizing the Pearl Harbor attack with the Southern operation. What action should he take if British reconnaissance planes or surface craft in these well-travelled sea lanes detected his huge invasion fleet with its convoys transporting thousands of troops and tons of supplies to Malaya?

Kondo would have preferred to shoot down any enemy scout planes before they could report his position. But Nagumo had been adamant that there must be no hostilities until the Pearl Harbor strike began. Yamamoto had agreed.

Yamamoto cautioned Kondo, "Don't begin your operation anywhere in the southern regions until it's clear that the air strike against Hawaii has been launched." If anyone discovered the Southern Fleet prematurely, Kondo must change course and "head back to Japan in a deceptive gesture to throw the British off balance."

Phase One in the Japanese advance was the capture of footholds in the Philippines, Borneo and Celebes to be used immediately as points of departure for the final assault on the "Malay Barrier" – the great arc of islands stretching from Sumatra to Timor.

Being north of the Japanese-held Marshall Islands, the American base at Wake would be an important staging area between Hawaii and the Philippines. Consequently the Japanese planned to capture this atoll early. Rear Adm. Sadamichi Kajioka would use a light cruiser-destroyer force to escort the invasion convoy of 450 men.

Vice Adm. Shigeyoshi Inoue's 4th fleet left the Inland Sea November 29 bound for the Bonin Islands 600 miles south of Tōkyō. December 4 they would sail from the Bonins to attack Guam. On the same day that the 4th left the Inland Sea, the main body of Kondo''s 2d Fleet left the Inland Sea for Maco, the Japanese naval base in the Pescadores. It would arrive December 2 and depart for the south December 4.

With only two destroyers and a tanker, Capt. Kanamo Konishi would sail from Tateyama for the apparently unimportant task of neutralizing Midway.

To avoid attracting attention, the Malayan force, under Vice Adm. Jisaburō Ozawa began leaving Japan in small units beginning November 20. The almost 100 vessels of the 3d Fleet, under Vice Adm. Ibo Takahashi, was based on Formosa, Palau and the Ryūkyūs. It would be organized into a Task Force of one carrier, five heavy cruisers, four light cruisers and more than 20 destroyers. There would be dozens of transports as well as patrol boats, mine sweepers and small craft.

Taking his own air power with him, Rear Adm. Takeo Takagi brought his Southern Philippine Support Force from the Inland Sea and headed directly for Palau, about 500 miles east of the Southern Philippines. From there he was to sail December 6 for Davao to begin the Philippine invasion.

Under Vice Adm. Nishizō Tsukahara, the Naval 11th Air Force of 360 planes, most on Formosa, plus 144 planes of the 5th Army, would support the Philippine invasion.

November 30, Vice Adm. Mitsumi Shimizu, C–n–C Sixth Fleet (submarines) arrived aboard his flagship *Katori* in Truk, a major naval base. From there he would leave December 2 to arrive in Kwajalein, in the Marshall Islands, December 5 to direct his Fleet.

This left a slender force, the China Area Fleet, Vice Adm. Mineichi Koga, to help the Army capture Hong Kong.

The Northern, 5th Fleet, Vice Adm. Hoshirō Hosogawa, was to patrol and defend the waters east of Japan.

At 2 p.m.,December 2, Sugiyama sent a cable to Terauchi: HINODE YAMAGATA, code for "The date for commencing operations (HINODE) will be December 8 (YAMAGATA).

Yet for all the meticulous planning there existed a flaw in the attack plan hidden from almost all eyes except that of Comdr. Tatsukichi Miyo.

The 25th Army's original plan for the landing at Kota Bharu envisaged the start of operations as midnight 7–8 December. The Army wanted to start disembarking halfway through the night of 7–8 December and to have completed the operation by dawn on the 8th. But, as we have seen, after being informed of the plan to attack Pearl Harbor the Army agreed to make the Kota Bharu landings after midnight on 7–8 December, the landing time 1:30 a.m. (Japanese time) to coincide with the expected 6 a.m. (Hawaii time) of the beginning of the Pearl Harbor attack.

Genda had originally agreed that the Pearl Harbor Striking Force was to attack just before dawn, that is about 6 a.m. But so many pilots had complained of the hazard of taking off in pitch–dark that at the last moment Genda had delayed the hours of the first strike to 8 a.m. Miyo learned of the changed hour for the attack only several days after the attack force left Hitokappu Bay.

Thereupon, Miyo concluded that if he changed to the new schedule, the information might fail to reach some commands and so the issuance would uncoordinate the Southeast Asia attack. Accordingly he remained silent about the change, even avoiding telling Rear Adm. Seiichi Ito, vice–chief of the Naval General Staff. Miyo took full responsibility for the decision upon himself.

No one had considered informing the British before attacking that relations were severed or that war was declared. So the chief evil that might result from

withholding the information of the delay in the Pearl
Harbor strike was that if the attack on the Malay peninsula
should precede it, as appeared likely, the British might
report the attack in time to alert the defenders of Pearl
Harbor.

Miyo was to say later, "I was resigned to leaving our
fate to Heaven."

Nagumo with his task force plowing its way across the
bleak northern Pacific had planned to use his three
submarines, under command of Capt. Hidemitsu Imaizumi, as
the eyes of the force. These submarines, 1-19, 1-21, and
1-23 each displaced about 2,581 tons, being much larger
than Kimmel's submarines. They had a high surface speed of
almost 24 knots and a cruising range of 14,000 miles. Each
had six torpedo tubes to port and starboard through which
to fire Japan's 24-inch oxygen-fueled torpedoes, torpedoes
that in range, speed and explosive power would more than
double the performance of the American models. Each
submarine carried a small one-man seaplane capable of 90
knots and a flight time of three hours. But now because of
low visibility and communications difficulties he feared
they might lost contact with the rest of the Fleet by
sailing ahead. Accordingly he placed them about two-thirds
of a mile starboard of the *Akagi*.

During the day the vanguard four destroyers scouted six
miles apart. The six carriers advanced behind this shield
in two parallel columns. Other destroyers guarded the
flanks of the column while tankers followed astern.

Behind all the other vessels the two fast battleships,
under command of Rear Adm. Gunichi Mikawa, crashed through
the heavy swells.

Fortune favored the task force in that the sea was
unusually calm for those latitudes at that season. Despite
occasional fog, the ships could refuel when necessary.

At night and during heavy overcast Nagumo brought his
ships closer together for easier communications. Since

there was strict blackout and radio silence, for most of the vessels the only guide was the wake of the ships ahead and an occasional blinker signal.

Working under security measures, the crews rose and retired with the sun. Being especially alert for American submarines, lookouts scanned the sea. During the first half of the trip one-fourth of the crews manned battle stations at all times. Aboard each carrier, six fighter planes stood constantly ready.

By day, training continued. Aboard the *Akagi*, Fuchida and all flight personnel studied the scale models of Oahu and Pearl Harbor. They drilled incessantly on recognizing enemy warships. Because in torpedo attack the main problem is the approach to the target, Fuchida and Lieut. Comdr. Shigeharu Murata, torpedo bomber leader of the First Air Fleet, exhorted the pilots of the torpedo planes to study the course of their approach with the utmost diligence.

Genda asked Lieut. Comdr. Shigeru Itaya, assigned to lead the first wave of fighter planes, "about his confidence" concerning the Zeros. Itaya replied, "On the basis of our experience on the continent and our estimated capability of the American fighter planes, I think one of our planes can handle three of theirs."

For the horizontal bombers, Genda had another word of advice. To Lieut. Izumi Furukawa, aerial observer, he pointed out "the depth of the water in Pearl Harbor is only 60 feet. Even if we achieve much damage the enemy can refloat the ships...if your bomb hits directly beside the turret and if it explodes in the powder magazine the ship will be reduced to fragments."

Furukawa doubted being capable of such accuracy.

Genda urged, "Do it with spiritual power."

In their own ways the others strove for perfection. Aboard the *Sōryū*, Petty Officer Noboru Kanai never doffed his flying jacket. Every morning and afternoon he climbed into his plane in its hanger and ran through the bombing

292

procedures.

Genda advocated repeated attacks. Knowing that Nagumo and Kusaka had already decided on a single attack he urged Nagumo, at every opportunity, to maintain an open mind and to be flexible in his approach to the problems. He exhorted Nagumo, above all, to launch repeated attacks until he rendered the enemy helpless and incapable of further menace to Japan.

Nagumo always replied, "Only one attack! Only one attack!" Nevertheless Genda nurtured the hope that repeated attacks might be made if fortune favored the Task Force. He prepared four different plans for repeat attacks to present for the approval of Nagumo if the first attack prospered. Each proposed the destruction of the United States Pacific Fleet and making it possible for Japan to capture the Hawaiian Islands.

Nagumo, however, was assailed by many fears. He feared that he might not receive the message cancelling the Pearl Harbor attack and so attack when Japan was supposed to be at peace. Ugaki, aboard the, *Nagato*, in the Inland Sea, was assured of no peace with the Allies when, at 5 P.M., December 2, he received the message: "Our Empire has decided to go to war against the United States, England and Holland early in December."

Ugaki immediately sent a message to the commanders in chief of each Fleet: "Decision made, but date and time will be ordered later."

When Nagumo received this message, his Fleet was approaching the halfway mark of the voyage. From that point one-half of the crew would maintain battle stations at all times.

At 10 P.M., when the First Air Fleet was about 940 miles north of Midway, Nagumo received another message: "Climb Mount Niitaka, 1208," which signified that the day of the attack, Japanese time, would begin at midnight December 8.

At 11:30 A.M., December 5, after refueling the entire Task Force, Supply Group Two – Tankers *Toho Maru* and *Nihon Maru* and their escort destroyer *Arare* – headed northwest to the rendezvous point where it would meet the Fleet as it returned from the attack. As the Group pulled away the *Toho Maru* signaled "Goodbye" and "We hope your brave mission will be honored with success."

December 6, Hawaii time, the Task Force had reached to about 600 miles north and slightly east of Oahu. At 5:30 P.M., the Force received a message from Yamamoto with the gist of his reply to the Emperor's rescript. Shortly thereafter he "respectfully related" the rescript itself. Thereupon all officers and men "firmly determined to fulfill the responsibility entrusted them by the Emperor by destroying the United States Fleet with utmost efforts."

An hour later the entire armada engaged in its final fueling, a time when it was least combat ready and most vulnerable to attack. Beneath cloudy skies, with the wind about 20 knots, the ships lay within range of Martin's B-17s but was too far from Pearl Harbor to attack it.

But the sea remaining fairly calm, the final refueling was successfully completed. By 8:30 A.M., Supply Group One – *Kenyo Maru*, *Kyokuto Maru*, *Shinkoku Maru* and *Kokuyo Maru*, with the destroyer *Kanami* as escort, broke away and headed northward.

At exactly 11:30 A.M., the Task Force swung due south to 180 degrees toward Hawaii and increased its speed to 20 knots. Ten minutes later the *Akagi* broke out the same "Z" flag Tōgō had hoisted at Tsushima.

Then the *Akagi* signaled the message from Yamamoto: "The rise and fall of the Empire depends upon this battle. Every man will do his duty."

The crew cheered.

In Honolulu, Yoshikawa encoded and sent the following message:

...At present there are no signs of barrage
balloon equipment. However, even though they have
made preparations, there are limits to the balloon
defense of Pearl Harbor because they must control
the air over the water and land runways of the
airports in the vicinity of Pearl Harbor, Hickam,
Ford and Ewa. ...in all probability there is
considerable opportunity left for a surprise attack
against these planes.
2. In my opinion the battleships do not have
torpedo nets. The details are not known. I will
report the results of my investigation..

As the fateful morning came, Genda pondered over a
telegram received at 1:50 A.M.

...Ships in port on 6th are: nine battleships,
three light cruisers, three seaplane tenders and
seventeen destroyers, in addition to four light
cruisers and two destroyers in the docks...All
heavy cruisers and carriers were out of the
harbor...

"It's regrettable," said Genda, "that the carriers are
not in port."
Those members of the crew whose particular task it had
been to attack the carriers as the most important target
echoed the sentiment. Further, the absence of the
carriers, contrary to normal weekends, raised the suspicion
that the Americans had detected the approach of the
Japanese Task Force and was preparing to ambush it.
But Yoshikawa's telegrams also reported:

... Oahu Island very calm and no blackout...It
appears that no air reconnaissance is being
conducted by the Fleet air arm.

The Japanese submarine fleet had already arrived at the target and completely encircled Oahu. In addition, certain submarines had been scouting the area of Lahaina Roads and Lanai Island in search of the American Fleet : *I-71* in the Alalakeiki Channel between Maui and Kahoolawe islands; *I-72* in Kalohi Channel, which separates the islands of Molokai and Lanai; *I-73* in Kealaikahiki Channel, the deep waters between Maui, Kahoolawe and Lanai.

A submarine report received at 7:03 P.M., December 6: "The enemy is not in Lahaina anchorage" had dashed the hope of sinking the United States Fleet past reclamation in Lahaina's depths.

The night was black; the carriers tossed in heavy seas. On each flight deck the maintenance men had lined up the aircraft in order of take-off for the first wave; in the hangars below the second-wave planes were lined up in the same order.

Intent on providing his pilots and flying crews with the latest information on the enemy and on sending all his aircraft aloft as smoothly as possible, each air officer, immediately after arising and dressing, picked up the latest intelligence concerning Oahu. Then he went on deck and ascertained that each of his planes was operational.

Some of the pilots, after having written farewell letters to home, had tossed and turned in their bunks and arisen as early as 3:30. Comd. Kyozō Ōhashi, senior staff officer Fifth Carrier Division, had spent most of the night in the operations room of the *Shokaku* listening to KGMB. There had been no hint from the program that the Americans were aware of the Task Force.

Aboard the *Akagi* Fuchida awoke about 5:00. He dressed with particular care, donning red underwear and a red shirt. He and Murata had purchased identical garments for the occasion. They reasoned that if they were wounded the blood would be less noticeable against the red material and so would be less apt to alarm the other flying officers.

Recently promoted to Commander, Fuchida found Murata, in flying togs, finishing breakfast in the officer's mess.

Likewise promoted a grade, Lieut. Comdr. Murata greeted with, "Good morning, Commander. Honolulu sleeps."

"How do you know?"

"The Honolulu radio plays soft music. Everything is fine."

After breakfasting, Fuchida reported to Nagumo in the operating room.

Fuchida saluted. "I'm ready for my mission."

Nagumo arose and grasped Fuchida's hand. "I have confidence in you."

Fuchida leading, they went toward the dimly lit ready room. On the way they met Genda. Fuchida grinned. Genda cuffed him on the shoulder in encouragement.

In the ready room of the *Akagi*, Capt. Kiichi Hasegawa was waiting with the other pilots who had gathered there for the final briefing. Since the room was too small to accommodate all, some pilots spilled over into the passageway.

The *Akagi* was 230 miles north of Oahu.

The blackboard showed the position of the ships in Pearl Harbor according to the 6 A.M. report of the preceding day. Air Officer Shōgo Masuda reviewed the attack plan. He emphasized morale, take-off and return. Fuchida spoke about strike methods, particularly stressing high-level bombing tactics.

Of the 183 planes that would be in the first wave, only 99 were to attack the ships in Pearl Harbor. The others were assigned targets and missions designed to gain air superiority so that the planes attacking Pearl Harbor ships could do so secure from enemy aerial attack.

The airmen who sere to attack the ships studied the board carefully. Murata briefed the torpedomen. Itaya emphasized to his fighters the control of the air. Last of all, Nagumo assured the fliers of his prayers and of his expectations for their success.

Fuchida called the men to attention. He saluted Hasegawa.

Hasegawa called, "Take off according to plan."

The men raced for their planes. Fuchida was the last to leave.

In the rough seas the ship pitched and rolled. In the predawn darkness white surf cast an occasional spray over the flight deck. The plane crews clung desperately to their planes to keep them from being flung into the sea.

Masuda said to Fuchida, "There's a heavy pitch and roll. What do you think of taking off in the dark?"

By pitch he meant the vertical motion of the ship's bow and stern; by roll he referred to the swaying.

Fuchida considered his fliers the best trained and most disciplined in the world. Like him, most were veterans of air combat in China. Each had averaged about 2,000 hours flight time.

He manifested his confidence in them now. "The pitch is greater than the roll. If this were a training flight, I would delay takeoff until dawn. If we coordinate the takeoffs with the pitching we can launch successfully."

He saluted the officers and went to his plane, the tail of which was striped with red and yellow to distinguish it as the commander's. Dawn was still an hour away.

As Fuchida left, Nagumo told Genda, "I have successfully brought the task force to the point of attack. From now the burden rests on your shoulders and on that of the rest of the fliers."

"Admiral, I'm sure the airmen will succeed."

Nagumo had an additional reason for being concerned about the foul weather. In fair weather the planes could launch on schedule and so reach their targets exactly on time — 8 A.M. Eight A.M. here would be 1:30 P.M. in Washington, 30 minutes after the note breaking off diplomatic relations was supposed to have been delivered.

Launching in this rough weather might take longer. So to reach the target on time they might need to launch earlier than scheduled. On the other hand, if the launching went smoothly they might reach target ahead of schedule since they could not afford to waste gasoline lingering over the fleet.

He decided the better option was an early launching.

At 5:30 A.M. the *Chikuma* and *Tone* had each catapulted into the murky sky a single-engined Zero-type scout seaplane. One was to reconnoiter Pearl Harbor; the other the Lahaina Anchorage. Each plane was to survey its assigned area for a quarter of an hour; then, having made sure its report would be correct, it would break radio silence. The need for last-minute, accurate information superseded the risk of detection.

The attacking planes were to receive the report of the scout planes while on the way to target. At 5:50 A.M. the six carriers, now some 220 miles north of Oahu, turned from their escort vessels, headed almost due east into a brisk wind and again increased speed to 24 knots. Combat pennants sped up the masts to wave beside the "Z" flags.

As each airman prepared to enter his cockpit, he tied around his head a white scarf, known as *hachimaki*. The hachimaki symbolized the desperateness of the project on which he was embarking. It was adorned with the characters for Hisshō (Certain Victory).

When Fuchida approached his bomber, the senior maintenance officer came to him with a specially-made white hachimaki.

"This is a present from the maintenance crew. Please take it along to Pearl Harbor."

Touched and pleased, Fuchida smiled, nodded and dexterously wrapped the hachimaki around his flying cap and secured it there. Already aboard was the pilot, Lieut. Mitsuo Matsuzaki and the radio operator, Petty Officer Shigenori Mazuki.

The weather had delayed the take-off 20 minutes from the time desired by Nagumo, but it would still be an early take-off. The warming motors of the planes vibrated their lighted flying lamps.

On the flight deck a green lamp swung in a circle signalling: "Take off!"

With Itaya in the lead, the fighters were to take off first. Since the flight deck was crammed with planes, only a short run was available to him for his take-off.

His motor began to roar. All eyes fixed on him as he began his run. The plane moved slowly, then increased its speed until he was speeding down the pitching, rolling deck. Just as his plane cleared the deck the ship pitched downward. His plane dipped almost to ocean level, then lifted and soared upward. The crew burst into a cheer.

As Itaya levelled off preparatory to beginning to circle, the next plane was already moving forward. The fighters from all six carriers took off. Led by Fuchida the high-level bombers followed; then the dive bombers led by Takahashi and then the torpedo bombers.

Within 15 minutes 183 planes were airborne. Fuchida signalled by taking his group of high-level bombers across the bow of the *Akagi;* with its orange and yellow signal lights flickering like fireflies in the darkness, the armada set course for Oahu.

One fighter had crashed on takeoff, but a destroyer quickly rescued the pilot. A second, from the *Kaga,* developed engine trouble and had to be left behind.

The fliers flew without parachutes. If during the attack the plane became too damaged to return to its carrier, the pilot was supposed to pick the best target and self-destruct by crashing on it. He was provided with a pistol and some survival gear to use if he found it necessary to ditch at sea.

Launched last of all were the fighter patrols that were to guard the Fleet in the absence of the other planes.

300

Then the crews worked frenziedly to prepare the second wave of assault planes for take-off.

The first wave flew toward its target at an altitude of about 9,800 feet. At the top level, under command of Fuchida, flew ten triangles of high-level bombers. To port, at some 11,000 feet, flew Takahashi's two groups of dive bombers. Murata's four groups of torpedo planes flew starboard at around 9,200 feet. Fore and aft, covering the entire force, flew Itaya's fighters.

As daylight broke, the rays of the sun pierced the clouds in streaks that made them resemble the naval ensign. Or so it seemed to Fuchida, who regarded the phenomenon as a good omen. He was in need of reassurance, for he did not expect to achieve surprise. He expected to lose half his men in the coming combat.

It was after 7:00 when he tuned in on KGMB and directed his pilot to home on this beam.

The music failed to relieve his pessimism. Had he known what had occurred earlier in British Malaya from the botched order for the hour to attack his pessimism might have deepened.

Vice Adm. Chūichi Nagumo, C-in-C 1st Air Fleet (right), bore t h e   p r i m a r y responsibility for Japanese success at Pearl Harbor.

19

THE FATEFUL DAY DAWNS

In Washington,about 11:30 on the evening of December 6, Roosevelt was able to reach Stark at his home. Roosevelt informed him of the information he had received from Magic. But since both had already concluded that Japan was "likely to attack at any time in any direction," Stark considered the phone call only a confirmation of this conclusion and not as something that required action from him.

In the meantime the Kramers had continued on their errand of delivering the message. From the White House they went to Hotel Wardman Park where Kramer delivered the message to Knox.

Just that evening, Knox had released to the press a glowing annual report of the Navy Department on the strength and readiness of the U.S. Navy. Now he took about 20 minutes to read the message Kramer had brought.

Security-minded and with his wife and a friend present, Knox avoided comment on what he had read. He did instruct Kramer to be at the State Department next morning where Knox, and presumably Stimson, would meet with Hull.

It was now 10:50 P.M. Mrs. Kramer drove her husband to the home of Capt. Theodore S. Wilkinson, director of Naval Intelligence in Arlington. Wilkinson was having a small dinner party that included Brig. Gen. Sherman Miles, ACS (Acting Assistant Chief of Staff) Intelligence, War Department, Beardall and two French officers.

Wilkinson came out to the car where Mrs. Kramer was waiting and brought her into the drawing room. There, while her husband retired with the Intelligence members to the library, she sipped coffee and drinks with those remaining.

In the library the Intelligence members read the message but only generalized that Japan seemed to be terminating negotiations. At 12:30, Kramer returned to his car. His wife drove him to his office where he returned the remaining copies of the message to the safe.

Learning from the watch officer that the 14th part of the message had not arrived, he had his wife drive him home.

When he returned to his office shortly after 7:30 Sunday morning, December 7, the 14th part of the message had been received and decrypted. Lieut. Francis M. Brotherhood handed it to him immediately.

It read:

7. Obviously it is the intention of the American Government to conspire with Great Britain and other countries to obstruct Japan's efforts toward the establishment of peace through the creation of a New Order in East Asia, and especially to preserve Anglo-American rights and interests by keeping Japan and China at war. This intention has been revealed clearly during the course of the present negotiations. Thus, the earnest hope of the Japanese Government to adjust Japanese-American relations and to preserve and promote the peace of the Pacific through cooperation with the American Government has finally been lost.

The Japanese Government regrets to have to notify hereby the American Government that in view of the attitude of the American Government it cannot but consider that it is impossible to reach an agreement through further negotiations.

Kramer gave copies of the intercept to McCollum and

Wilkinson, one of whom would give it to Stark. Kramer then put his copies in the loose-leaf binder for delivery.

Just as he was about to leave, Lieut. Alfred V. Perring came in with two more Purple intercepts he had just decrypted. Unlike the long note, which was in English throughout, these intercepts had been sent in Japanese and so had required further processing.

Though it was the Navy's day to process the transcripts, Kramer's translators had the Sunday off. He had no time to spare for the task. He asked Bryant to take the telegrams over to Signal Intelligence Service for translation and to tell Doud to send them back as soon as the task was completed.

Shortly after 9:30, Kramer left the Navy Building for the State Department. He delivered the intercept to Knox in the reception room of Hull's office about 9:55 and then returned to the Navy Building.

When he arrived, about 10:20, he found ready translated what was to become known as the One O'Clock Message. It read:

> **Will the Ambassador please submit to the United States Government (if possible to the Secretary of State) our reply to the United States at 1 P.M. on the 7th, your time.**

A second intercept read:

> **Please destroy at once the remaining cipher machine and all machine codes. In like manner also dispose of secret documents.**

Kramer had had experience as a navigator in Central America and navigation was one of his hobbies. He delayed long enough to figure out on a navigator's plotting circle what the time would be at the various danger spots in East

Asia and the Pacific when Nomura was scheduled to appear at the State Department with the note.

He told Chief Ship's Clerk Harold L. Bryant that 1:00 P.M in Washington would be 2:00 A.M. in Manila and 7:30 A.M. in Hawaii.

Though he was later to say that the intercept did not suggest to him an attack on Hawaii, his taking the immediate trouble of figuring the relationship of the time of delivery to the time in Hawaii indicates he was apprehensive about the area. He had served for about two years as executive officer and navigator of a destroyer based at the submarine base at Pearl Harbor. He knew that at the time he had served there a larger percentage of the crew were ashore on Sunday than other days of the week when ships were in port. Furthermore, 7:30 A.M. had been the normal time for the piping of the crew to breakfast when the ships would be most vulnerable.

Kramer said that the time of delivery "tied with the sun and (Japanese) movements in progress elsewhere." The time of delivery might have been set to coincide with the beginning of "some amphibian landing operations."

Kramer immediately instructed Bryant to prepare another set of folders for immediate delivery. Bryant had them ready in about five minutes. Kramer delivered one set to McCollum at Stark's office, pointing out the relationship of the delivery time for the message to the developments of the past week or so in the Southwest Pacific, with reference to Malaya and the Kra Peninsula.

He left the Navy Building and arrived at the State Department about 10:40 where he delivered a set of the intercepts to John F. Stone, Hull's personal assistant, again mentioning the significance of the time for the delivery of the official Japanese note, with mention of the hour in Hawaii.

He then went to the White House. There in Gen. Watson's office he found Beardall to whom he delivered the

intercepts. Kramer told him that the Japanese note was to
be delivered at one o'clock, which could be the time set
for the launching of Japanese military operations.

Beardall took the intercepts upstairs to Roosevelt's
quarters. Roosevelt was still in bed, reading the
newspapers.

Roosevelt accepted the intercepts and quickly read
through them.

The President said, "It looks like the Japs are going
to break off the negotiations."

Beardall failed to mention that Nomura had orders to
deliver the message at one o'clock; nor did he mention that
Kramer thought the hour of delivery might coincide with the
launching of Japanese military operations. Apparently
unperturbed, Roosevelt thanked Beardall and returned the
intercepts to him.

Beardall then left for the Navy Building to which
Kramer had already returned.

It was now past 10 o'clock — around 4:30 A.M. in
Hawaii. Stark was in his office, an arm's length from the
telephone. The Navy seldom used the scrambler telephone
for secret information because Rear Adm. Leigh Noyes, Chief
of the Communications Division, had warned it could not be
depended upon for security.

All his top associates except Turner were with him.
Though none of them believed the Japanese would dare to
strike at Pearl Harbor, Wilkinson and the others thought of
the Japanese concentrations in the Marshalls as a probable
threat to Oahu. In the deferential manner of their
relationship they suggested that Stark take action.

Wilkinson said, "Why don't you pick up the telephone
and call Adm. Kimmel?"

Stark reached for the phone. But as his hand closed on
it he recalled that it was only 4:55 A.M. in Hawaii, an
ungodly hour to disturb the sleep of Kimmel. He also felt
he should avoid directing and supervising the detailed

administration of commanders in the field. He did not believe Pearl Harbor endangered.

He shook his head and replaced the phone. "No. I'll call the President first."

Though the call reached the President's switchboard promptly, the operator said the President's line was busy. Stark replaced the phone.

Bratton arrived at the Munitions Building at 9 A.M. and found the 14th part of the Japanese note awaiting him. He had been disinclined to make much of the 14-part note and this final piece of it failed to alter his opinion. He was later to say, "This was primarily of...immediate interest to the Secretary of State, not to the Secretary of War or the Chief of the General Staff."

As he was reading the 14th part, Doud handed him the intercept of the one o'clock Message.

Bratton detected an ominous significance in the one o'clock Message. It activated the 14-part message. Though Sunday was not a normal working day for the diplomatic corps it asked for delivery that day. No other directive from Tōkyō to its Washington embassy had ever specified a precise time for a meeting.

Bratton concluded that the one o'clock message was an authentic execute of the Winds Code received on the 5th, indicating an early break with Great Britain. He knew enough about the United States military conversations with the Dutch and British to assume that such a break must also mean a break with the United States.

He did not think the Japanese were going to attack Pearl Harbor, if only because Pearl Harbor had been given a war warning and according to the war plan the ships were consequently expected to be at sea. Nevertheless he felt that the message merited sending a warning to the field commanders in all Pacific areas.

Since he was unauthorized to send the warning, he hurried off to find someone who was. Intercept in hand, he

raced next door looking for Miles, then to the front office
looking for Marshall.

Neither was in so Bratton ran back to his own office
and, on his own initiative, phoned Marshall at his quarters
in Fort Meyer.

An orderly answered the phone and told Bratton that the
general had left the house about 10 minutes before to go
horseback riding.

"Well, you know generally where he goes. Do you think
you could get ahold of him?"

"Yes, sir, I think I can find him."

"Please go out at once. Get assistance if necessary
and find Gen. Marshall. Tell him who I am and ask him to
go to the nearest telephone – that it is vitally important
that I communicate with him at the earliest practicable
moment."

Bratton then called Miles at home and told him what he
had done. "You had better come down at once," he told
Miles, "Gen. Marshall may want to see you and talk with
you."

Then he phoned Gerow and advised him to come to his
office as fast as possible.

On Sunday mornings, Marshall usually rode his horse
King Story for an hour, following the winding bridle paths
of Rock Creek Park in the District of Columbia. On this
Sunday, however, he chose to ride for an extra 20 minutes,
riding to the Virginia side of Potomac Park. Consequently
the orderly sought him in vain.

Only after Marshall returned to his quarters did he
receive the message from Bratton. By then it was 10:25–
4:55 in Hawaii.

Marshall phoned Bratton. In guarded language, Bratton
explained that he had "a most important" message that
required the immediate presence of the general. Assuming
that Marshall was phoning from a booth somewhere, he
suggested that he remain there while Bratton sent a car to

308

take the message to him at once.

"No," said Marshall, "don't bother to do that.   I'm coming down to my office. You can give it to me there."

Bratton figured it would take Marshall ten to 15 minutes to reach the office. Intercepts in hand, he waited for him in the hall.   But Marshall showered, changed clothes and then sent for his limousine, which was parked at the Munitions Building on the other side of the Potomac.

When Marshall finally arrived, he bypassed Bratton, went directly to his office and began reading the 14-part message aloud – this being his first opportunity to familiarize himself with it. Bratton entered, held out the one o'clock message and said it was the most important message and Marshall should see it immediately. Marshall simply droned on with the 14-part message.

Only when he had completely read through the 14-part message did Marshall look at the one o'clock message.

In the meantime other members of his staff had drifted in – Miles, Gerow and Col. Charles W. Bundy. Marshall polled them one by one as to their interpretation of the one o'clock message. They agreed it indicated that the Japanese intended to attack somewhere in the Pacific at, or shortly after, one o'clock.

No one mentioned the time of the message as relating to Hawaii, but Miles urged an immediate warning to the Philippines, Panama, the West Coast and Hawaii.   All concurred in sending an additional alert by the fastest possible means.

Marshall drew a piece of scratch paper toward him and wrote out the requested information in longhand. Then he picked up the phone and, in a guarded way, informed Stark of his intention.

Stark had been discussing the one o'clock message with Capt. Roscoe E. Schuirmann, Navy liaison officer with the State Department.   Stark told Marshall that "we had sent them so much already" that he "hesitated to send more."

After hanging up on Stark, Marshall listened to further urging to send the message. The phone rang. It was Stark. He asked that Marshall add the words "Inform the Navy" to his message.

Stark also asked whether Marshall could get out the message quickly, explaining that the Navy system, under pressure, was very fast. Marshall assured him he could have the message delivered quickly without Navy assistance.

At the bottom of the pencilled message Marshall added "Inform the Navy." He handed the sheet to Bratton. "Take it to the Message Center and see that it gets dispatched at once by the fastest safe means."

As Bratton went out the door, Gerow called after him, "If there is any question of priority, give the Philippines first priority."

Despite the urgency no one seemed to seriously consider telephoning.

Hearing Bratton in the code room, Lieut. Col. Edward F. French, in charge of the War Department Signal Center, went to investigate. He found the excited Bratton, message in hand, trying to get action.

Bratton handed the message to French. "The Chief of Staff wants this sent at once by the fastest safe means."

French looked over the message. "Well, will you help me get this into readable script? Neither I nor my clerk can read Gen. Marshall's handwriting."

Bratton read the message to a clerk, who typed it out.

Bratton glanced at his watch; it was already 11:58. He asked French how long it would take to deliver the message.

"It will take about 30 or 40 minutes for it to be delivered to the person to whom it is addressed."

Of course, after delivery it must be deciphered, decoded and put into the hands of the addressee.

At 12:00 noon the first message went to the Caribbean Defense Command. At 12:06 the word went out to MacArthur in the Philippines. At 12:11 to the Presidio on the West

Coast.

An obstacle interposed to the delivery of the message to Hawaii. When French checked with his Signal Center, he discovered the atmospheric conditions had blocked off the channel to Honolulu since about 10:30.

The preceding day he had learned that RCA (Radio Corporation of America) was installing a teletype circuit to Hawaiian Headquarters. So unwilling to inform the Navy that their channel to the Naval Radio Station at Aiea, Hawaii, on the outskirts of Honolulu, was open while the Army line was dead, French decided to send the dispatch to Western Union, who would forward it to RCA. It was then 12:18; 6:48 in Hawaii.

Western Union sent the telegram by cable from Washington to San Francisco, relayed it to the RCA office there by pneumatic tube, who then radioed it to RCA in Honolulu. There the message, addressed to "Commanding General Hawaiian Department, Fort Shafter, T.H.", but bearing no mark to indicate it was special or urgent, was received and pigeonholed at 7:33 A.M.

Back in Washington, about the time Bratton was receiving the phone call from Marshall, just returned from his horseback ride, Stark and Knox had begun their meeting with Hull. Hull was certain the Japanese were planning some deviltry; all wondered where the blow was to fall.

At 11 A.M., Hull's office received a phone call from the Japanese embassy asking for the 1:00 o'clock appointment, which was granted.

The Japanese ambassadors were as concerned as those in the State Department. They also expected some deviltry and suspected they were being used as a cat's paw to help perpetrate it. In addition they had been assigned the stupendous task of typing out, without a qualified typist, the note for presentation to the State Department at 1 P.M.

From the preceding evening the Japanese embassy – a dainty, cream-colored building on Massachusetts Avenue had been swarming with friends and trusted newspapermen attracted by the ominous portents of the situation. They overflowed to the basement rumpus room where they played billiards or listened to the radio as they waited.

In the Code Room when the 13 telegrams containing the first 3000-odd words of the note had arrived that evening they had been given to Senior Telegraph Officer Masara Horiuchi for decrypting. But the clerks had managed to complete only eight parts of the note when they were called away to attend a farewell dinner that Counselor Sadao Iguchi was giving for First Secretary Hidenari Terasaki who was about to leave for his new post in Buenos Aires. They returned from the dinner at 9:30, slightly fuddled from the sake they had drunk there. Horiuchi and the five code clerks: Takeshi Kajiwara, Hiroshi Hori, Tsukao Kawabata, Kenichirō Kondo and Juichi Yoshida returned to their decrypting. Shortly before midnight they finished all 13 parts.

After ordering Horiuchi to keep his staff on hand to await the arrival of the final part of the note, Senior Secretary Shiroji Yuki, accompanied by Kurusu, took the copy to Nomura's private quarters. In the meantime, with acid he had obtained from the naval attache two days before, Horiuchi had his staff destroy the remnants of the three other cipher machines. They completed the task at 3:00 A.M. December 7.

Since the final part of the note had still not arrived, Counselor Iguchi let the clerks go home to sleep, keeping only Kondo to stand watch.

Nomura had delayed the typing of the incomplete note. During the night nothing had been done on it.

Beginning at 7:00 A.M., and continuing for an hour, telegrams marked "urgent" began arriving from the RCA office. But except for Kondo, sound asleep on a cot in the Code Room, no clerk was at the embassy to decode them. Counselor Iguchi awakened Kondo and told him to call back his colleagues. Grumbling over the summons, they returned at 10 A.M.

Disposing of some ceremonial dispatches, the clerks came to the more important telegrams. At 10:40 they came to No. 902, Part 14 of the note and decrypted it in 20 minutes. Then they started on No. 907, the one o'clock message, which had been delivered at 8 A.M.

Together with the transcript of the 14th part of the note in English, Secretary Yuki took the telegram upstairs to an outer office in Nomura's quarters where Okumura was bent over a typewriter struggling to copy the other parts. Okumura had been at the task since 8 A.M., pecking out the letters and making slow progress. By 11:00 he had completed 13 parts, but deciding there were too many errors, he began retyping.

When Okumura had only 136 words of the final passage untyped, Nomura had Junior Interpreter N. Enseki arrange for a 1:00 P.M. appointment with Hull.

It was 12:30 when Okumura finished the typescript. He took it to an adjoining room where Yuki and Tsutomu Nishiyama proofread it and found a few more errors. They returned the transcript to Okumura for retyping.

Since it was clear that the corrections could not be made in time for the ambassadors to keep the 1:00 o'clock appointment, Enseki again phoned and asked that the appointment be postponed until 1:30.

After conferring with Hull, Stone told Enseki that "the secretary will expect the ambassadors as soon as their preparations are completed."

20

THE POISED HAMMER FALLS

In Tōkyō, Grew had first learned of Roosevelt's message to the Emperor through a broadcast from San Francisco. Late that same evening, December 7 – Tōkyō time – he received a short triple-priority telegram from Hull explaining that a telegram was then being encoded that contained a message from the President. Grew was to communicate the message to the Emperor at the earliest possible moment.

The message arrived in Tōkyō at noon December 7. There an order had gone out to delay all foreign cables on an alternating schedule – ten hours one day, five hours the next. Sunday, December 7, Japanese time, happened to be the day scheduled for ten hours. So despite the TRIPLE PRIORITY stamp, it was 10:30 that evening when Grew received the cable.

He had already communicated to the Foreign Minister that he wished to exercise his privilege as ambassador extraordinary by being received by the Emperor. Now he had his aide, Eugene H. Doonan, telephone Tōgō's secretary and ask for an immediate interview.

Vexed by the delay in receiving the message, but determined to carry out the letter of his order, Grew, message in hand, about 11:50 p.m. arrived at the official residence of the Foreign Minister. There he told Tōgō that he had a personal message from Roosevelt to the Emperor. He read it aloud.

Tōgō said he would study the message. Grew asked if this intention indicated doubt that the Foreign Minister might ask an audience with the Emperor for the American ambassador. Tōgō replied he would present the request to the throne.

It was then 12:30 a.m., December 8.

At 12.40 a.m., after Grew had left, Tōgō telephoned Kido and asked his advice on how to handle the matter. Kido said that even at midnight the Emperor would grant an audience. First, however, Tōgō must carefully deliberate with Tōjō as to procedure for the presentation and to the diplomatic effect of the delivery.

Tōgō had the letter translated into Japanese. Then he called on Tōjō. Tōjō asked whether the message contained "anything new." Tōgō replied that it contained nothing new.

"Well then, nothing can be done, can it?"

Tōjō had no objection to the Foreign Minister taking the letter to the Emperor. Together the two worked out a reply.

Tōgō got up to leave. "It seems a pity to go around disturbing people in the middle of the night."

Tōjō found a mitigating feature in the disturbance. "It's a good thing the telegram arrived late. If it had come a day or two earlier we would have had more of a to-do."

Tōjō knew in outline of events occurring elsewhere that seemed likely to nullify the effect of Roosevelt's telegram.

The convoy that was to invade Malaya – the Malaya Force – had left Sama Harbor on Hainan Island December 4 under command of Vice Adm. Jisaburō Ōzawa. His flagship: *Chōkai.* Eighteen transports, behind a screen of cruisers and destroyers, carried 20,000 men of Yamashita's 25th Army.

The 5th Division, under Maj. Gen. Matsui was to secure Singora and Patani and then immediately push into Malaya. The 56th Division under command of Maj. Gen. Hiroshi

Takumi, and known as the Takumi Force, was to land at Kota Bharu.

The primary task of both these forces was to achieve Japanese air mastery over Malaya.

If we look at a map of Southeast Asia, we see the Malay Peninsula appearing like a serpent from its lair along the Thailand–Burma border, its snakelike head pointed toward Sumatra, Java and the Lesser Sunda Islands that curl along the southern border of the Dutch East Indies. At the snout of the snake head, where the two-pronged tongue would protrude, was the British fortress of Singapore, bristling with guns pointing seaward.

The Allies considered Singapore impregnable.

By capturing the airfield at Victoria Point, a vital staging post in the journey from India to Malaya, the Japanese also intended to prevent the British from reinforcing by air from India to Malaya. Victoria Point is on the far side of the Isthmus of Kra at its narrowest point, so the 143d Infantry Regiment of the 55th Division, the Uno force, was to land at a number of points on the Isthmus, cut across it and seize the air field.

The Imperial Guards Division, under Lt. Gen. Nishimura, was to dispose of Thailand. Stationed in Cambodia, the division was to cross the Thai frontier into Battambang Province, ceded by Thailand earlier in the year, and from there move directly on Bangkok. If possible, they were to achieve this objective peaceably.

Although admittedly difficult to achieve, secrecy of design was to be sought. The first security scare had come December 5 when the destroyer *Uranami* discovered a Norwegian vessel ahead of and to starboard of the convoy.

The Norwegian vessel was enroute from Bangkok to Hong Kong. Vice Adm. Takeo Kurita ordered the Norwegian vessel to sail eastwards until the convoy had passed. He also signalled the *Uranami* to smash the Norewegian's wireless before releasing the vessel.

At 1:40 the following afternoon a greater danger appeared in an aircraft on the distant horizon when the convoy was 93 miles southeast of Cape Cambodia. It appeared and disappeared between clouds so that the Japanese were at first unable to ascertain if it were hostile.

Soon it was identified as British. It was a Hudson from the Australian squadron stationed at Kota Bharu and piloted by Flight–Lieut. Ramshaw.

Ramshaw came up to the convoy, circled and then began to shadow it, keeping out of range of the anti–aircraft guns. He reported his finding. Kota Bharu reported the sighting to Air Headquarters, Far East, who flashed the news to London.

For an hour Ōzawa agonized over whether to order the Australian plane shot down and so risk beginning hostilities with Great Britain sooner than planned. When he finally decided to take the risk his order was issued too late; the Australian had escaped.

On the 7th, one of Ōzawa's sea scout planes, piloted by 2d Lieut. Ōgata, sighted a British Catalina, patrol flying boat, 20 miles WNW of Panjang Island in the Gulf of Siam. The Malaya Force was then 60 miles west of that position. The plane was coming up to the Japanese rendezvous point in the Gulf of Siam, Point G, where the convoy would disperse and the deception maneuvers would cease. Ōgata judged that the Catalina would discover the convoy within 30 minutes.

Ōgata slipped under the Catalina, opening fire as he did so. Until that moment the Catalina appeared not to have seen him, but it immediately returned fire. So began the first exchange of fire between Japanese and British.

Ōgata succeeded in luring the Catalina eastward, away from the convoy. He was unsure if unaided he could shoot it down. Soon ten Japanese fighters arrived and disposed of the Catalina.

Though 25 minutes had elapsed between the Japanese

sighting of the Catalina and the time it was shot down, Singapore had not received a report.

Without further incident the Malaya Force reached Point G and began to split up for a five-pronged attack, with Kota Bharu the southernmost point and most difficult objective. The cruiser *Sendai*, the 19th Destroyer Division, three minesweepers and three transports were assigned to the task.

Defended by two newly completed airdromes close by, Kota Bharu would be the only landing on British territory. Capture of the British aircraft network in the area was vital for the success of the operations across the border of the 25th Army.

Since the possibility of British attacks by air, by torpedo bombers and submarines could not be gauged beforehand, the Tōkyō Agreement between Army and Navy had left consideration of Kota Bharu to the commander on the spot – Adm. Ōzawa. He had to decide whether the landing should synchronize with those in Thailand; he chose a simultaneous landing

At 4:30 P.M., about 120 miles north of Kota Bharu, the *Uranami* discovered another Norwegian ship, a 1,350 ton merchantman. The Japanese boarded her. Suspecting she was carrying out intelligence for the British, the Japanese made the crew take to the lifeboats and scuttled their ship.

At 7:25 P.M., when the escort was about 60 miles from Kota Bharu, a Blenheim, fast medium-range bomber, appeared. The *Uranami* opened fire; the Blenheim made off.

The Japanese assumed that both the Norwegian vessel and the Blenheim had reported hostile action and that, consequently, a surprise landing was impossible.

At 11:55 P.M., December 7, the Takumi Force was anchoring off Kota Bharu. Despite cloud, visibility was fair. The Japanese could see lights on shore and the harbor light at Tumpat. But as the transports cast anchor,

318

all the shore lights went out.

A strong east wind caused a heavy swell that capsized some of the first boats the Japanese lowered, tipping the Japanese infantry into the sea. But by 1:35 A.M. the first wave of assault troops was speeding towards shore in 20 landing craft. Shortly after 2:00, the watchers on the ships saw signals near the landing points. Shots rang out; flares went up. The Pacific War had begun.

It was 6:30 A.M., December 7 in Hawaii, 15 minutes from the time the first wave of Japanese planes had left their carriers to attack Oahu and 2 A.M. in Tōkyō where Roosevelt's message to the Emperor had yet to be delivered.

About this time, under a starlit sky, Tōgō set out for the palace, where he found Kido waiting for him.

Clad in naval uniform, the Emperor received Tōgō at 3 A.M. The Emperor listened to the reading of the message and approved the refusal that the Prime Minister and Foreign Minister had worked out.

An hour and 45 minutes had passed since the attack on Kota Bharu had begun. News had begun to come in from the attack force in Hawaii.

It was not only the untimely attack on Kota Bharu that might have alerted the Americans, there had been a number of incidents off Oahu that might have put them on their guard.

The Japanese were to launch their five 79-foot, two-man midget submarines at 11 P.M., December 6. They had orders to steal into Pearl Harbor and once the attack began to circle Ford Island, where the major ships were moored, and assist in sinking them. Theoretically, after accomplishing their mission, they were to rendezvous with the *I* class submarines seven miles off Lanai Island. But no one, including those who had volunteered for the mission, expected them to return. Certain that theirs was a suicide mission, the participants arranged for the distribution of their personal effects.

Four of the five midgets cast off on schedule at 11 P.M., so close to Oahu they could see the lights of downtown Honolulu. The fifth midget, borne by the mother submarine *I-24* and designated submarine *C*, had developed gyrocompass trouble. Its commander, Ensign Kazuo Sakamaki and his petty officer, Kyogi Inagaki, had spent two hours vainly attempting to fix it.

The skipper of the mother submarine, *I-24*, Lieut. Comdr. Hiroshi Hanabusa, spoke: "We are about to carry out the Hawaiian operation as scheduled. All hands be ready."

He turned to Sakamaki.   "Ensign Sakamaki, we have arrived at our destination, but your gyrocompass is not working. What are you going to do?"

"I'm going ahead."

"On to Pearl Harbor!" shouted Hanabusa.

"On to Pearl Harbor!" echoed Sakamaki.

Under submerged conditions, 10 miles south of Pearl Harbor, the *I-24* released the midget.

These midgets were to be the first portents of the scheduled attack.

At 3:42 A.M. the waning moon, in its last quarter, peeked through the broken overcast to light up the area about one and three-quarter miles south of the entrance buoys from Pearl Harbor where the minesweepers *Condor* and *Crossbill*, sisterships, plied their mechanical brooms.

The *Condor* had just emerged from the approach channel to Pearl Harbor when something in the darkness "about 50 yards ahead off the port bow" attracted the attention of Ensign R.C. McCloy, officer of the deck. He called to Quartermaster Second Class R. C. Uttrick and asked his opinion.

Uttrick peered through the binoculars and said, "That's a periscope, sir, and there aren't supposed to be any subs in this area."

At 3:57 A.M., by yardarm blinker, McCloy notified the destroyer *Ward*: "Sighted submerged submarine on westerly course, speed 9 knots."

The four-stack *Ward* was a relic, the last of the WW I models. All but a few of the crew were Naval Reservists whose only other sea duty had been on Lake Superior aboard an ancient gunboat, *Paducah*. The *Ward* had been steaming two miles one way and two miles back outside Pearl Harbor for nearly a year. In all that time this sighting seemed to be the first of particular interest.

The *Ward* officer of the deck, Ensign Eugene L. Platt, grabbed the inter-com and roused the commander, 35-year-old Lieut. William W. Outerbridge, who had retired to his cabin.

Outerbridge had been born in Hong Kong to a British merchant captain and a girl from Ohio. After the death of the captain, the American girl returned home with her child. Outerbridge entered Annapolis, Class of 1927. Then he spent 14 years inching his way up to his present rank.

Until a few days before he had been executive officer of the destroyer *Cummings*, where all the officers were Academy men except one reservist. Now he was the only Academy man on a ship full of reservists. The *Ward* was his first command, and this evening was his first night-patrol aboard her.

Neither he nor Platt were able to see the reported periscope, but he sounded general alarm and to the gong of the summons the crew tumbled from their bunks and took up battle stations. The *Ward* proceeded to the position of the *Condor* and stood as close to her as possible without risking fouling her sweeping gear, but without result.

For the next hour the *Ward* crisscrossed the choppy seas searching for the periscope. The men on deck caught no sight of it; the sonar men below decks were unable to pick up any sound of it. In doubt whether the *Condor* had actually seen a submarine, Outerbridge queried her again: "What was the approximate distance and course of the submarine that you sighted?"

"The course was about what we were steering at the time, 020 magnetic and about 1000 yards from the entrance apparently headed for the entrance."

Outerbridge then realized he had been searching in the wrong direction. He turned westward, but still doubting that a submarine had been sighted, he again asked the *Condor*, "Do you have any additional information on the sub?"

"No additional information."

"When was the last time approximately that you saw the submarine?"

"Approximate time 0350, and he was apparently heading for the entrance."

Outerbridge thanked them for the information and asked them to notify the *Ward* if they had any more information. He had the search go on in the restricted area outside the buoys. He released the crew from their battle stations; most returned to their bunks. He retired to the emergency cabin and went to sleep.

The incident was logged but not relayed to headquarters.

At 4:58 the protective net at the Pearl Harbor entrance swung open to admit the two minesweepers. It would remain open until 8:40. The *Condor* had probably sighted a midget submarine and it may have entered the harbor with the two minesweepers and was now resting on the bottom of Pearl Harbor awaiting the expected attack that she would attempt to assist.

Outerbridge was awakened by the relieving deck officer, Lieut. (j.g.) O. W. Goepner calling, "Captain, quick! Come out on the bridge."

Seaman H. E. Raenbig, the *Ward's* helmsman, had sighted something questionable near the target repair ship *Antares*. He reported that the *Anatares*, inbound with a steel barge under tow, had a suspicious object astern. He asked Quartermaster H.F. Gearin to use his binoculars for a better view.

Gearin immediately saw that the black object astern of the *Antares* was not hanging on the hawser of the repair ship but moving in line with it. He showed it to Goepner who said it looked like a buoy to him but to keep watching it.

Gearin did so and about a minute later reported he thought it was a small conning tower. At this point a Navy patrol bomber began circling overhead. Convinced the helmsman was right, Goepner summoned Outerbridge.

In robe and pajamas, Outerbridge came on deck to find the false dawn breaking beyond the Koolau Range giving sufficient light for visibility. Following the pointing fingers of the bridge crew, he could see the dim outline of a small submarine slipping along half submerged in the wake of the *Antares* and her tow, the conning tower of a type unknown to him.

Outerbridge signalled full speed ahead and sounded general quarters again to summon the crew to battle stations. He headed the old destroyer straight for the gap between the barge and the conning tower, now some 400 yards off the *Ward's* starboard bow.

At this point the *Antares* also took note of the strange object following her. She blinkered that she felt she was being followed.

The pilot of the plane circling the object, Ensign William Tanner, from Kaneohe Naval Air Base, thought he was observing an American submarine in distress. He dropped two smoke pots to mark its position.

Without the smoke pots the submarine was not only visible to those on deck but the sound of it was audible to the sonar men below who recognized the echoing ping of a submerging submarine. Outerbridge assessed the situation to himself, "She is going to follow the *Antares* in."

At 100 yards he ordered, "Commence firing."

At 6:45 A.M. the bow gun of the *Ward* fired. The shot

went too high. The crew made quick corrections. At about 50 yards the Number 3 gun sent a shell crashing into the midget, just below the base of the conning tower.

A brilliant flash came from the stricken submarine. It heeled over and began losing its forward speed. Probably the two crewmen aboard had been killed instantly. The submarine was sucked alongside the *Ward* then writhed and spun in its wake as it sank.

Outerbridge ordered a depth charge attack. Chief Torpedoman W. C. Masakawitz rolled the explosive ashcans off the fantail; they detonated under the submarine's bow.

A geyser of green water erupted, followed by a boiling eruption of oil and bubbles. Aloft, Tanner reflected on his orders: "Depth bomb and sink any submarines found in the defensive area without authority." He saw the *Ward* attacking the submarine; he dropped two depth bombs of his own.

Both destroyer and patrol plane circled the area, carefully searching it through binoculars. They saw only a mass of oily scum. At first sonar picked up echoes, but they sank lower and lower and died away in the 200 fathoms of water.

Thinking he had dropped his bombs on an American submarine, Tanner bitterly reported his action to the Kaneohe Naval Air Station.

Outerbridge was confident he had sunk an enemy submarine. At 6:51 A.M. he radioed the 14th Naval District watch officer: We have dropped depth charges upon sub operating in defensive sea area."

After sending the report, he decided that it was insufficiently clear. If he only reported that he had dropped depth charges, headquarters might think he had done so mistakenly on a blackfish or whale. So at 6:53 he sent a second report: "We have attacked fired upon and dropped depth charges upon submarine operating in defensive sea area."

Then he saw a white fishing sampan lying in the defensive area contrary to regulations. He turned the *Ward* around and chased after the sampan, which sped toward Barber's Point. When he finally caught up with the sampan someone aboard it waved a white flag. He thought the signal odd, even though the sampan might have heard some firing.

At 7:03; the *Ward* established sound contact on a second submarine. The *Ward* dropped more depth bombs. At 7:06 it sighted a black oil bubble 300 yards astern.

Meanwhile the Army was receiving clues to the portending assault. At the time the *Ward* had depth-bombed the second midget, the Opana Mobile Radar Station at Kahuku Point registered the approach of an air armada.

The Army Aircraft Warning System (AWS) consisted of an information center at Fort Shafter and elsewhere on Oahu, several mobile radars (SR-270's) mounted on trucks and located at Kawailoa, Kaawa, Koko Head, the rear of Fort Shafter and at Kahuku Point. The one at Kahuku, known as Opana, 230 feet above sea level and on the northernmost point of the island, was the one most likely to pick up the enemy flight.

The mobile radars had been received only in August 1941. They had been operating on a training basis for several months, not on a 24-hour basis since no liaison officers had been assigned to them.

On the morning of December 7 the AWS radar centers were manned from 4 to 7 A.M. Believing that these hours would be the most likely for an attack by aircraft taking off from carriers, Short had effected them after receiving the war-warning message of November 28. By limiting the hours of operation, he also limited the wear and tear on the equipment.

This morning Privates Joseph L. Lockard and George E. Elliott had gone on duty at Kahuku at 4:00 A.M. When 7:00 A.M., the hour to shut down arrived, the breakfast truck they had been anticipating had still not arrived. Elliott, the plotter, wanted more instruction; Lockard, the operator and more experienced, kept the warning system open while he gave the instruction.

Elliott was at the controls at 7:02 A.M. when "something completely out of the ordinary" appeared on the screen. The oscilloscope had suddenly picked up an image so peculiar that Lockard thought something must be wrong with the set.

A quick check showed the set was operating normally. Lockard took over from Elliott and decided that what showed on the oscilloscope "must be a flight of some sort."

Elliott went to the plotting board. At 7:02 the flight appeared at 5 degrees northeast of azimuth at 132 miles. They reckoned it as an enormous flight of "probably more than 50" planes. Elliott suggested phoning the reading to the Information Center. Lockard demurred; normal operating hours had ended. Elliott persisted: it being a nonscheduled exercise it would be a good test for the Information Center.

After they had discused the action for seven or eight minutes the scope showed the blip to be about 20 or 25 miles nearer Oahu. Lockard gave in and told Elliott to phone in the information.

The Information Center was at Fort Shafter, several miles east of Pearl Harbor and 30 miles from Opana.

At 7:06 Elliott tried the headphones that connected directly with one of the spotters at the Information Center. The line was dead.

Then he tried the regular Army circuit. Finally he got the information switchboard operator, Private Joseph McDonald, who worked in a small cubicle just outside the plotting room.

Elliott said, "There's a large number of planes coming in from the north, three degrees east."

Thinking no other was left at the Information Center,

Army Aircraft Plotting Room of Information Center, Fort Shafter, Oahu, Hawaii. Photographed Feb. 5, 1942

McDonald wrote down the message and turned around to time it by the big clock on the plotting room wall. Through the open door he noticed Lieut. Kermit Tyler sitting alone at the plotting table.

Tyler had been commissioned in the Air Corps and had arrived in Hawaii about ten months previously. The second ranking officer in the 78th Pursuit Squadron, he had been assigned to this task at Fort Shafter Information Center only once before. On that occasion the only other person there had been the telephone operator, so Tyler had learned little. On another occasion, on a tour for officers, he had been taken through the Center and picked up the general principles of the project.

As he had driven to Fort Shafter through the darkness this morning, he had listened to the Hawaiian music emanating from his car radio and originating in KGMB. A bomber-pilot friend had told him that when KGMB broadcast all night it was a good indication that a flight of Army planes would be coming in from the mainland. They used the beam to home on.

This morning there had been about five or six plotters placing plots (arrows) on the board. None of them were officers. Again he had received little instruction. About 7 A.M. they had folded up their equipment and left.

Now McDonald took his written message to Tyler, explaining that it was the first time he had received anything like it.

McDonald asked, "Do you think we ought to do something about it?" They did not get much practice and this seemed "an awful big flight."

Tyler was unimpressed. Having listened to the music of KGMB on the way to Fort Shafter, he took it for granted that the flight seen from Opana must be American planes—either planes flying in from the mainland or, about as likely, Navy planes flying in after having left their carriers.

McDonald returned to the switchboard and called back Opana. Lockard answered: he was as excited as Elliott had been. The blips looked bigger than ever; the distance was shrinking fast: 7:03 A.M., 113 miles; 7:15, 92 miles. At least 50 planes must be speeding toward Oahu at almost 180 miles per hour.

When McDonald told him Tyler thought everything was all right, Lockard protested, "Hey, Mac!" Explaining that he had never seen so many planes, so many flashes on the screen, Lockard asked to speak directly to Tyler.

McDonald returned to Tyler. "Sir, I would appreciate it very much if you would answer the phone."

Tyler took the phone and listened patiently while Lockard gave him "all the information...the direction, the mileage and the apparent size of whatever it was..." the biggest sighting he had ever seen.

Tyler was still convinced the planes were American. He told Lockard, "Well, don't worry about it." Security reasons prevented him from explaining his conclusions.

It was about 7:20 A.M.

His spirits dashed, Lockard thought they might as well shut down the set; Elliott wanted to practice further. They followed the flight on in: 7:25 A.M., 62 miles; 7:30 , 47 miles; 7:29, 22 miles. At this point they lost the flight in the "dead zone" caused by the hills around them.

At 7:30 they made the last report of the sighting: 41 degrees, 20 miles.

In the meantime Outerbridge's 6:53 A.M. message about sinking a submarine was getting attention at Naval Headquarters. The watch officer that morning was Lieut. Comdr. Harold Kaminski, a reservist who had been in the Navy off and on ever since being an enlisted man in the World War. Regularly in charge of net and boom defenses , he took his Sunday turn as duty officer like everyone else.

Due to delays in decoding, paraphrasing and typing, it was 7:12 before Kaminski received Outerbridge's message.

Then, on his own responsibility he sent the ready-duty destroyer *Monahan*, by visual signal, the message: "Get under way immediately and contact U.S.S. *WARD* in defensive sea area."

Then he phoned the information to Capt. John B. Earle, chief of staff of the 14th Naval District.

It was the first time Earle had heard of a Navy ship firing at such a contact; he was astonished. Nevertheless he thought it was just one more of the submarine sightings that had been turning up recently. He said he would inform Bloch and told Kaminski to verify the dispatch and to inform the Commander-in-Chief Pacific (CINPAC) duty office and Comdr. Charles Momsen, 14th Naval District operations officer.

At 7:15 A.M. Early had Bloch on the phone. The two men spent five or ten minutes trying to decide if the message was reliable. They decided to await further developments.

Meanwhile Kaminski had notified CINCPAC headquarters at the submarine base. The assistant duty officer, Lieut. Comdr. Francis Black received the call about 7:20. Black relayed the report to the duty officer, Comdr. Vincent Murphy, who was dressing in his quarters.

Murphy said, "While I'm finishing dressing, call him (Kaminski) and see what he's doing about it and whether or not he's called Adm. Bloch."

Black tried to call Kaminski, but though he dialed repeatedly Kaminski's line was always busy. Black informed Murphy.

Murphy said, "All right, you go to the office and start breaking out the charts and position of the various ships; I'll dial one more time and then be over."

Murphy phoned; the line was still busy. He then phoned the operator and instructed him to tell Kaminski to call him immediately and to break into any conversation Kaminski might be having "unless it was of supreme importance."

As Murphy entered his office the phone was ringing:

Lieut. Cmdr. Logan Ramsey of Patrol Wing Two reported he had just received word from the duty officer on Ford Island, Lieut. Dick Ballinger, that one of their planes "on intertype tactics" had "sunk a submerged submarine one mile off the entrance to Pearl Harbor."

Murphy replied, "That's funny, we got the same sort of message from one of the destroyers on inshore patrol."

Ramsey had scarcely hung up when Kaminski called Murphy to report the action of the *Ward*. Murphy telephoned Kimmel; he had him on the line at 7:40.

Kimmel had arisen about 7:00 to prepare for a scheduled golf game with Short. He had neither shaved nor breakfasted, but he replied, "I will be right down."

The U.S.S. Ward (below) under command of Lieut. William W. Outerbridge (right) began the defense of Pearl Harbor by dropping depth charges on a Japanese midget submarine.

21

BETWEEN HAMMER AND ANVIL

When Kimmel was promising to come right down to
headquarters at 7:40 A.M., December 7, Honolulu was waking
to another splendid day, bright and cool in a city still
unspoiled by the highrise buildings, freeways and other
marks of overpopulation that would mar it later. It was a
time of optimism, too, for the defense money the Federal
government was pouring into strengthening its outpost in
the Pacific - for barracks, housing, storage and all the
appurtenances of defense was bringing prosperity to the
residents. Those working on the projects were earning more
than they ever had before and the money flowed from their
pockets into that of the merchants in town who had
decorated the downtown streets with colored lights and were
preparing for the most lavish Christmas ever.

True there was a threat of war in the Far East. The
residents received this information from their morning
paper, the *Honolulu Advertiser*, in screaming headlines. In
reference to Rep. Martin Dies, chairman of the Un-American
committee, the *Advertiser* blared November 10: **Dies Says
War With Japan within three or four Weeks or Entire Matter
Settled.** In another story: **Withdrawal of U.S. Marines from
Shanghai "prelude to American action in Pacific": Sao Taon
Pao said.** In another: **Threat of U.S. - Japan War
Emphasized by Spokesmen. Dies, Sterling Expect Fight to
Start Soon.**

November 30 the front page of the Advertiser blazoned:
**Japanese May Strike Over Weekend!   KURUSU BLUNTLY WARNED
NATION READY FOR BATTLE.   U.S. PATROL ON BURMA ROAD MEANS**

WAR – JAPAN.   America is Warned to Keep Hands Off.

The *Advertiser* of December 2 reported that the vanguard of the British eastern fleet was sighted on the horizon from Singapore at 2:30 P.M., headed, as far as could be seen, by two heavy-tonnage battleships and a long line of smaller craft.   "Public enthusiasm was at a pitch even surpassing that at the time of the first contingent of Australian troops arrival last February."

December 2: **'BLAST JAPAN OFF SEAS' URGE.   NIPPON TOLD TO SINK U.S. SHIPS.   May Declares Congress Will Vote For War.**

May was Rep. Andrew J. May, chairman of the House military affairs committee.   In Washington he urged Roosevelt to tell the Japanese that unless they renounced their ambitions for an empire in South Asia the United States "will blast them off the land and blow them out of the water.

"If American planes could be used to guard the Burma Road they could also be used to bomb Tokyo.   That would be guarding the Burma Road, wouldn't it?"

Few residents seemed to need reassurance, but the *Advertiser* gave it to them anyway in an editorial pointing out that the Japanese Navy was inferior to the American. The newspaper also featured a story showing the military on guard to protect Hawaii.

The nation itself had been reassured by the Knox statement of the preceding day.   December 7, *The New York Times* headlined the story: **NAVY IS SUPERIOR TO ANY SAYS KNOX**

Accustomed to this newspaper fare, the average resident of Oahu thought of the enemy as insignificant and far away. He gave no thought to the prospect of the war erupting on his doorstep.

The troublous state of the world had been a blessing to Hawaii and was expected to continue until America entered the affray far beyond its frontiers and brought peace to the world on American terms. The residents never dreamed of an enemy fleet in Hawaiian waters, only 200 miles distant, where Nagumo on the bridge of the *Akagi* gazed in the direction in which his planes had disappeared. Surprised and pleased by the nearly flawless takeoff, he could overlook the circumstance that his planes would arrive over their targets ahead of schedule. Ignorant that the war had already begun in Malaya, he was consequently unconcerned that the British had had ample time to warn their American ally.

As noted, Fuchida did not expect to achieve surprise anyway. But as he neared Oahu, guided by the music from KGMB, which seemed to be operating normally, and with no fighters coming to intercept him, it began to appear that he might, after all, achieve surprise.

At exactly 7:35 came the report from the *Chikuma* scout plane that had hovered over Pearl Harbor to ascertain the situation. "Enemy formation at anchor; nine battleships, one heavy cruiser, six light cruisers are in the harbor."

At 7:38 he reported the meteorological conditions at Pearl Harbor: "Wind direction from 80 degrees, speed 14 meters, clearance over enemy fleet 1700 meters, cloud density 7."

Almost immediately afterward the *Tone* scout plane reported: "The enemy fleet is not in Lahaina Anchorage." The report disposed of the Japanese hope of sinking the American ships in the deep waters of Lahaina and scrapped the alternative plans Genda and Fuchida had painstakingly worked up and reviewed at Hitokappu Bay. The Japanese must destroy the Fleet at Pearl.

Fuchida had planned to fly over the northeastern mountains to attack, but listening to the radio he heard this weather forecast:

"Averaging partly cloudy, with clouds mostly over the mountains. Cloud base at 3500 feet. Visibility good. Wind north, 10 knots."

333

He could not have imagined a more favorable weather situation. Since Oahu was only partly cloudy, there would be breaks in the clouds over his targets. But since the clouds over the mountains were at 3500 feet it would be wiser to pass to the west of the island and approach from the south.

Suddenly the clouds broke and he saw a long white line of coast at Kahuku Point. He told Pilot Matsuzaki, "This is the north point of Oahu."

He ordered, "Tenkai!" (Take attack positions.)

Though the image may not have occurred to Fuchida, the shape of Oahu may be likened to the head of an elephant, with Kahuku point, the top of its skull. Down the center, in a southeasterly direction, runs the corrugated trunk— the Koolau Range – its tip ending at Makapuu Point, as if drinking from the blue ocean there.

East of the trunk, an excrescence on the tusk, was Kaneohe Naval Air Base. A little below was Bellows Air Force Station.

West of the trunk, on the plateau between the Waianae and Koolau Ranges, were the Army base of Schofield Barracks and the Air Force base of Wheeler Field. West of that is the wrinkled ear – the Waianae Range. If Fuchida descended the skull on the western side he would pass the small Army air base at Haleiwa, the Naval Air Station at Barber's Point, just below the tip of the ear, and arrive at the prime target, Pearl Harbor. He had made meticulous plans to deal with all of the points of potential resistance except Haleiwa. He himself would concentrate his attack on Pearl Harbor.

The group deployed. Fuchida picked up his rocket pistol.

According to plan, one flare from the rocket pistol would signal that surprise had been achieved. At this signal, Murata's torpedomen would start their downward glide while Itaya's fighters sped on to seize control of

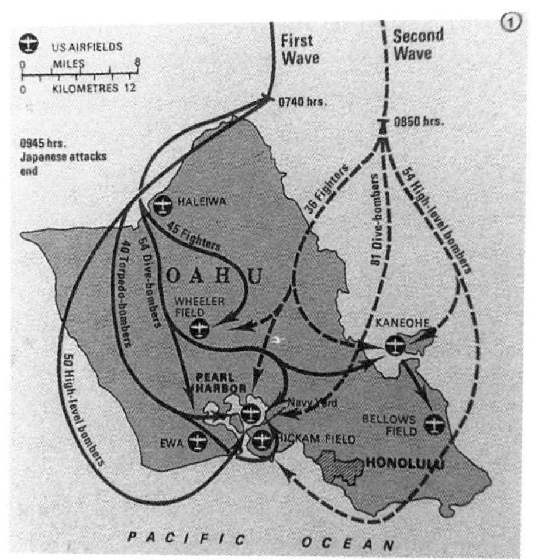

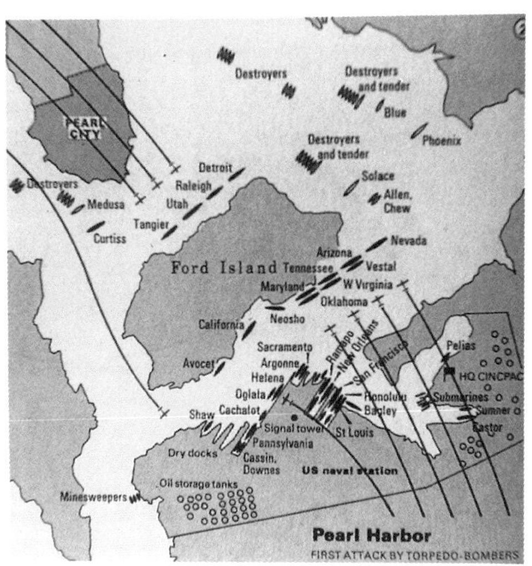

(Top) Map showing the approach routes of the two waves of attacking Japanese planes. (Bottom) Disposition of American ships in Pearl Harbor as seen by the attackers.

the air. The slow torpedo bombers would thus have a clear path to their targets. The dive and high-level bombers would follow.

At 7:40 a.m., seeing no fighters in the air or any other indication that his group had been detected, Fuchida fired a single flare. Then he noted that one of the fighter group leaders, Lieut. Masaharu Suganami, must have failed to observe the signal; his planes had failed to take the required formation. After awaiting about 10 seconds, Fuchida fired another flare to alert Suganami.

The leader of the dive bombers, Lieut. Comdr. Kakuichi Takahashi, saw this second flare and misjudged it to be the signal for failure to achieve surprise. With his 51 dive bombers he immediately swooped for an attack on Ford Island, Pearl Harbor and nearby Hickam Air Field.

Realizing that Takahashi had erred, Murata could only lead his fleet of 40 torpedo planes to the target as quickly as possible.

Fuchida ground his teeth in vexation over this botching of the carefully worked out plan. But he soon saw that the order of attack was unimportant.

Nevertheless, his 50 high-level bombers would attack last. Now he led them westward, cut across the westernmost tip of Oahu and then seaward again, circling to approach Pearl Harbor from the south. As he rounded Lahilahi Point, midway down the edge of the elephant's ear, he studied Pearl Harbor through binoculars.

Seen from the air, Pearl Harbor resembles a large lake emptying through its channel into the Pacific. The Waipio Peninsula divides the harbor into two parts. The larger part, if the Middle and East Lochs are regarded as one, is the side nearer Honolulu to the east.

In the center of this eastern section is Ford Island, which the Navy used as an air base. Around Ford Island on this Sunday morning, like pendant beads suspended from a necklace, were the moored ships. On the eastern side the battleships *Oklahoma* and *Maryland*, *West Virginia* and *Tennessee* were moored in pairs, the *California* moored singly. The battleship *Arizona* was moored next to Ford Island with the repair ship *Vestal* moored on the outer side.

On the western side was the battleship *Utah*, often misidentified in accounts of the attack as only a target vessel, but which was also designated and staffed as an anti-aircraft training ship. There were also the light cruisers *Raleigh* and *Detroit* and seaplane tender *Tangier*.

Altogether there were 97 ships in the harbor that morning.

Fuchida was astounded at what he saw. Later he was to write:

> **Below me lay the whole U.S. Fleet in a formation I would not have dared to dream of in my most optimistic dreams. I have seen all German ships assembled in Kiel Harbor. I have also seen the French battleships in Brest. And finally I have frequently seen our own warships assembled for review before the Emperor, but I have never seen ships, even in the deepest peace, anchored at a distance less than 500 to 1,000 yards from each other. A war fleet must always be on the alert since surprise attacks can never be fully ruled out. Had these Americans never heard of Port Arthur?**

At 7:49 A.M., Fuchida told Mazuki, "Notify all planes to launch attacks." Mazuki immediately began to tap out the order in plain code: "To, to, to, to..."

Correctly interpreting the attack signal to mean that his torpedo planes were to lead the attack, Murata strove to reach his targets before the dive bombings would obscure them with smoke. At 7:57 the torpedo planes began launching torpedoes at the battleships.

To intercept the anticipated fighter resistance, the Japanese fighter planes had approached the island in two groups — one from the northwest, the other from the northeast. Finding few planes to combat, the Japanese strafed the airfields where the neatly lined-up American planes were open targets.

Fuchida's high-level bombers proceeded on west of Oahu, seeing only Japanese planes in the air and no sign of air combat. He passed Barber's Point airfield, at the base of the elephant's jaw bone, but believing there were no planes there, and observing no antiaircraft fire, he continued on without swerving. Ships in Honolulu Harbor seemed asleep; the radio broadcasts were continuing normally.

Feeling he had achieved surprise and that success was assured, he directed Mazuki to wire: "We have succeeded in making a surprise attack. Request you relay this report to Tokyo."

Fuchida's ten squadrons formed into a single column, the lead plane in each squadron manned by a specially trained pilot and bombardier.

The pilot and bombardier of Fuchida's squadron were considered the best in the Japanese Navy; Fuchida gave permission for their plane to take the lead. As the group began its bombing run, antiaircraft fire erupted, filling the sky with dark gray bursts of smoke like dirty cotton balls. Fuchida's plane trembled from near misses then bounced as if struck.

Mazuki said, "The fuselage is holed to port. A steering control wire is damaged."

The plane was still under control, however, and flying at 3300 feet headed for the battleship *Nevada* anchored just ahead of the *Arizona*. Fuchida concentrated on the bomb under the lead plane. He pulled the safety bolt from the bomb release lever of his own plane and grasped the handle.

Antiaircraft fire again shook his plane; he saw the bomb fall from the third plane. Fuchida ordered the plane to return to its carrier but the pilot replied, "Fuel tank destroyed, will follow you," which meant he chose to die by crashing his plane on the best available target.

This time when the bombardiers should have released their loads the planes ran into clouds that obscured the targets. Waving his hands to indicate they had passed the release point, the bombardier indicated that the group must reform to try again. The squadron circled back over Honolulu to come in for another attempt. This time as they closed on Pearl Harbor other groups were making their runs and dropping bombs.

A colossal explosion rent the air. A huge column of dark red smoke erupted to 1,000 feet above the *Arizona*. A shock wave rocked the plane. Fuchida called to Matsuzaki.

"Yes, Commander," came the reply, "the powder magazine must have exploded. Terrible indeed!"

Five armor-piercing bombs had fallen on the *Arizona*. One of the bombs had crashed through the deck near the Number 2 turret, starting a fire. Apparently fed by oil from the forward tanks, the fire had spread rapidly and reached the powder magazine.

The magazine exploded at 8:10 A.M. Less than nine minutes afterward the ship settled to the bottom, trapping more then 1,000 of the crew in the hull.

A portent of the impending disaster had appeared to Lieut. Comdr. Logan C. Ramsey, operations officer under Bellinger, about 7:55 A.M. While awaiting authentication of the submarine sinking he stood near a window of the Ford Island command center watching the color guard prepare to hoist the flag. Hearing the scream of a plane diving over the station, he turned to Lieut. Richard Ballinger and said:

"Dick, get that fellow's number, for I want to report him for about 16 violations of the course and safety regulations."

As the plane went into its dive, each man looked out separate windows following its course.

"Dick, did you get his number?"

"No, but I think it was a squadron commander's plane because I saw a band of red on it."

"Check with the squadrons and find out which squadron commander's planes are in the air."

"I saw something black fall out of that plane when it completed its dive."

At precisely 7:57 an explosion reverberated from the hangar area.

"Never mind the squadron commander, Dick. That was a Jap plane and a delayed action bomb."

Ramsey raced across the corridor to the radio room and ordered all radiomen on duty to send out in plain English: **"AIR RAID, PEARL HARBOR. THIS IS NO DRILL."**

The message went out at 7:58. Kimmel's headquarters followed with a similar one.

After Murphy had phoned Kimmel at 7:40, he received a call from Kaminski reporting the *Ward's* encounter with the sampan. He had already reported the matter to Earle, who deduced from the information that the *Ward* would not be escorting an innocuous sampan if there were a submarine about. Murphy, however, thought the information about the sampan justified another call to Kimmel. He phoned him at 7:50.

As Murphy talked to Kimmel, a yeoman burst into the room, crying, "There's a message from the signal tower saying the Japanese are attacking Pearl Harbor and this is no drill."

Murphy relayed this message to Kimmel. Then he told the communications officer to radio the Chief of Naval Operations, the C-n-C Atlantic Fleet, the C-n-C Asiatic Fleet and all the forces at sea: **AIR RAID ON PEARL HARBOR. THIS IS NO DRILL.**

The message went out at 8:00 a.m. Adm. Bellinger had radioed a similar message to all ships in the harbor at 7:58.

When Kimmel received Murphy's second message, he ran out to his yard and stood there watching the planes make their torpedo runs. The wife of Capt. John Earle joined him.

She said quietly, "Looks like they've got the *Oklahoma*."

"Yes, I can see they have."

The CINCPAC official car screeched to a stop. Kimmel ran to it and jumped in. As the car moved off, Capt. Freeland Daubin, who commanded a squadron of submarines, leaped on the running board. Earle's station wagon followed.

Kimmel arrived at CINCPAC headquarters within five minutes – between 8:05 and 8:10. In moments the backbone of his fleet was destroyed – *Arizona*, *Oklahoma* and *West Virginia* sunk...*California* sinking; *Maryland* and *Tennessee* bottled up by wrecked battleships alongside.

As word of the fate of his battleships reached him, a groan escaped Kimmel. Comdr. Maurice E. Curts, communications officer beside him, Kimmel stood by the window looking out. A spent bullet crashed through the glass, struck Kimmel on the bosom of his white uniform, leaving a dark splotch, and dropped to the floor.

He picked up the bullet and murmured sorrowfully, "It would have been merciful if it had killed me."

Short was equally despondent. From his quarters in Fort Shafter he had been listening to the Bedlam coming from Pearl Harbor and had decided the Navy must be having some kind of battle practice. When the explosions increased, he went out on his lanai for a look. He saw a lot of smoke to the west. Lieut. Col. Walter C. Philips appeared. Hickam and Wheeler had phoned – this was "the real thing."

The telegram from Marshall addressed to Short had

arrived at RCA on South King Street, near Iolani Palace, at 7:33 A.M., three minutes past the 1 P.M. Washington deadline. Since there was nothing on the message to indicate priority, the clerk filed the message in a pigeon hole marked for Kalihi, the district of Honolulu that included Fort Shafter just beyond its western border.

The messenger to whom the message would be assigned for delivery, Tadao Fuchikami, 23, had been killing time talking to acquaintances on the parking lot across the street. He was a plumber by trade, but a recent appendix operation diverted him from heavy work, so he had bought an Indian motorcycle and gone to work as messenger for RCA. He was accustomed to enterting Fort Shafter every day with messages.

After he checked in for work, but before he began his deliveries, the RCA station at Kahuku phoned that it had seen Japanese planes overhead and that they were attacking. All at Honolulu RCA were skeptical of the report. But when Fuchikami left the building and looked toward Pearl Harbor he could see smoke arising.

Still only half-believing the report of the Japanese attack, he mounted his motorcycle and started out. He heard nothing above the roar of the motorcycle. As he passed the Fish Market near Aala Park he saw it thronged with the usual Sunday morning shoppers. Though they had been warned of the Japanese attack they refused to believe it and continued their routine affairs.

When he had gone a little farther, Fuchikami saw a Japanese plane, presumably a Zero, pursuing and firing on an American P-40 in the direction of Pearl Harbor. For the first time he gave credence to the report of the Japanese attack. It did not occur to him to postpone his deliveries.

He had telegrams to deliver on the route towards Fort Shafter; he took care of them first. He went up Kalihi Valley to deliver one. Returning he found his egress

Five armor piercing bombs had fallen on the Arizona (above). Fire spread to the powder magazine, which exploded at 8:10 A.M. Here the ship is settling to the bottom, trapping more than 1,000 of the crew in the hull.

The magazine of the Destroyer Shaw (above) explodes in a crescendo of flame and smoke.

Stunned personnel observe the wrecking of the Naval Station.

Crew evacuating the stricken, sinking California (above).

barred by a sandbag emplacement with a mounted machine gun.

The soldiers in the emplacement told him there were reports of Japanese parachutists landing and that his green RCA uniform looked like a military uniform. He might be mistaken for an invader. They told him to go home.

As the son of Japanese immigrants he might, in the circumstances, have particularly looked like an invader. But neither then nor later in his rounds did anyone refer to his ancestry.

Disregarding the order to go home, he went on toward Fort Shafter, which was nearby. At the corner of King and Middle Streets he ran into another checkpoint, this one swarming with policemen. They were preventing cars from passing through so the road was jammed. Fuchikami rode his motorcycle on the sidewalk. The police asked his mission. Learning that he had a message for Fort Shafter, they let him pass.

At Fort Shafter the sentry waved him in without question. There, sometime after nine, he left his message; apparently it went unlogged until 11:45.

When Fuchida had cried, "Tora! Tora! Tora!" to signal he had achieved surprise, the second wave of 170 planes was about halfway to Oahu. Like the first wave, the second flew at staggered altitudes for greater maneuverability and better interception of enemy aircraft, though at this point they had met no enemy aircraft to intercept. The first wave had destroyed or damaged most of them on the ground.

The second wave, under Lieut. Comdr. Shigekazu Shimazaki, of the *Zuikaku*, arrived at Oahu about 10 miles east of Kahuku Point, at 8:40. Unlike the first wave, the second was to approach its targets from east Oahu.

The first wave was still in action. The newcomers could see the puffs of antiaircraft fire exploding in the sky and the high-level bombers floating in single file above Pearl Harbor. The second wave was ordered to circle to avoid interference with the first wave.

342

At 8:54 as the first wave retired the second was ordered to attack. Led by Lieut. Comdr. Takashige Egusa, 81 dive bombers flew over the Koolau Range to attack Hickam Field and Pearl Harbor. Fifty-four high-level bombers attacked Kaneohe Naval Air Base, Bellows Field and Hickam. Some fighters were supposed to secure air supremacy for the Pearl Harbor attack, but finding no opposition veered off to assist in the attacks on Wheeler Field and to assist the high-level bombers elsewhere.

Of the 353 planes attacking Oahu, 199 had been assigned to gain air superiority, a task in which they had been mightily assisted by the blunder of Short in parking his planes wing tip to wing tip, in plain view, where they became open targets. When the fighters sprayed these planes with incendiary bullets the stricken planes spread fire and destruction to their neighbors.

The sky was so covered with clouds and smoke that the second wave had trouble finding its targets. Also ship and ground antiaircraft fire was now heavy. The swift American response to the attack surprised the Japanese who having been taught to always take the offensive were accordingly less well trained in defensive tactics.

The Japanese considered the ships putting up the stiffest repelling fire to be the least damaged, so they concentrated their attacks on them. The Japanese then observed the *Nevada* trying to get under way to leave the harbor; the planes converged on her in the hope of sinking her in the channel and thus bottling up the harbor. Dive bombers came at her from every direction, smothering her with hits. Fires spread rapidly through her and she began to settle in the water. As she approached the floating drydock, signal flags from the Naval District Headquarters warned her to stay clear of the channel.

The skipper accordingly ran her aground at Hospital Point, at the base of the channel. There the tide turned her around to face the direction from which she had come.

With smoke covering so many targets, the Japanese turned on the largest undamaged target remaining, the Fleet flagship *Pennsylvania*, in Drydock 1. During the first attack, the drydock had been flooded to prevent the battleship from surging forward and crushing the destroyers if the dock gates were destroyed. The flooding raised the battleship to dockside, allowing her antiaircraft guns to be put in action.

The Japanese succeeded in putting only one bomb in the *Pennsylvania* but repeatedly struck the destroyers. Japanese fighters and bombers also raked over the airfields throughout the island, except for Haleiwa.

At 9:02, Egusa's dive bombers made a direct hit on the *Pennsylvania* in dry dock. At 9:07 a high=level bomber scored a strike. A direct hit exploded in the forward magazine of the destroyer *Shaw* as she floated in drydock, nearly ripping off her whole bow. The dive bombers attacked the destroyers *Cassin* and *Downes* so fiercely they had to be abandoned; shortly thereafter magazine and torpedo explosions shook them from bow to stern. At 9:08 a dive bomber scored a hit on the destroyer *Raleigh*, already damaged by the first wave of the attack.

About 10:04, Egusa's bombers, racks empty, flew off to strafe Ewa, Hickam and Ford Island.

The second wave cost the Japanese 14 dive bombers and six fighter planes. One of these fighter planes, though damaged, flew towards its carrier as far as Niihau Island where it crashlanded. The pilot lived there for six days before he was killed by natives. (See Beekman: *The Niihau Incident*.) Many others had been hit but escaped.

Fuchida hovered over the scene, assessing the damage and rounding up stragglers. His badly shot-up plane had circled for about two hours. In the three hours he had been over the area he had not encountered a single enemy plane. As he mulled over this he was startled by a fighter plane approaching and banking from side to side, evidently

344

to display the Rising Sun on its wings. He saw it was from the *Zuikaku* and must have been here since the first wave. Wondering if any other fighters had been left behind, he ordered Matsuzaki to go to the rendezvous point for a final check. There he found a second fighter.

He led the two fighters back to their carriers.

To facilitate the return of his planes, Nagumo had brought his carriers to within 190 miles of Oahu. Throughout the morning the weather had worsened. High seas and tricky winds made landings difficult. The pilots were tense and tired. Some made bad landings. Deck crews had to push a few badly damaged craft into the sea to clear the landing area for fuel-short planes circling overhead.

Fuchida was the last to land. There refueled and rearmed planes were lined up on the flight deck in preparation for the enemy if he counterattacked. All flying officers recovered aboard the *Akagi* reported at once to Air Officer Cmdr. Shōgo Masuda.

On the flight deck near the bridge, with the aid of Lieut. Shigeharu Murata, Masuda tabulated the results on a large blackboard.

When Fuichida's plane landed about noon, Genda wrung his hand. then Genda rushed back to the bridge. A sailor rushed to Fuchida with the message that Nagumo wanted to see him at once.

Despite the message, Fuchida carefully examined the blackboard and listened to the reports of about 15 flying officers as he sipped a cup of tea. Their observations tallied with his. He felt he could render a fairly accurate assessment of the results of the attack.

Another messenger informed Fuchida that he was to report to Nagumo and to hurry. Fuchida went to the bridge where he found Rear Adm. Ryūnosuke Kusaka, Hasegawa, Oishi, Genda and a few other staff officers gathered around Nagumo. Fuchida had planned to give a formal briefing, but Nagumo broke in:

"The results — what are they?"

"Four battleships sunk; four battleships damaged." He listed by berth and type the other ships his airmen had sunk.

"Do you think the U.S. Pacific Fleet will be unable to come out from Pearl Harbor within six months?"

"The main force of the U.S. Pacific Fleet will be unable to come out within six months."

Nagumo beamed and nodded.

Kusaka asked, "What do you think the next targets should be?"

"The next targets should be the dockyards, the fuel tanks and an occasional ship."

Kusaka asked about the possibility of an American counterattack. Both Genda and Fuchida assured him that the Japanese controlled the air over both Oahu and the sea.

Oishi asked, "Is the enemy in a position to counterattack the task force?"

Fuchida said, "I believe we have destroyed many enemy planes, but I don't know whether we have destroyed all of them. Probably the enemy could still attack the Fleet."

Nagumo asked, "Where do you think the missing U.S. carriers are?"

Fuchida was unsure. He thought they were probably training at sea, but no doubt by now the carriers had received word of the attack and would be looking for the Japanese task force.

This opinion obviously awakened unpleasant associations in the mind of Nagumo, who had already observed that a carrier could succumb to a single bomb hit.

Oishi asked the opinion of Genda.

"Let the enemy come," said Genda, "If he does, we will shoot down his planes."

When the question of the extent of the damage inflicted on airfields and air bases arose, Fuchida said, "All things considered we have achieved a great amount of destruction, but it would be unwise to assume that we have destroyed everything.   There are still many targets remaining that should be hit.   Therefore I recommend that another attack be launched."

Nagumo demurred.   Later he would list the reasons for his demurral. They were:

1. The first attack had inflicted all the damage hoped for, another attack could not be expected to greatly increase the extent of the damage.

2. Even though taken by surprise, enemy return fire had been surprisingly prompt;   another attack would meet stronger opposition and Japanese losses would be disproportionate to the additional destruction that might be inflicted.

3. Intercepted enemy messages indicated at least 50 large enemy planes were still operational; the Japanese did not know the whereabouts of the enemy carriers, cruisers and submarines.

4. To remain within range of enemy land-based planes was disadvantageous, especially since Japanese air reconnaissance was extremely limited.

Genda urged, "Stay in the area for several days and run down the enemy carriers."

The tankers could be called down from the north to refuel the fleet.   Eventually the enemy carriers would be located and destroyed. Then the Task Force could sail home by way of the Marshall Islands, attacking Pearl Harbor repeatedly as it sailed west of Oahu.

Nagumo, who had been opposed to the operation from the first, felt it had already succeeded beyond expectations.

He and Kusaka agreed the operation had been 80 percent successful; the other 20 percent was unworthy of the risk involved.

The second wave had inflicted less impressive loss on the enemy than the first and had paid three times the price. Further, in addition to the 29 missing planes, 74 had been damaged. Though Nagumo did not yet know it, he had lost all of his midget submarines.

Kusaka, who had opposed the operation in the beginning and had believed that the Japanese should have concentrated all their forces in the main theater of operations, counselled against remaining. He wanted to move men and ships as quickly as possible to the main theater in Southeast Asia.

Sitting in the command post, eating his first meal since the predawn breakfast, Fuchida heard the command: "Preparations for attack cancelled." The *Akagi* broke out her signal flags to advise the Task Force to retire to the northwest.

Fuchida rushed to the bridge to protest. He saluted Nagumo and asked, "Why are we not attacking again?"

Kusaka intervened, replying so firmly that he discouraged further question. "The objective of Pearl Harbor has been achieved. Now we must prepare for other operations ahead."

Bitter and angry, Fuchida saluted and stalked off. Fuchida believed that since Japan lacked the resources for a prolonged war, it should smite the enemy with all its power at the very beginning, smiting him again and again with all the nation's resources.

His anger would not down. For the rest of the voyage home he spoke to Nagumo only when duty and courtesy demanded that he do so.

Most of the survivors of the attack agreed that another attack was practicable from the standpoint of aircraft condition and morale of personnel. The pilots aboard the

348

Akagi asked Genda for an explanation of the decision of Nagumo to retire without having launched a third strike.

Genda listed the following reasons: The strike had already achieved its expected result of immobilizing the American Fleet for six months thus giving the Japanese a free hand in Southeast Asia; a second attack would risk considerable damage to the Task Force; the Task Force did not know the position of the American carriers.

Despite rationalizing the order to retire, Genda tagged Nagumo as a "miscast misfit," but he blamed Nagumo less for being miscast than he did the Personnel Section of the Navy Ministry.

The Task Force steamed back towards Japan. Some vessels would be detached from it en route to assist in the assault on Wake Island.

In the anchorage at Hashirajima, aboard the flagship *Nagato*, Yamamoto had spent the eve of battle playing shōgi – Japanese chess – with staff officer Yasuji Watanabe. They finished the game earlier than usual.

Yamamoto and his staff officers bathed and retired to their cabins for a nap. Not long after midnight, most of the staff officers were up and assembled in small groups in the operation room.

The four walls were plastered with large maps of the entire Pacific area and charts of various zones of Southeastern Asian waters. On a table were a large globe and still more charts; on a smaller table were files of operational orders and radio messages. Across the passage from the *Nagato's* operating room lay the radio room. To enable the officers to hear messages as they came in, a cord led from the radio room, across the passage, to a receiver on an operations room table. Eyes shut, Yamamoto sat in a folding chair at the back of the room, before a big table.

News came of the successful landing of the Army at Khota Bharu. There followed a report of a successful landing at Batan, a 35-square-mile island of the Philippines in the Luzon Strait, midway between Formosa and Luzon.

Senior Staff Officer Kameto Kuroshima glanced at the clock on the bulkhead. "It should be coming in any minute now."

The radio operator broke into the room and shouted to Akira Sasaki, the staff officer on duty, "Sir – the repeated *to* signal!"

Sasaki turned to Yamamoto. "As you hear, sir, the message was sent at 0319 hours."

Yamamoto opened his eyes wide and nodded. He asked the radio operator, "Did you get the message direct from the plane?"

The Operation Room had and had thus set a record for a long-distance reception of a plane message.

There followed reports from the attacking units:

"Surprise attack successful."

"Enemy warships torpedoed; outstanding results."

"Hickam Field attacked; outstanding results."

The radio was also picking up uncoded radio messages from the American side: "SOS – attacked by Jap bombers here..." "Oahu attacked by Jap dive-bombers from carrier..." "Jap – this is the real thing."

After the second wave of the attack, the officers sat down to breakfast. There was laughter among them and an unusual amount of talk.

Yamamoto did not share their high spirits. After the meal he called Shigeru Fujii to his side and said, "...the government says that it cut the time between handing over the final ultimatum and the launching of the attack to thirty minutes...From the cables that have come in so far, it looks as if the Attack Force has kept its side of the bargain. But there would be trouble if someone slipped up and people said it was a sneak attack...make a thorough check."

22

THE SOLEMN RECKONING

Responsible for firing the first American shot of the Pacific War, Outerbridge had received a request for "additional details" of his action at 7:37. At 7:55 the *Ward* was still at General Quarters. Outerbridge was on the bridge with his executive officer, Lieut. Comdr. Dowdy.

Looking toward Pearl Harbor, Dowdy said, "They are making a lot of noise over there this morning, Captain."

"Yes, I guess they are blasting the new road from Pearl to Honolulu."

"Look at those planes. They are coming straight down."

Outerbridge looked.

Dowdy added, "Gosh, they are having an attack over there."

Outerbridge replied, "They certainly are."

Tyler who had told Elliott and Lockard not to worry about the planes they saw approaching was still at the Fort Shafter Information Center when he heard the first explosions. He strolled outside. For a moment he watched planes coming down on Pearl Harbor in what appeared to be "Navy practice at Pearl." Then somewhat closer he heard a few bursts of antiaircraft fire.

He remained though his watch was over. A few minutes after eight he received a call: "There's an air attack at Wheeler Field."

This time Tyler knew what to do. He recalled the headset operators.

Elliott and Lockard, who had tried to alert Tyler, found the pickup truck arriving to take them to breakfast about the time they had lost the Japanese flight about 20 miles from the island in the "dead zone" caused by distortion from the back wave of the mountains.   They boarded the truck for the nine-mile ride to their camp at Kawailoa.

They left Opana at 7:45. On the way to Kawailoa they noticed all the men from their camp driving at top speed in the opposite direction – men fully equipped with field packs and helmets. But it was only after they arrived at their camp, about eight, that they learned that the Japanese had attacked.

About the time Ramsey had reported the American Naval plane dropping a bomb on a submarine off Pearl Harbor—7:30 A.M. in Hawaii, 1:00 P.M. in Washington – Knox returned to his office in the nation's capital following his conference with Hull and Stimson.   Stark and Turner joined him.

Breaking off their discussion, they walked out of Knox's office and entered that of his confidential assistant, John H. Dillon. As they stood by Dillon's desk a naval commander appeared at the door with the Pearl Harbor dispatch: WE ARE BEING ATTACKED. THIS IS NO DRILL.

Knox read the dispatch as incredulity and consternation spread over his features. "My God, this can't be true! This must mean the Philippines!"

Stark checked with CINCPAC, the office of origin. "No, sir," reported Stark, "This is Pearl."

It was necessary to report to the President.

At 1:47 P.M., when he received the phone call from Knox, Roosevelt was having lunch in his Oval Room study with Hopkins, talking "about things far removed from war..."

Like Knox, Hopkins was at first incredulous. There must be some mistake. Surely the Japanese would not attack Oahu.

Roosevelt recapitulated his efforts to keep the country

out of war and spoke of his unwavering desire to complete his administration without war. If the report were true the Japanese would have relieved him of making a decision contrary to his wishes.

He credited the report. It was just the kind of unexpected thing the Japanese would do — at the very time they had been discussing peace in the Pacific they had been plotting to dispel it.

At 2:05 Roosevelt phoned Hull, who was closeted with his legal adviser, Green H. Hackworth and Ballantine. Roosevelt said, "Cordell, Knox has just called with the report that the Japs have attacked Pearl Harbor."

Hull asked, "Has it been confirmed?" and added, "I'd like you to have it confirmed and call me back before I receive Nomura and Kurusu. They're outside in the waiting room."

Hackworth left at 2:20. Now convinced of the veracity of the attack report, Hull asked Ballantine to bring in the two ambassadors.

The Japanese bowed their way in. Okumura had finished his typing at 1:50. Waiting downstairs in the main hall of the Embassy, Nomura and Kurusu received the note from Yuki, climbed into their limousine and drove to the Old State Building. They reached the diplomatic waiting room as Roosevelt was phoning news of the attack to Hull.

Nomura presented the note, explaining that he had been instructed to deliver it at one o'clock sharp. He apologized that difficulties in decoding and transcribing had delayed him.

Hull replied that he was receiving the note at two o'clock.

He pretended to read the document and then said:

I must say that in all my conversations with you during the last nine months, I have never uttered one word of untruth. This is borne out absolutely

by the record. In all my 50 years of public
service, I have never seen a document that was more
crowded with infamous falsehoods and distortions on
a scale so huge that I never imagined until today
that any Government on this planet was capable of
uttering them.

Lifting his hand to cut off any protest from Nomura,
Hull nodded toward the door. The envoys walked out, heads
down, Nomura evidently under great emotional strain.

When Roosevelt phoned him, Stimson was having a late
lunch at Woodley.

"Have you heard the news?"

"Well," said Stimson, "I have heard the telegrams which
have been coming in about the Japanese advances in the Gulf
of Siam."

"Oh, no, I don't mean that. They have attacked Hawaii.
They are now bombing Hawaii."

Stimson expected the attack to end in a major victory
for America. He felt relieved that the indecision was over
and that a crisis had come that would unite America for the
coming struggle. At 2:28 Stimson phoned the President
confirming the attack.

Marshall learned of the attack at 2:30 when Col. John
R. Deane, secretary of the General Staff, phoned him at his
quarters.

In the White House, about 3 P.M., the President's
advisers gathered around him. Most of the information they
were receiving came from Stark in the Navy Department, his
voice revealing his "shocked unbelief." Grace Tully took
down the fragmentary and shocking reports in shorthand,
typed them up and relayed them to Roosevelt. As she
transcribed, Beardall, Rear Adm. Ross T. McIntire and
others anxiously read the script from over her shoulder.
The confusion and noise around the President proved so
distracting that she retired to use the phone in his

bedroom.

Roosevelt remained more calm than anyone else. But at each new message he tightened his lips and grimly shook his head revealing rage beneath his calmness.

He telephoned Joseph B. Poindexter, governor of Hawaii.

The 72-year-old Poindexter, a widower, had been a U.S. District Court judge in Honolulu. First appointed governor in 1934, he had been in office ever since. He lived with his daughter, Helen, in the gubernatorial mansion Washington Place on Beretania Street, across from Iolani Palace in which he had his office.

At 9:30 A.M., Hawaii time, an anti-aircraft shell had exploded near the driveway of his residence. Fragments had cut through the shrubbery and killed a pedestrian across the street. After he had gone to his office in Iolani Palace, an anti-aircraft shell burst in the corner of the grounds there.

Over radio station KGU, at 11:15 A.M, he proclaimed a state of emergency. His proclamation effected the M Day Act passed by a special session of the Territorial Legislature barely two months before the attack.

At 12:10 Short visited him and asked for martial law. Short feared the Japanese would attempt a landing the following morning aided by local saboteurs. Poindexter promised an answer in an hour and phoned Roosevelt. At 12.40 the call had come through.

Poindexter told Roosevelt the Japanese had attacked; about 50 civilians had been killed. Hawaii badly needed food and planes. Roosevelt replied that planes and a cargo of food had already been ordered. Poindexter reported that Short asked for martial law; Roosevelt approved the request. Poindexter said there was danger from the local Japanese.

Though Short was under great strain, Poindexter was calm. Poindexter signed the declaration of martial law. But after Short had left, Poindexter said of his signing that he had never in his life hated doing anything so much.

The police placed the Japanese Consulate under guard at noon.

With the declaration of martial law, Army Intelligence, aided by FBI and police, began arresting residents considered dangerous. Thirteen squads of officers shared cards already prepared with the names and addresses of Japanese suspects. Within three hours nearly every Oahu suspect had been picked up and placed in custody at the Immigration Station. They included 370 Japanese, 98 Germans and 14 Italians.

The courts were closed. A military judiciary was created to hear civilian cases.

Despite his later calmness, while talking to the President the governor had almost shrieked into the phone. To the men around him, Roosevelt said, 'My God, there's another wave of Japanese planes over Hawaii right this minute."

The defenders had continued to fire after the Japanese left, in some cases shooting at their own planes.

Hull arrived for a Cabinet meeting, his face "as white as his hair."

Roosevelt discussed troop and air force dispositions with Marshall. Marshall assured him he had ordered MacArthur to execute "all the necessary movement required in event of an outbreak of hostilities with Japan."

The President urged Hull to keep the South American republics informed and to maintain rapport with them. He directed Stimson and Knox to place guards around arsenals, munition factiories and bridges. He did not want a military guard around the White House.

After the Cabinet meeting the leaders of the Senate entered. Roosevelt gave the assembled legislators what information he had. They sat in dumbstruck silence. He began to outline how the Japanese attack began.

"In other words at dark last night, they might very

well have been four hundred or five hundred miles away from the Island and therefore out of what might be called a good patrol distance. Senator Thomas T. Connally had been listening in mounting rage.

Connally had wholeheartedly supported the administration's foreign policy. He had stated that the United States should maintain a "policy of resistance" to the conquest of the democracies by dictators. Becoming chairman of the Senate's Foreign Relations Committee in the summer of 1941, he had thereafter devoted most of his energies to supporting Roosevelt's war program. Now he boiled over.

"Hell's fire, didn't we do anything!"

"That's about it," said Roosevelt.

Connally turned on Knox. "Well, what did we do?"

Knox began to answer, but Connally interrupted. "Didn't you say last month that we could lick the Japs in two weeks? Didn't you say that our Navy was so well prepared and located that the Japanese couldn't hope to hurt us at all? When you made those public statements, weren't you just trying to tell the country what an efficient Secretary of the Navy you are?"

At 4 P.M. Hull was presiding over a conference at the State Department when a report came that Japan had declared war on the United States. In Tōkyō, where the report originated, Grew had received a phone call from Tōgō's secretary, Toshikazu Kase.

Kase said he had been trying to telephone ever since 5 A.M. but had been unable to get through to the Embassy.

Grew hurriedly dressed and set out, arriving at the official residence about 7:30. In formal dress, the Foreign Minister entered the reception room almost immediately. The manner of Tōgō was grim, but Grew had always found him to be sphinxlike so saw nothing unusual in the other's demeanor. In a gesture of finality, Tōgō slapped a document on the table.

Tōgō spoke in Japanese. Kase interpreted; he would later send the text in handwriting.

"His Majesty has expressed his gratefulness and appreciation for the cordial message of the President. He has graciously let known his wishes to the Foreign Minister to convey the following to the President as a reply to the latter's message:"

Some days ago, the President made inquiries regarding the circumstances of the augmentation of Japanese forces in French Indochina to which his Majesty had directed the Government to reply. Withdrawal of Japanese forces from French Indochina constitutes one of the subject matters of the Japanese-American negotiations. His Majesty has commanded the Government to state its views to the American Government also on this question. It is, therefore, desired that the President will kindly refer to this reply.

Establishment of the peace in the Pacific and consequently of the world has been the cherished desire of his Majesty for the realization of which he has hitherto made the Government to continue its earnest endeavors. His Majesty trusts that the President is fully aware of this fact.

Tōgō then said that the document he was about to hand to the ambassador, a memorandum of 13 pages in English, dated December 8, had been communicated by Adm. Nomura to Mr. Hull, breaking off the conversations. Tōgō said he had seen the Emperor and that the memorandum constituted the Emperor's reply to the President's message.

Grew asked if this disposition of the case meant that his request for an audience with the Emperor had been rejected. He pointed out that according to international usage the ambassador had access to the sovereign to whom he is accredited; when he requests it, the Japanese ambassador in Washington is frequently received by the President. The critical situation between Japan and America justified the granting of Grew's request for an audience.

Tōgō replied that he had neither desire nor intention to stand between the Throne and the American ambassador. He then made a little speech, thanking Grew for his cooperation during the conversations and for his efforts toward maintaining Japanese-American friendship.

As usual, he descended to the ground floor with Grew and saw him off at the door.

After returning to the Embassy, Grew learned of the outbreak of hostilities through a *Yomiuri* bulletin received there.

About 11 A.M. Ohno of the Foreign Office arrived at the Embassy and asked to see Eugene H. Dooman, counselor of the Embassy. Dooman was absent because the police had already closed the gate and denied him entrance. So instead Ohno saw First Secretary Edward S. Crocker.

Ohno took a document from his pocket and said, "I am instructed to hand to you, as representing the Embassy, the following document, which I shall first read to you."

He read in English as follows:

> **I have the honor to inform Your Excellency that there has arisen a state of war between Your Excellency's country and Japan beginning today.**
> **I avail myself of this opportunity to renew to Your Excellency the assurances of my highest consideration.**

Crocker said, "This is a very tragic moment."

"It is; and my duty is most distasteful."

Ohno then read an English translation of a statement concerning the Embassy and the suspension of its functions.

From that moment Grew and his staff were locked in the Embassy compound.

At 11:40 the rescript of the Emperor was read:

> We, by the grace of Heaven, Emperor of Japan, seated on the throne of a line unbroken for ages eternal, enjoin upon our loyal and brave subects: We hereby declare war on the United States of America and the British Empire...Eager for the realization of their inordinate ambition to dominate the Orient...both America and Britain...obstructed by every means our peaceful commerce and finally resorted to direct severance...The situation being such as it is, Our Empire for its existence and self-defense has no other recourse but to appeal to arms...

The Emperor had not written the above message, but is said to have asked that the following be included:

> Now, unfortunately, it has come – truly unavoidable and far from Our Wishes – that Our Empire has to cross swords with America and Britain.

Shortly afterwards Tōjō spoke on the radio. Echoing the general theme of the royal document, he claimed that Japan had done her best to prevent war. But Japan had not lost a war in the 2,600 years of its history. He proclaimed, "I promise you final victory."

Yamamoto was less sanguine. At 8:00 A.M., the commanders and chiefs of staff of the units remaining at Hashirajima assembled aboard the *Nagato* for an account of the situation and an assessment of results achieved.

Taken together, the reports so far received suggested that all the warshsips at anchor in Pearl Harbor had been put out of action. However, to allow for cases where the same damage had been sighted and reported by more than one plane, the staff officers reduced the numbers to what seemed a more probable figure.

Yamamoto advised them to take an even more conservative view. Accordingly they cut the figures by about 60 percent, considerably underestimating the actual damage wrought. Even so, the results were impressive.

Nevertheless, Yamamoto persisted in his gloom.

He said, "We have failed to destroy the American carriers, and the American broadcast says Japan attacked Pearl Harbor 55 minutes before delivering notification. The character of the American people being what it is, nothing can infuriate them more. I fear we have only awakened the sleeping giant and filled him with a terrible resolve."

In its recorded music program that day, NHK broadcast Beethoven's Fifth Symphony, interspersing it with repeated announcements proclaiming, "The Imperial Navy has finally gone into action."

When Winant had arrived at Chequers the afternoon of December 7, he found Churchill pacing up and down outside the entrance. Twenty minutes earlier his guests had gone in to lunch. Winant had come because he knew of the Japanese convoys proceeding toward the Isthmus of Kra. He knew the Japanese were on the road to war and he wanted to be with Churchill at this critical moment.

Since the defeat of France in June 1940, the British, almost alone, had held out against Germany. Now it had an ally in Russia, but the Germans were at the portals of Moscow; no one could foresee how successful might be the Russian counteroffensive launched the preceding day. With another formidable foe ready to attack the British in the Far East, the situation was indeed critical.

Churchill turned to Winant and asked if he thought there was going to be war with Japan.

"Yes."

With unusual vehemence, Churchill declared, "If they declare war on you, we shall declare war on them within the hour."

"I understand, Prime Minister. You have stated that publicly."

"If they declare on us, will you declare on them?"

"I can't answer that, Prime Minister. Only the Congress has the right to declare war under the United States Constitution."

They went to lunch together. Most of the guests left early. Those who remained spent a quiet afternoon.

In the evening, a few minutes before nine, they went into the dining room. Being unwell, Mrs. Churchill did not come down to dinner. Guests included Harriman; Harriman's daughter, Kathleen; Pamela Churchill, Maj. Gen. Sir Hastings Ismay, chief of staff to the Minister of Defense; Comdr. C.R. Thompson and Churchill's principal private secretary, John Martin.

Looking grim, Churchill sat in complete silence, sometimes with his head in his hands. It was his custom to listen to the nine o'clock broadcast, which usually gave the fullest summary of the day's news. Just before the hour struck, Churchill roused himself and called out to Sawyers, the butler, to put the radio on the table.

The radio was a small $15.00 portable Hopkins had sent after returning to the United States. Churchill turned it on by raising the lid.

There came forth a jangle of music, then news of a tank battle in Libya in which the British forces had not done well. The announcer read the headlines and then began a more detailed summary of the day's happenings.

> The news has just been given that Japanese aircraft have raided Pearl Harbor, the American naval base in Hawaii. The announcement of the attack was made

**in a brief statement by Pres. Roosevelt. Naval and
military targets on the principal Hawaiian island
of Oahu have been attacked. No further details are
yet available.**

Those present stared at each other in amazement.
Churchill jumped to his feet and started toward the door.
"We shall declare war on Japan."

Following him, Winant protested, "Good God, you can't
declare war on a radio announcement."

Churchill halted and stared at Winant. "What shall I
do?"

"I will call up the President by telephone and ask him
what the facts are."

Churchill nodded, "And I shall talk to him too."

At that moment, Martin appeared at the door and said
excitedly that the Admiralty was on the phone for the Prime
Minister. Winant and Harriman followed Churchill into his
office. The Admiralty confirmed that Pearl Harbor had been
attacked.

In a few minutes Winant had Roosevelt on the line.
Roosevelt confirmed the report. Winant said he had a
friend with him who wanted to speak to the President.

Winant added, "You will know him as soon as you hear
his voice."

"Mr. President," said Churchill, "what's this about
Japan?"

Still in conference with his war cabinet, Roosevelt
said, "It's quite true. They have attacked us at Pearl
Harbor. We are all in the same boat now."

Then, according to Churchill, those at Chequers
returned to the dining room "and tried to adjust our
thoughts to the supreme world event which had occurred,
which was of so startling a nature as to make even those
who were near the centre gasp."

Parliament would not have met until Tuesday. But

Churchill was so intent on making good his promise to declare war within the hour that he put his office to phoning members scattered about the island so that he might convoke Parliament the next day. He took this action even though it would be only later that night that he would receive the report that the Japanese had also attacked the British in Malaya.

He also thought of Chiang Kai-shek who had been appealing to him for aid on the ground that if Japan could crack Chinese resistance it would attack Great Britain. Chiang had written to him, "If the Japanese can break our front here we shall be cut off from you, and the whole structure of your own air and naval coordination with America and the Netherlands East Indies will be gravely threatened in new ways and from a new direction."

Now Churchill wired Chiang:

The British Empire and the United States have been attacked by Japan. Always we have been good friends; now we face a common enemy.

Like the Americans, Churchill underestimated the military prowess of the Japanese. The initial response to the attack at the United States State Department had been that the Japanese had been exceedingly stupid to attack Hawaii. But when the damage they had wrought began to become evident, there was less talk of the Japanese being stupid.

But Churchill was unpossessed of this information when he formed his opinion after the phone call to Washington. From the point of view of Churchill, the attack on Pearl Harbor was an act of madness through which the Japanese courted destruction.

Churchill believed that the British Empire and the Soviet Union with the United States possessed two or three times the force of their opponents. He "went to bed and slept the sleep of the saved and thankful."

Night had fallen in Berlin when the foreign-broadcast monitoring service first picked up the news of the sneak attack on Pearl Harbor. When an official of the Foreign Office Press Department telephoned the news to Ribbentrop he refused to believe it and was angry at having been disturbed. He said the report was "probably a propaganda trick of the enemy." He ordered that he be left undisturbed until morning.

Finally persuaded of the truth of the report, Ribbentrop, at 9:10 P.M., phoned Ciano in Rome. Ribbentrop was joyful over the news, so happy that Ciano felt constrained to congratulate him. When Ciano informed Mussolini, Mussolini was also happy.

Ciano, however, was unsure the development was to the advantage of the Axis. From his point of view it would prolong the war, enabling the United States to bring its great productive power into full effect.

Hitler was at his military headquarters, the Wolf's Lair, trying to cope with the major offensive the Russians had launched against the German troops beleaguering Moscow. Receiving the news of the Pearl Harbor attack, he slapped his thighs in delight.

Crying, "The turning point!" he raced from his bunker and through the icy darkness to break the news to Field Marshal William Keitel and Gen. Alfred Jodl.

There a disconcerting thought assailed him. "How strange that with Japan's aid we are destroying the positions of the white race in the Far East – and that Britain is fighting in Europe with those swine the Bolsheviks."

The head Bolshevik, Josef Stalin, must have been relieved that the attack against America rendered unlikely an assault by Japan against Russia. He would have been happier yet at the prospect of his major enemy, Hitler, making common cause with Japan and so bringing the United

States into the war as an ally of Russia.

Back in Hawaii many of the residents had observed the attack from the hills of Honolulu and similar vantage points. A hint of the repercussion the attack was to have on the islands had come when Poindexter invoked the powers conferred on him by the Hawaii Defense Act.

At 2:58 P.M. Maj. Robert J. Fleming handed the decoded message of Marshall to Short. It read:

The Japanese are presenting at 1 p.m. Eastern Standard Time today what amounts to an ultimatum. Also they are under orders to destroy their code machines immediately. Just what significance the hour set may have we do not know, but be on the alert accordingly.

Enraged, Short threw the message into a wastebasket.

When an Army courier delivered a copy of Marshall's message to Kimmel, Kimmel told him the message was no longer of the slightest interest. He threw it into a wastebasket.

Roosevelt had dinner in his study with his son, James, Grace Tully and Hopkins, with Hopkins looking "like a walking cadaver, just skin and bones." The President neither talked about Pearl Harbor nor complained about the situation.

At 10:30 he gathered his official family about him in the Oval Room, with Hopkins the only non-Cabinet member present. Roosevelt sat at his desk while the others formed a ring around him. He briefed them on developments and read the draft of the address he planned to deliver to Congress the next day.

Waiters brought in beer and sandwiches. At 12:30 Roosevelt said he was going to bed and dismissed the others.

So fell the curtain on that memorable day, with the

tragi-comedy of the luckless submariner, Kazuo Sakamaki,
still to be played out.

*Hawaii Gov. Joseph B. Poindexter.   He had never hated
anything so much as surrendering civil law to martial.*

23

ALL THE WORLD AT WAR

The defenders had destroyed most of the Japanese midget submarines; none had damaged the defenders. One midget that escaped damage was that of the ill-fated Ensign Kazuo Sakamaki.

Sakamaki's vessel, with the broken gyrocompass, almost sank when launched. By desperate maneuvering he and Inagaki managed to keep it from passing below its maximum depth of 100 feet. He tried to steer toward the lights of Oahu by navigating through his 6-foot fixed periscope. The *Ward* picked up the submarine by sonar and dropped five depth charges on it.

The depth charges failed to destroy the submarine, but Sakamaki fell, bumped his head, lost consciousness and ran his vessel on a reef. The accident damaged one torpedo but failed to explode it. Sakamaki backed the submarine off the reef, but possibly dazed by the noxious fumes from the submarine's batteries ran aground again.

Again he broke free, but the pounding from the depth charges and repeated groundings had damaged both the steering and torpedo-firing mechanisms. He and Inagaki succumbed to battery fumes and the submarine drifted out to sea.

When they regained consciousness they saw an island. Sakamaki thought it was distant Lanai; in truth it was Rabbit Island, close to the southeastern shore of Oahu.

Again the submarine ran up on a reef. To prevent the "secret weapon" from falling into American hands the two set its self-destruct mechanism and jumped into the water for the mile swim to the beach. The utter futility of their mission culminated in the failure to detonate of the charge they had set to destroy the submarine.

Between five and six o'clock the morning after the Pearl Harbor attack, Cpl. David Akui, born in Hawaii, was stationed at Waimanalo Beach building a defensive machine-gun emplacement along the northeast shore of Bellows Field. He saw an object bobbing up and down in the ocean. At first he thought it was a turtle, but when a large wave broke over it he clearly saw the arms and head of a man.

Akui grabbed his rifle and captured the unconscious Sakamaki as he floated ashore. Inagaki was later found dead in the surf.

But at the cost of this one prisoner, the midget submarines and 29 planes, the Japanese had sunk or seriously damaged 18 ships. They had plundered the Americans of the battleships *Arizona*, *Oklahoma* and *Utah* and the destroyers *Cassin* and *Downes*. They had sunk or caused to be beached the battleships *West Virginia*, *California* and *Nevada* and the minelayer *Oglala*. They had damaged the battleships *Tennessee*, *Maryland* and *Pennsylvania*; the cruisers *Helena*, *Honolulu* and *Raleigh*; the destroyer *Shaw*, the seaplane tender *Curtiss* and the repair ship *Vestal*.

They had destroyed 188 planes and damaged 159, killed 2,403 American military personnel and wounded 1,113. To this toll was added the damage the defenders inflicted on themselves as a result of the attack – shooting down planes from the American carrier *Enterprise* as they came in to land as well as B–17s from the anticipated flight from the mainland. The defenders were responsible for most of the 68 civilians killed and 35 wounded – most by antiaircraft shells with unset fuses that exploded on impact with the ground in nearby Honolulu; and for local fishermen machine-gunned by trigger-happy American fliers who, the morning after the attack, mistook the fishermen for invaders.

Of the 40 or so shells that had fallen on Honolulu only one was Japanese and that apparently fell there by accident. It fell in the middle of a deserted downtown street, causing some property damage but injuring no one.

Churchill, of course, was still ignorant of this debacle when he awoke December 8 to take action against Japan.

Under the British Constitution the Crown declares war on the advice of Minister; Parliament is confronted with the decision. Churchill was consequently able to more than keep his word to the United States. Great Britain declared war upon Japan before the American Congress could act. The Royal Netherlands Government likewise speedily declared war on Japan.

Having received the authorization of the War Cabinet for the immediate declaration of war on Japan, Churchill so informed the Japanese ambassador by the following message:

Sir:

On the evening of December 7th His Majesty's Government in the United Kingdom learned that Japanese forces without previous warning either in the form of a declaration of war or of an ultimatum with a conditional declaration of war had attempted a landing on the coast of Malaya and bombed Singapore and Hong Kong.

In view of these wanton acts of unprovoked aggression committed in flagrant violation of International Law and particularly of Article 1 of the Third Hague Convention relative to the opening of hostilities, to which both Japan and the United Kingdom are parties, His Majesty's Ambassador at Tokyo has been instructed to inform the Imperial Japanese Government in the name of His Majesty's Government in the United Kingdom that a state of war exists between our two countries.

I have the honour to be, with high consideration,

Sir,

Your obedient servant,

Winston S. Churchill

In his history of the war, Churchill adds: "Some people did not like this ceremonial style. But after all when you have to kill a man it costs nothing to be polite."

Parliament met at 3 P.M. Despite the shortness of the notice he had given, the House was full. He addressed the House:

> It is of the highest importance that there should be no underrating of the gravity of the new dangers we have to meet, either here or in the United States. The enemy has attacked with an audacity which may spring from recklessness but which may also spring from a conviction of strength. The ordeal to which the English-speaking world and our heroic Russian Allies are being exposed will certainly be hard, especially at the outset, and will probably be long, yet, when we look around us over the sombre panorama of the world, we have no reason to doubt the justice of our cause or that our strength and will-power will be sufficient to sustain it.

> We have at least four-fifths of the population of the globe upon our side. We are responsible for their safety and for their future. In the past we have had a light which flickered, in the present we have a light which flames, and in the future there will be a light which shines over all the land and sea.

Both Houses unanimously voted for the declaration of war.

Roosevelt had asked that Mrs. Woodrow Wilson accompany Mrs. Roosevelt to the joint session of Congress he was scheduled to address on the morning of December 8. So when he was wheeled in she was there, elegantly dressed, her hands in white gloves, beside the wife of the President who most resembled and most admired her husband.

Roosevelt began to speak:

Yesterday, Dec. 7, 1941 — a date which will live in infamy — the United States of America was suddenly and deliberately attacked by the naval and air forces of the empire of Japan...

The attack yesterday on the Hawaiian Islands has caused severe damage to American naval and military forces. Very many American lives have been lost. In addition American ships have been reported torpedoed on the high seas between San Francisco and Honolulu.

Yesterday the Japanese Government also launched an attack against Malaya.

Last night Japanese forces attacked Hong Kong.

Last night Japanese forces attacked Guam.

Last night Japanese forces attacked the Philippine Islands.

Last night the Japanese attacked Wake Island.

This morning the Japanese attacked Midway Island.

Japan has, therefore, undertaken a surprise offensive extending throughout the Pacific area. The facts of yesterday speak for themselves. The

President Franklin D. Roosevelt asks Congress to declare war on Japan.

people of the United States have already formed
their opinions and well understand the implication
to the very life and safety of our Nation...
Hostilities exist. There is no blinking at the
fact that our people, our territory and our
interests are in grave danger.

He concluded by asking Congress to declare that "since
the unprovoked and dastardly attack" a state of war "has
existed between the United States and the Japanese Empire."
Though interrupted by frequent bursts of applause, the
speech had lasted only six-and-a-half minutes.There was no
debate such as had occurred between April 2 and April 6,
1917 when President Wilson had asked for a declaration of
war against Germany. Within 33 minutes after the President
finished speaking Congress brought in its verdict. The
Senate approved the declaration 82 to 0; the House 388 to
1.
The lone dissenting vote was cast by Miss Jeannette
Rankin of Montana, who in 1917 had also voted against war.
Whereas in 1917 she had had supporters, now her nay vote
was greeted with boos and hisses.
Though some advisers had urged him to do so, Roosevelt
had mentioned neither Germany nor Italy in his address.
But he spoke of them in detail in his fireside chat to the
nation the evening after Congress declared war on Japan.
He declared:

...the sudden criminal attacks perpetrated by the
Japanese...provide the climax of a decade of
international immorality...Powerful and resourceful
gangsters have banded together to make war upon the
whole human race.

The United States was fighting alongside "other free
peoples...to maintain our right to live among our world

neighbors in freedom and common decency, without fear of assault." ...The course Japan had begun in Manchuria in 1931 now "parallelled the course of Hitler and Mussolini in Europe and in Africa."

Roosevelt included in his indictment attacks "without warning" in Europe and North Africa by Hitler and Mussolini. Hitler's victims included 14 countries, beginning with his occupation of Austria in 1938 and continuing through the invasion of Russia in June 1941. The international "gangsters" were involved in conquests "all of one pattern."

During these later years the United States had built up the American war production machinery so that it could be used to help defend any nation "resisting Hitler or Japan..." There was no "security" for any country or person" in a world ruled by the principles of gangsterism." War "conducted in the Nazi manner is a dirty business."

In conclusion, Roosevelt said that "Germany and Italy, regardless of any formal declaration of war, consider themselves at war with the United States at this moment just as much as they consider themselves at war with Britain or Russia." The United States would be ill-served if she eliminated a dangerous Japan and "found that the rest of the world was dominated by Hitler and Mussolini."

The speech came close to an unofficial declaration of war on Germany and Italy. Roosevelt hoped they would declare war on America and thus relieve him of the onus of the request.

Such a course was urged by the Japanese Ambassador to Berlin, Gen. Hiroshi Ōshima even before the attack on Pearl Harbor and likewise by the Japanese ambassador to Rome. Ōshima met with Ribbentrop at one o'clock the day after the Pearl Harbor attack and urged him to have Germany and Italy immediately issue formal declarations of war on America. Ribbentrop told him that Hitler was in the midst of a conference at General Headquarters (the Wolf's Lair in

East Prussia) discussing how the formalities of declaring war could be carried out so as to make a good impression on the German people. Ribbentrop would communicate the wish of the Japanese to Hitler and do what he could to have it carried out properly.

Ribbentrop also informed Ōshima that on that very morning Hitler had issued orders to the German Navy to attack American ships whenever and wherever it might meet them.

That evening Hitler set out for Berlin. He arrived there at 11 o'clock on the morning of December 9. Ribbentrop informed him that since Japan was obviously the aggressor Germany need not declare war on America under the Tripartite Pact.

Hitler said, "If we don't stand on the side of Japan, the Pact is politically dead. But that is not the main reason.

"The chief reason is that the United States already is shooting against our ships. They have been a forceful factor in this war and through their actions have already created a situation of war."

Hitler also said that the United States would now make war on Germany. From Hitler's point of view, German prestige required Germany to beat America to a declaration of war. So he ordered the German charge d'affaires in Washington to present the text of a note from Berlin to the State Department on Dec. 11, 1941 at 3:30 P.M., German time, which would be 9:30 A.M. Washington time. The note summed up Germany's reasons for a declaration of war, ending with the charge that America, starting with violations of neutrality, had "finally proceeded to open acts of war against Germany. It has thereby virtually created a state of war."

At the time of the delivery of the note, Hitler went before the German Reichstag in the Kroll Opera House, Berlin, to air his grievances in greater detail. In the meantime he had had opportunity to judge the caliber of his new military ally and the judgment was favorable.

Not only had the Japanese inflicted a disgraceful defeat on the Americans at Pearl Harbor, they were carrying everything before them. December 8, according to the Western calendar, they had destroyed 100 enemy aircraft in the Philippines. December 10 they had landed in the N. Philippines and captured the American island of Guam and the British islands of Tarawa and Makin, besides sinking the British battleship *Prince of Wales*, on which Roosevelt had met with Churchill, and the British cruiser *Repulse*.

Never in the history of warfare had there been so perfectly timed and coordinated an assault as that the Japanese had launched in Southeast Asia and the Pacific.

Hitler was a vengeful man, and now he had reason to feel a measure of confidence as he vented his resentment against the man, Roosevelt, who had taunted him, frustrated him and provided massive aid to Great Britain when it had appeared that without that aid the United Kingdom would have fallen. Hitler said:

> **Permit me to define my attitude to that other world which has its representative in that man who, while our soldiers are fighting in snow and ice, very tactfully likes to make his chats from the fireside, the man who is the main culprit of this war...**
>
> **I will pass over the insulting attacks made by this so-called President against me. That he calls me a gangster is uninteresting. After all, this expression was not coined in Europe but in America, no doubt because such gangsters are lacking here. Apart from this, I cannot be insulted by Roosevelt, for I consider him mad, just as Wilson was...First he incites war, then falsifies the causes, then odiously wraps himself in a cloak of Christian**

hypocrisy and slowly but surely leads mankind to
war, not without calling God to witness the honesty
of his attack – in the approved manner of an old
Freemason...

Roosevelt has been guilty of a series of the
worst crimes against international law. Illegal
seizure of ships and other property of German and
Italian nationals was coupled with the threat to,
and looting of, those who were deprived of their
liberty by being interned. Roosevelt's ever
increasing attacks finally went so far that he
ordered the American Navy to attack everywhere
ships under the German and Italian flags, and to
sink them – this in gross violation of
international law. American ministers boasted of
having destroyed German submarines in this criminal
way. German and Italian merchant ships were
attacked by American cruisers, captured and their
crews imprisoned.

In this way the sincere efforts of Germany and
Italy to prevent an extension of the war and to
maintain relations with the United States in spite
of the unbearable provocations which have been
carried on for years by President Roosevelt have
been frustrated... National Socialism came to
power in Germany in the same year Roosevelt was
elected President...He took over a state in very
poor economic condition, and I took over the Reich
faced with complete ruin, thanks to democracy...
While an unprecedented revival of economic life,
culture and art took place in Germany under
National Socialist leadership, President Roosevelt
did not succeed in bringing about even the
slightest improvement in his own country...This is
not surprising if one bears in mind that the men he
had called to support him, or rather, the men who

had called him, belonged to the Jewish element, whose interests are all for disintegration and never for order...He guessed that the only salvation for him lay in diverting public attention from home to foreign policy...He was strengthened in this by the Jews around him...

Thus began the increasing efforts of the American President to create conflicts...For years this man harbored one desire – that a conflict should break out somewhere in the world

Hitler recited what he identified as Roosevelt's efforts in bringing about the desired conflict, beginning with the Quarantine Speech Roosevelt had made in Chicago in 1937.

Now he is seized with fear that if peace is brought about in Europe his squandering of millions of money on armaments will be looked upon as plain fraud, since nobody will attack America – and then he himself must provoke this attack upon his country.

I think you have all found it a relief now that, at last, one State has been the first to take the step of protesting against this historically unique and shameless ill-treatment of truth and of right...The fact that the Japanese Government, which has been negotiating for years with this man, has at last become tired of being mocked by him in such an unworthy way fills us all, the German people and, I think, all other decent people in the world, with deep satisfaction...The President of the United States ought finally to understand – I say this only because of his limited intellect– that we know that the aim of his struggle is to destroy one state after another...

As for the German nation, it needs charity
neither from Mr. Roosevelt nor from Mr. Churchill,
let alone from Mr. Eden. It wants only its rights!
It will secure for itself this right to live even
if thousands of Churchills and Roosevelts conspire
against it...
I have therefore arranged for passports to be
handed to the American charge d'affaires today, and
the following —

At this point the Hitler's words were drowned by the
deputies of the Reichstag leaping to their feet and
cheering.

Shortly afterward, at 2:30 P.M., Ribbentrop received
Leland Morris, the American charge d'affaires in Berlin,
read out to him the German declaration of war and curtly
dismissed him.

The same day in Berlin Germany, Italy and Japan signed
a tripartite agreement declaring "their unshakable
determination not to lay down arms until the joint war
against the United States and England reaches a successful
conclusion" and not to conclude a separate peace.

The same day, from his balcony on the Palazzo Venezia,
Mussolini spoke on "this day of solemn decision in the
history of Italy" that was now united with "heroic Japan."
He told the cheering hundreds in the plaza below him that
the successful assault in the Pacific had demonstrated the
spirit of the soldiers of the Rising Sun. It was "a
privilege to fight alongside them."

The Axis having thus neatly relieved him of the
responsibility of first declaring war, Roosevelt, the same
day, gained a declaration of war against Germany and Italy
without a dissenting vote in either chamber. This time
Rep. Rankin voted "present."

Canada and Costa Rica had declared war on Japan
December 7. December 8, China, which had been waging war

against Japan without a formal declaration, now formally declared war on Germany, Italy and Japan.   The same day the Free French declared war on Japan, as did Honduras, San Salvador, Guatemala, Haiti and the Dominican Republic. December 9, Cuba and Nicaragua declared war on Japan. December 11, Cuba, Costa Rica, Nicaragua, Guatemala and the Dominican Republic declared war on Germany and Italy.

So now the whole world was engaged in war — war more destructive and hideous than any mankind had ever experienced.

Principal Characters

Beardall, Capt. John R.
Naval aide to President
Roosevelt

Bratton, Col. Rufus S.
Chief, Far East Section, G-2

Chamberlain (Arthur) Neville
British prime minister 1937-
1940

Churchill, Winston
British prime minister from
May 1940

Elliott, Pvt. George E.
Radar Station Operator

Fuchida, Comdr. Mitsuo
(fōō chē' dä mē tsōō' ō)
Leader, air attack on Pearl
Harbor

Genda, Comdr. Minoru
(gen' dä mē nō ' lōō)
Air staff officer,
Japanese First Air Fleet

Grew, Joseph C.
U.S. ambassador to Japan

Harriman, (William) Averell
Roosevelt's special envoy to
Britain

Hirohito (hē lō hē' tō)
Emporer of Japan

Hitler, Adolf
German dictator

Honma, Lieut. Gen Masaru
(hōn' mä mä sä' lōō)
Commander Japanese 14th
Army

Hopkins, Harry Lloyd
Advisor to President Roosevelt

Hull, Cordell
Secretary of State

Kimmel, Adm. Husband E.
Commander in Chief,
U.S Pacific Fleet

Knox, W. Frank
Secretary of the Navy

Konoye, Prince Fumimaro
(kō nō' yä fōō mē mä' lō)
Prime Minister of Japan, July
1940-October 1941

Kramer, Lieut. Comdr. Alvin D.
On loan from Far Eastern
Section, ONI, to Translation
Section, Communications
Division, Navy Department

Kurusu, Saburo
(kōō lōō' sōō sä bōō' lō)
Special Japanese envoy to
Washington

Layton, Lieut. Comdr. Edwin T.
Intelligence officer, Pacific Fleet

Lockard, Pvt. Joseph L.
Radar Station operator

Marshall, Gen. George C.
Chief of Staff, U.S. Army

Matsuoka, Yosuke
(mä tsōō ō' kä yō sōō' kä)
Japanese Foreign Minister
July 1940-July 1941

Miyo, Comdr. Tatsukichi
(mē' yō tä tsōō kē' chǐ)
Member, Operations Section,
First Bureau, Japanese General
Staff

Mussolini, Benito
Italian dictator

Nagano, Adm. Osami
(nä gä' nō ō sä' mē)
Chief, Japanese Naval General
Staff

Nagumo, Vice Adm. Chuichi
(nä gōō' mō chōō ē' chǐ)
Commander in Chief, Japanese
First Air Fleet

Nomura, Adm. Kichisaburo
(nō mōō' lä kē chē sä' bōō lō)
Japanese Ambassador to the
United States

Onishi, Rear Adm, Takijiro
(ō' nē shē tä kē jē' lō)
Chief of Staff, Japanese 11th Air
Fleet.

Outerbridge, Lieut. William W.
Captain, Ward

Poindexter, Joseph R.

Governor of Hawaii
Ribbentrop, Joachim von
  German foreign minister
Richardson, Adm. James O.
  Commander in Chief,
  U.S. Fleet 1940
Roosevelt, Franklin D.
  President of the United States
Schulz, Lieut. Lester Robert
  Assistant to Capt. Beardall
Short, Lieut. Gen. Walter C.
  Commanding general,
  Hawaiian Department
Stalin, Joseph
  Soviet dictator and supreme
  commander
Stark, Adm. Harold R.
  Chief of Naval Operations (CNO)
Stimson, Henry R.
  Secretary of War
Sugiyama Gen. Gen
  (sōō gē yä' mä gen)
  Commander 1st Imperial Army,
  also of home Defense Army and
  Army Chief of Staff
Terauchi, Gen. Count Hisaichi
  (tä lä ōō' chē hē sä ē' chē)
  Commander in Chief, Japanese
  Southern Army
Tōgō, Shigenori
  (tō' gō shē gä nō' rē)
  Foreign minister, Tōjō Cabinet
Tōjō, Gen. Hideki
  (tō' jō hē dä' kē)
  War minister, Konoye Cabinet;
  Prime minister, Oct. 18, 1941
Toyoda, Vice Adm. Teijiro
  (tō yō' dä tä ē jē' lō)
  Foreign minister, third Konoye
  Cabinet
Tyler, Lieut. Kermit
  Pursuit officer, Fort Shafter
  Information Center
Ugaki, Rear Adm. Matome
  (ōō gä' kē mä tō' mä)

Chief of Staff,
Japanese Combined Fleet, from
Aug. 10, 1941
Welles, Sumner
  Undersecretary of State
Wilson, Woodrow
  President of the United States,
  1913-1921
Winant, John Gilbert
  U.S. Ambassador to Great
  Britain
Yamamoto, Adm. Isoroku
  (yä mä mō' tō ē sō lō' kōō)
  Commander in Chief, Japanese
  Combined Fleet
Yamashita, Lieut. Gen. Tomoyuki
  (yä mä shē' tä tō mō yōō' kē)
  Commander in Chief,
  Japanese 25th Army

BIBLIOGRAPHY

Allen, Gwenfread, *Hawaii's War Years*, University of Hawaii
Press, 1950
Allen, Louis, *Singapore 1941-1942: The Politics and Strategy of
the Second World War*, Univ. of Delaware Press, 1977
Adams, Henry H., *Harry Hopkins: A Biography*, G. P. Putnams'
Sons, 1977
Agawa, Hiroyuki,*The Reluctant Admiral: Yamamoto and the
Imperial Navy*, Kodansha International, 1982
Ashley, Maurice, *Churchill As Historian*, Charles Scribner's
Sons, 1968
Bailey, Thomas A., *Woodrow Wilson and the Great Betrayal*,
Quadrangle, 1945
Bliven, Bruce, *The World Changers*, John Day Co., 1965
Blond, Georges, *Admiral Togo*, Macmillan, 1960
Blum, John Morton, *Woodrow Wilson and the Politics of Moral-
ity*, Little, Brown, 1956
Blum, John Morton, *Roosevelt and Morganthau*, Houghton
Mifflin, 1970
Brackman, Arnold C. *The Last Emperor*, Scribners, 1975
Broad, Lewis, *Winston Churchill: The Years of Achievement*,
Hawthorn Book, 1963
Browne, Courtney, *Tojo: The Last Banzai*, Rinehart and Win-
ston, 1967
Busch, Noel F., *The Emperor's Sword: Japan versus Russia in
the Battle of Tsushima*, Funk & Wagnalls, 1969
Bailey, Thomas A. and Paul B. Ryan, *Hitler versus Roosevelt:
The Undeclared Naval War*, The Free Press, 1979
Baker. Leonard, *Roosevelt and Pearl Harbor*, Macmillan, 1970
Baldwin, Hanson W., *Crucial Years: 1939-1941*, Harper & Row,
1976
Barker, A. J., *Pearl Harbor*, Ballantine, 1969
Bartlett, Bruce R., *Cover-up: The Politics of Pearl Harbor, 1941-
1946*, Arlington House, 1978
Bendiner, Elmer, *A Time for Angels*, Knopf, 1975
Borg, Dorothy and Shumpei Okamoto, *Pearl Harbor as History*,
Columbia University Press, 1973
Butow, R. J. C., *The John Doe Associates*, Stanford University
Press, 1974
Cadogan, Sir Alexander, *Diaries of Sir Alexander Cadogan,
1938-1945*, G.P. Putnam's Sons, 1971
Caffrey, Kate, *Out in the Midday Sun: Singapore 1941-1945*,
Stein and Day, 1973
Calvocoressi, Peter and Guy Wint, *Total War: the Major New
History of WW II (two volumes)*, Ballantine, 1973
Carter, Violet Bonham, *Winston Churchill: An Intimate Portrait*,
Harcourt, Brace and World, 1965
Cassels, Lavender, *The Archduke and the Assassin: Sarajevo,
June 28th 1914*, Dorset Press, 1984
Close, Upton, *Behind the Face of Japan*, D. Appleton-Century,

1942

Coffey, Thomas M. *Imperial Tragedy: Japan's Experience of War*, World Publishing, 1970

Costello, John, *The Pacific War, 1939-1945*, Quill, 1981

Churchill, Winston S. *Second World War, (first three of six volumes)*, Houghton Mifflin, 1948

Clark, Blake, *Remember Pearl Harbor*, Modern Age Books, 1942

Clark, Ronald, *The Man Who Broke Purple: The Life of Col.William F. Friedman*, Little, Brown and Co.,1977

Collier, Richard, *1940: The Avalance*, Dial Press,1979

Collier, Richard, *Duce! A Biography of Benito Mussolini*, Viking Press, 1971

Collier, Richard, *The Road to Pearl Harbor: 1941*, Atheneum, 1981

Colvin, Ian, *The Chamberlain Cabinet*, Taplinger, 1971

Cohen, Stan, *East Wind Rain*, Pictorial Histories Pub. Co., 1981

Congdon, Don, editor, *Combat WW II: Pacific Theater of Operations*, Arbor House, 1958

Coolidge, Olivia, *Winston Churchill and the Story of Two World Wars*, Houghton Mifflin, 1960

Coox, Alvin D., *Tojo*, Ballantine, 1975

Country Beautiful Editors, *A Man of Destiny: Winston S. Churchill*, Country Beautiful Foundation, 1965

Davis, Kenneth S., *FDR: The Beckoning of Destiny, 1882-1928*, G.P. Putnam's Sons, 1971

DeGaulle, Charles, *War Memoirs: The Call to Honour, 1940-1942*, Viking Press, 1955

Downing, David, *The Devil's Virtuosos: German Generals at War 1940-5*, St. Martin's Press, 1977

Esposito, Brig. Gen. Vincent J., *Concise History of World War II*, Frederick A. Praeger, 1964

Farago, Ladislas, *The Broken Seal: The Story of "Operation Magic"*, Random House, 1967

Feis, Herbert, *Road to Pearl Harbor*, Atheneum, 1950

Fellowes-Gordon, Ian, *he Magic War: The Battle for North Burma*, Charles Scribner's Sons, 1971

Fertig, Howard, *Germany and Japan: A Study in Totalitarian Diplomacy 1933-1941*, Martinus Nijhoff, 1958

Fleming, Kate, *The Churchills*, Viking Press, 1975

Freud, Sigmund and William C. Bullitt, *Thomas Woodrow Wilson: A Psychological Study*, Houghton Mifflin, 1967

Goebbels, Joseph, *Goebbels Diaries: 1939-1941*, Penguin, 1982

Graves, Eleanor and David E. Scherman, *Life Goes to War: A Picture History of World War II*, Simon & Schuster, 1981

Graff, Robert D. and Robert Emmett Ginna; text by Roger Butterfield, *FDR*, Harper & Row, 1962

Greene, Theodore P. *Wilson at Versailles*, D.C. Heath and Co., 1957

Greer, Thomas H., *What Roosevelt Thought: The Social and Political Ideas of Franklin D. Roosevelt*, Michigan State

University Press, 1958

Grew, Joseph C. *Ten Years in Japan*, Simon & Schuster, 1944

Guillain, Robert, *I saw Tokyo Burning: An Eyewitness Narrative from Pearl Harbor to Hiroshima*, Doubleday, 1981

Hara, Capt. Tameichi, etc. *Japanese Destroyer Captain*, Ballentine, 1961

Harriman, W. Averell and Elie Abel, *Special Envoy to Churchill and Stalin, 1941-1946*, Random House, 1975

Hart, B.H. Liddell, *The German Generals Talk*, Morrow Quill, 1979

Heiber, Helmut, *Goebbels*, Hawthorn Books, 1972

Hitler, Adolf, *Mein Kampf*, Houghton Mifflin, 1971

Holmes, W. J. *Double-Edged Secrets: U.S. Naval Intelligence Operations in the Pacific during WW II*, Naval Institute Press, 1979

Humble, Richard, *Japanese High Seas Fleet*, Ballantine, 1973

Humble, Richard, *United States Fleet Carriers of WW II in Action*, Blandford Press, 1984

Ickes, Harold L., *The Secret Diary of Harold L. Ickes: The Lowering Clouds 1939-1941*, Simon and Schuster, 1954

Ienaga, Saburo, *Pacific War: 1931-1945*, Pantheon Books, 1978

Ike, Nobutake, *Japan's Decision for War: Records of the 1941 Policy Conferences*, Stanford University Press, 1967

Jansen, Marius B., *Japan and China: From War to Peace, 1894-1972*, Princeton University, 1975

Johnson, David, *The London Blitz: The City Ablaze Dec. 29, 1940*, Stein and Day, 1981

Kanroji, Osanaga, *Hirohito: An Intimate Portrait*, Gateway Publishers, 1975

Kennedy, Capt. Malcolm D., *The Estrangement of Great Britain and Japan, 1917-35*, Univ. of California Press, 1969

Kimmel, Husband E. *Admiral Kimmel's Story*, Henry Regnery Co., 1955

Kojima, Noboru, *Jōroku-nen Jūni-gatsu Hachi-nichi: Taiheiyō Sensō: Hawai Dai-Kūshū Made*

Krauss, Rene, *Winston Churchill*, Lippincott, 1941

Langer, Walter C., *Mind of Adolf Hitler: The Secret Wartime Report*, New American Library, 1972

Lash, Joseph P., *Roosevelt and Churchill 1939-1941*, W.W. Norton, 1976

Layton, Rear Adm. Edwin T., *"And I was There"*, Quill: William Morrow, 1985

Lee, Asher, *Goering, Air Leader*, Hippocrene, 1972

Leeds, Christopher, *Italy Under Mussolini*, Wayland, 1972

Lewin, Ronald, *Churchill As Warlord*, Stein & Day, 1973

Lewin, Ronald, *The American Magic*, Farrar, Straus Giroux, 1982

Lindley, John M., *Carrier Victory: The Air War in the Pacific*, Elsevier-Dutton, 1978

Loewenheim, Harold D. and others editor, *Roosevelt and Churchill: Their Secret Wartime Correspondence*, Saturday Review Press, 1975

Lord, Walter, *Day of Infamy*, Bantam, 1957

Lord, Walter, *The Miracle of Dunkirk*, The Viking Press, 1982

Machray, Robert, *Little Entente*, Howard Fertig, 1970

Macksey, Kenneth, *Kesselring: The Making of the Luftwaffe*, David McKay Co., 1978

Makels, Lee Arne, *Japanese Attitudes Towards the United States Immigration Act of 1924*, Stanford University, 1973

Maggregor-Hastie, Roy, *Day of the Lion: The Life and Death of Fascist Italy, 1922-1945*

Massie, Robert K., *Nicholas and Alexandra*, World Books, 1968

Mayer, S.L., Editor, *The Rise and Fall of Imperial Japan, 1894-1945*, Military Press, 1984

Miale, Florence R. and Michale Selzer, *This Nuremberg Mind: The Psychology of the Nazi Leaders*, Quadrangle, 1977

Middlebrook, Martin and Patrick Mahoney, *Battleship: The Sinking of the Prince of Wales and the Repulse*, Charles Scribner's Sons, 1979

Miers, Earl Schenk, *Story of Winston Churchill*, Wonder Books, 1965

Mikesh, Robert C., *Zero Fighter (Rei-sen)*, Jane's, 1981

Mitchell, Richard H., *Thought Control in Prewar Japan*, Cornell University Press, 1976

Moran, Lord, *Churchill: Taken from the Diaries of Lord Moran*, Houghton Mifflin, 1966

Morin, Relmin, *East Wind Rising: A Long View of the Pacific Crisis*, Alfred A. Knopf, 1960

Morison, Samuel Eliot, *The Two-Ocean War*, Ballantine, 1963

Mosley, Leonard, *Hirohito, Emperor of Japan*, Prentice-Hall, 1966

Mosley, Leonard, *Marshal: Hero for Our Times*, Hearst Books, 1982

Mussolini, Rachele, *Mussolini: An Intimate Biography by His Widow*, William Morrow, 1974

Nakamura, Masatoshi, *Hawai Mikikan Ni-jū-ku-ki*, (29 Planes that Failed to Return*, Konnichi no Wadai-sha

Nakamura, Masatoshi, *Tora, Tora, Tora: Ware kishō ni seikō seri*, Konnichi no Wadai-sha, 1968

Nalty, Bernard C., *Tigers Over Asia*, Elsevier-Dutton, 1978

O'Connor, Dr. Raymond, *The Japanese Navy in World War II*, U.S. Naval Institute, 1969

Okumiya, Masatake, Jirō Horikoshi and Martin Caidin, *Zero: The Story of Japan's Air War in the Pacific: 1941-45*, Ballantine, 1956

Parkinson, Roger, *Origins of World War Two*, Wayland, 1970

Parkinson, Roger, *Tormented Warrior: Ludendorff and the Supreme Command*, Stein and Day, 1979

Payne, Robert, *Life and Death of Adolf Hitler*, Prager, 1973

Peare, Catherine Owens, *The FDR Story*, Thomas Y. Crowell,

1962

Peck, Ira, *The Battle of Britain*, Scholastic Book Services, 1970

Perkins, Frances, *The Roosevelt I Knew*, Harper Colophon, 1946

Pelz, Stephen E., *Race to Pearl Harbor: The Failure of the Second London Naval Conference*, Harvard University Press, 1974

Piccigallo, Philip R., *The Japanese on Trial: Allied War Crimes Operations in the East, 1945-1951*, Univ. of Texas Press, 1979

Pimlott, John, *World War II in Photographs*, Military Press, 1984

Pitt, Barrie, *Churchill and the Generals*, Bantam, 1981

Pogue, Forrest C., *George C. Marshall: Ordeal and Hope 1939-1942*, Viking, 1966

Potter, John Dean, *Yamamoto: the man who menaced America*, Paperback Library, 1965

Prange, Gordon W. *Tora! Tora! Tora!*, Reader's Digest 1966

Prange, Gordon W., etc., *At Dawn We Slept*, Penguin, 1981

Prange, Gordon W., *Target Tokyo: The Story of the Sorge Spy Ring*, McGraw-Hill, 1984

Rauch, Basil, *Roosevelt From Munich to Pearl Harbor*, Creative Age Press, 1950

Rauschning, Hermann, *Hitler Speaks*, Thornton Butterworth, 1939

Reischauer, Edwin O., *The United States and Japan*, Harvard University, 1957

Rich, Norman, *Hitler's War Aims*, W.W. Norton, 1973

Richardson, Stewart, *The Secret History of WW II, ...Cables and Letters of Roosevelt, Stalin and Churchill*, Richardson & Steirman, 1986

Roetter, Charles, *The Art of Psychological Warfare: 1914-1945*, Stein and Day, 1947

Roosevelt, Elliott and James Brough, *The Roosevelts of Hyde Park*, Putnam, 1973

Roosevelt, Elliott and James Brough, *Roosevelts of the White House*, Putnam, 1975

Ross, Ishbel, *Power with Grace: The Life Story of Mrs. Woodrow Wilson*, G. P. Putnam's Sons, 1975

Sakai, Saburo, *Samurai: Flying the Zero in WW II*, Ballantine, 1957

Schlesinger, Arthur M. Jr., *Crisis of the Old Order: The Age of Roosevelt 1919-1933*, Houghton Mifflin, 1957

Schofield, Vice Adm. B.B., *The Attack on Taranto*, Naval Institute Press, 1973

Sheehan, Ed, *One Sunday Morning*, Island Heritage, 1961

Sherwood, Robert E., *Roosevelt and Hopkins*, Universal Library, 1948

Shillony, Ben-Ami, *Revolt in Japan: The Young Officers and the February 26, 1936 Incident*, Princeton University Press, 1973

Shirer, William L., *Rise and Fall of the Third Reich*, Simon and Schuster, 1960

Shiroyama, Saburo, *War Criminal: the Life and Death of Hirota*

Koki, Kodansha, 1977

Smith, Gene, *When the Cheering Stopped: The Last Years of Woodrow Wilson*, Time, 1964

Spector, Ronald H. *Eagle Against the Sun: The American War With Japan*, Vintage, 1985

Speer, Albert, *Inside the Third Reich*, Macmillan, 1970

Stafford, Comdr. Edward P., *The Big 'E': The thrilling story of the U.S.S. Enterprise*, Ballantine, 1962

Stanley, Col. Roy M., *Prelude to Pearl Harbor: War in China 1937-41*, Charles Scribner's Sons, 1982

Steichen, Edward and Tom Maloney, *U.S. Navy War Photographs*, Crown, 1956

Stimson, Henry, *On Active Service in Peace and War*, Harper & Brothers, 1948

Smith, S.E., *United States Navy in WW II*, Ballantine, 1966

Stephan, John J. *Hawaii Under the Rising Sun: Japan's Plans for Conquest After Pearl Harbor*, Univ. of Hawaii Press, 1984

Sulzberger, C. L., *American Heritage Picture History of WW II*, American Heritage, 1966

Sunderman, Maj. James F., *World War II in the Air: The Pacific*, Bramwell House, 1962

Taylor, A.J.P., *The War Lords*, Penguin, 1977

Taylor, Lawrence, *A Trial of Generals: Homma, Yamashita, MacArthur*, Icarus Press, 1981

Terasaki, Gwen, *Bridge to the Sun*, Univ. of North Carolina Press, 1957

Theobald, Rear Adm. Robert A., *The Final Secret of Pearl Harbor*, Devin-Adair, 1954

Togo, Shigenori, *The Cause of Japan*, Simon & Schuster, 1956

Toland, John, *The Rising Sun: The Decline and Fall of the Japanese Empire, 1936-1945*, Random House, 1970

Toland, John, *Hitler: The Pictorial Documentary of His Life*, Doubleday, 1978

Trefousse, Hans Louis, *What Happened at Pearl Harbor? Documents Pertaining to the Japanese Attack*, College and University Press, 1958

Tuchman, Barbara W. *The Guns of August: The Drama of August 1914*, Macmillan, 1962

Ulam, Adam Bruno, *Stalin: the man and his era*, Viking, 1973

Vinacke, Harold M., *A History of the Far East in Modern Times*, F.S. Crofts, 1941

Warner, Denis and Peggy, *The Tide at Sunrise: A History of the Russo-Japanese War 1904-1905*, Charterhouse, 1974

Way, Peter, *Codes and Ciphers*, Crescent Books, 11977

Westwood, J.N. , *The Illustrated History of the Russo-Japanese War*, Henry Regnery Co., 1974

Welsh, Douglas, *The USA in World War 2: The Pacific Theater*, Galahad Books, 1982

Wheeler, Richard, *A Special Valor: The U.S. Marines and the Pacific War*, New American Library, 1983

White, Theodore H. and Annalee Jacoby, *Thunder Out of China*,

William Sloane Associatesx, 1946
Whittle, Tyler, *The Last Kaiser: A Biography of Wilhelm II,
German Emperor and King of Prussia*, Times Books, 1977
Willmott, H.P. *Pearl Harbor*, Prentice-Hall, 1983
Willmott, H.P. and others, *Greatest Battles of World War II*,
Galahad Books, 1981
Wilson, Dick, *When Tigers Fight: The Story of the Sino-Japanese War, 1937-1945*, Viking, 1982
Wilson, Theodore A., *The First Summit: Roosevelt and Churchill
at Placentia Bay 1941*, Houghton Mifflin, 1969
Winant, John Gilbert, *Letter From Grosvenor Square*, Houghton
Mifflin, 1947
Wistrich, Robert *Who's Who in Nazi Germany*, Macmillan, 1982
Wohlstetter, Robert, *Pearl Harbor: Warning and Decision*,
Stanford University Press, 1962
Yoshida, Shigeru, *Japan's Decisive Century: 1867-1967*,
Praeger, 1967
Young, Brigadier Peter, *World Almanac Book of World War II*,
World Almanac Publications, 1981
Zacharias, Rear Adm. Ellis M., *Secret Missions*, Paperback
Library, 1965

Newspapers
Honolulu Advertiser,
Honolulu Star-Bulletin
The New York Times

INDEX

on *Panay;* accepts Japanese
assurances, 96;

  bio. 94; 152, fol.;

  gives Nomura note objecting
to meeting of Konoye and
Roosevelt, 192; 224, 234,
237, 238;

  gives "comprehensive basic
proposal" to Japanese
ambassadors, 238;

  washes hands of negotiation,
257, 271, 311 fol., 314;
353 fol.

Hyde Park, 14

I-10, 253

I-19, 291

I-21, 291

I-23, 291

I-24, 320

I-71, 296

I-72, 251, 296

I-73, 251, 296

I-74, 252

Iguchi, Sadao, 312

Ikawa, Tadao, 159, 160

Illustrious, 114

Imaizumi, Capt. Hidemitsu, 291

Imaizumi, Capt. Ijirō, 263

Imamura, Gen. Hitoshi,
  given command of 16th
Army, 245

Immigration policy (Western),
73-74

Imperial Conference,
  decides to prepare for war
with Allies, 190-192, 218;
  formalizes war decision, 241,
fol.

Imperial Way (Kōdōha), 82

Inagaki, Petty Officer Kyogi,
321, 368-369

Indianapolis, 283

Influence of Sea Power Upon History, The (Mahan), 15

Ingersoll, Capt. Royal E.,

sent to confer with Admiralty, 92

Inoue, Junnosuke, Finance
Minister, assassinated, 75

Inouye, Rear Adm. Shigeyoshi,
253, 289

Inukai, Prime Minister
Tsuyoshi, assassinated, 76

Ishiwara, Maj. Kanji, 32

Ismay, Maj. Gen. Sir Hastings,
362

Isuzu, 175

Itagaki, Seishiirō, 32

Italian Fleet, 114-115

Itaya, Lieut. Comdr. Shigeru,
292, 297 fol.; 334 fol.

Ito, Rear Adm. Seichi, 298

Iwakuro, Col. Hideo, 160

Iwasaki family, 75

Japan,
  history of rejection of West,
67, 68;
  recognizes government of
Wang Ching-wei, 103;
  proposal for Allied agreement, 149;
  calls on Chiang to surrender,
155;
  plan for war with West, 158;
  attacks Indochina, 158;
  officially recognizes Wang
Ching-Wei government,
159;
  officially withdraws from
Washington Naval Treaty
and lays keels of giant
Yamato and *Musashi,* 178

Japanese Air Force, 180

Japanese plan for world domination, 16-17

Jodl, Gen. Alfred, 365

Joffre, Marshal Joseph, 22

Joseph, Louis, 27, 28

Junnosuke Inoue, 75

KGMB, 327, 323

PICTURE CREDITS

Associated Press: 206/7; three preceding 341
Brown Bros: 88
Central Press Photos: 51T
European: 51B
Franklin D. Roosevelt Library: Frontispiece,
24TL, 97, 146/147, 216
Hawaii State Archives: 367
Kyodo Photo Service: 187, 219R
Library of Congress: 24TR and 24B
National Archives: 120, 327, 330, 340, 373
Naval Historical Center: 239R
Real War Photos: 82, 167
Robert Hunt Library: 247L
United Press International: 230R
U.S. Navy Photo: 96, 194LC, 340
Ushio: 194T